IMAGES
of America

SHERIDAN COUNTY

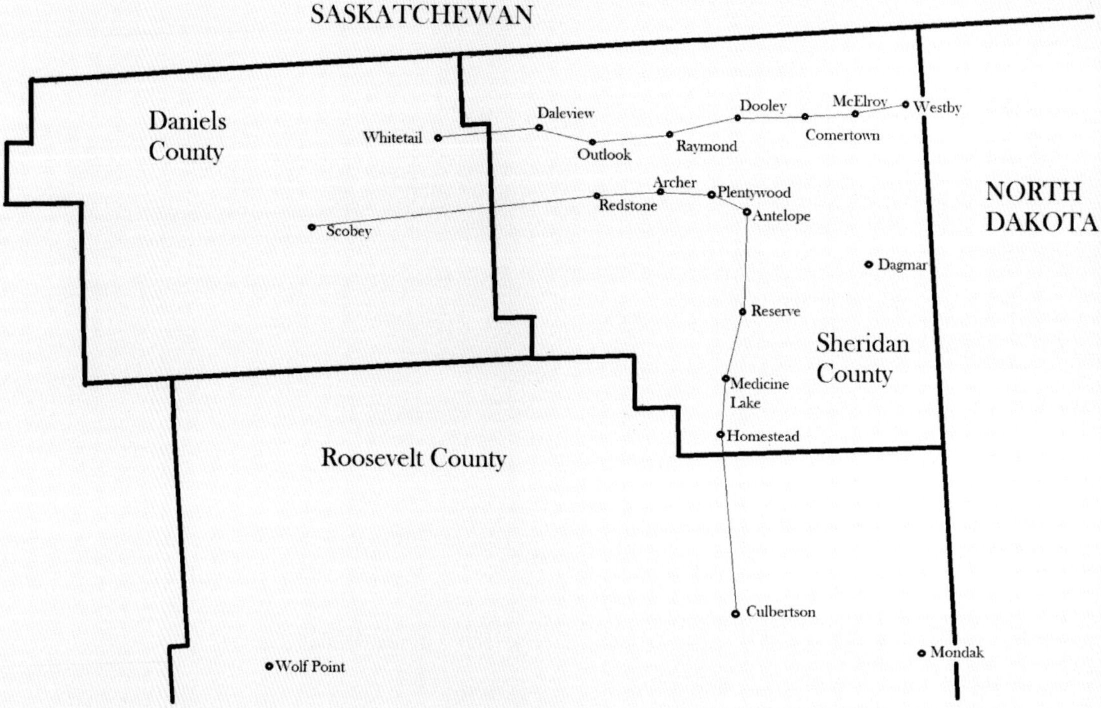

This map represents Sheridan County's borders, towns, and railroads in the early 1920s, after Daniels and Roosevelt Counties were carved from it. At the time of its statehood in 1889, the entire eastern third of Montana was shared between Dawson and Custer Counties. Valley County was partitioned from Dawson in 1893, and included land as far west as Malta, with the Missouri River forming its southern boundary. Sheridan County was created in 1913, with Roosevelt County being partitioned from it in 1919 and Daniels County in 1920. (Courtesy of Verlaine McDonald.)

ON THE COVER: A threshing crew works on John Shoal's homestead during the harvest season of 1913. (Courtesy of Heather and Mark Shoal.)

IMAGES
of America

SHERIDAN COUNTY

Helen Wagnild Stoner and Verlaine Stoner McDonald
Foreword by Joe Nistler

ARCADIA
PUBLISHING

ISBN 978-0-7385-9605-1

Published by Arcadia Publishing
Charleston, South Carolina

Printed in the United States of America

Library of Congress Control Number: 2012939911

For all general information, please contact Arcadia Publishing:
Telephone 843-853-2070
Fax 843-853-0044
E-mail sales@arcadiapublishing.com
For customer service and orders:
Toll-Free 1-888-313-2665

Visit us on the Internet at www.arcadiapublishing.com

To Sheridan County's residents, past and present.

CONTENTS

Foreword

"Between the blizzards, and the July heat and 40-below temperatures, you people in Sheridan County are either tougher or crazier than most Americans." Those were the words of Sheridan County native Gerry Nathe of Virginia in 2011. Nathe, whose family has farmed on the western side of Sheridan County for three generations, was commenting on the reasons Sheridan County residents stay where they are. There are some inherent positives of living in Sheridan County: wide-open spaces, minimal population and pollution, no rush-hour traffic jams, lots of oil, durum wheat, and cattle production.

For the most part, the current residents of Sheridan County are the descendants of the early-20th-century homesteaders who gambled that they could make a decent living on 160 or 320 acres of dryland farm. In actuality, about one in six farmers stuck around for at least 20 years. Drought, the Great Depression, sinking grain prices, grasshoppers, cutworms, and hail sent a high percentage of homesteaders packing.

The national desperation of the 1930s was magnified in Sheridan County by overwhelming poverty, crop failure, the continuing activity of the local Communist Party, plus a bootlegging industry that made a mockery of both local law enforcement and Prohibition.

Ironic as it might seem, Sheridan County was in a perfect position in the 1940s and 1950s to take advantage of expanding food demands during and after World War II. The rapid development of the oil industry was a highlight of Sheridan County life in the 1960s and 1970s. The short-lived oil boom temporarily doubled the size of Plentywood, propelled a hot economy, and created a wealth of nightlife and activities for both local residents and visitors from Saskatchewan and North Dakota.

By 2011, the economy of Sheridan County had awakened from a few decades of slumber. Durum prices rose to $15 per bushel, oil to $100 per barrel, and cattle sold for $1.20 per pound, adding up to a level of prosperity rarely seen since the county was created in 1913. After 100 years, Sheridan County's economic roller coaster is still moving; it remains to be seen if the ride will be smooth or bumpy.

And whether the county's people see themselves as tougher, crazier, or more fortunate than most Americans, well, you need to ask them yourself.

Acknowledgments

We extend our gratitude to the dozens of current and former Sheridan County residents who submitted more than 400 photographs for this book. We wish it had been possible to include all of them. We are also grateful for all of the information and anecdotes provided in letters and telephone calls that helped us prepare captions for the images.

Thank you, to John Poultney, who invited us to make a proposal to Arcadia Publishing for a book on Sheridan County, and to our acquisitions editor, Elizabeth Bray, who has skillfully shepherded us through the publication process.

A number of friends deserve special acknowledgement: Joe Nistler, *Sheridan County News*; June Johnson, Sheridan County clerk and recorder and Mary Lynch, clerk and recorder's office; Sheila Lee, Sheridan County librarian; Doug Smith, Sheridan County planner; Pat Tange, Sheridan County Museum curator; and LeRoy Brenteson, Tammy Burgess, Virginia Carpenter, Kathy and Marv Eberling, Phyllis Gabbard, Dave Golterman, Ardelle Hart, Ken Keldsen, Marbea Lane, Elice Nelson, Dona Osksa, Heather and Mark Shoal, Tim Syme, Albert Walikonis, and Myrtle Waller.

Finally, we are especially grateful to Andy McDonald. He was the first to suggest this mother-daughter collaboration, sacrificed time from his own book project to care for Carlyn and Maryn as we did our work, and offered a keen eye in editing the text.

INTRODUCTION

Since I left Montana to go to college, I've come home to Sheridan County about 50 times. Over the course of those almost 30 years, I've noticed an interesting trend. In the last decade or so, whenever I have mentioned that I am planning a trip to Montana, the reactions have ranged from a kind of vague admiration, expressed in statements like, "Oh, I've heard it's just beautiful there," to outright swooning and obvious envy.

This is a remarkable departure from what I experienced in the 1980s. I'll never forget the response of a college acquaintance when I mentioned where I grew up. He said, "Montana. Let's see. Isn't that somewhere over by Minnesota?" In retrospect, I should have told him that, yes, it is over by Minnesota in the same way that Boston is by Washington, DC, or New York is by North Carolina. All of these places are roughly 450 miles apart.

The college student's misunderstanding was not an isolated instance of someone who failed his high school geography class; there was, for a long time, a profound lack of knowledge about our state, and not only whether it bordered Minnesota. My own family encountered this firsthand in the 1960s, when some relatives from Wisconsin decided to drive out for a visit. When they arrived and began to unload their luggage, we observed that much of their trunk space was consumed by five-gallon cans of gas. They had somehow formed the impression that there weren't many filling stations out on the wild frontier and that it would be safest to haul their own fuel.

Since the 1990s, the world has come to know our state more fully, mainly as a result of the media. Books and films such as *A River Runs Through It* and *The Horse Whisperer* have featured the gorgeous scenery of Montana. But our corner of the state does not look like the places portrayed in the movies, and there are still many Montanans who notice that the writers of newspaper articles and television news broadcasts seem to think that eastern Montana begins and ends in Billings. On a good day, they might mention Miles City or Glendive.

In fact, there is a rich and colorful past and present in the northeastern part of Montana, and this book is another attempt to add to a growing body of work that more fully captures Sheridan County's history. It includes relatively few images having to do with the more notorious aspects of our history, mainly because those events have recently become well publicized. Instead, this book is a collection of photographic images portraying the lives of Sheridan County people, their work, families, homes, pastimes, and the ways they celebrated living in what many of us consider the best part of America.

—Verlaine Stoner McDonald

One

The Early Years

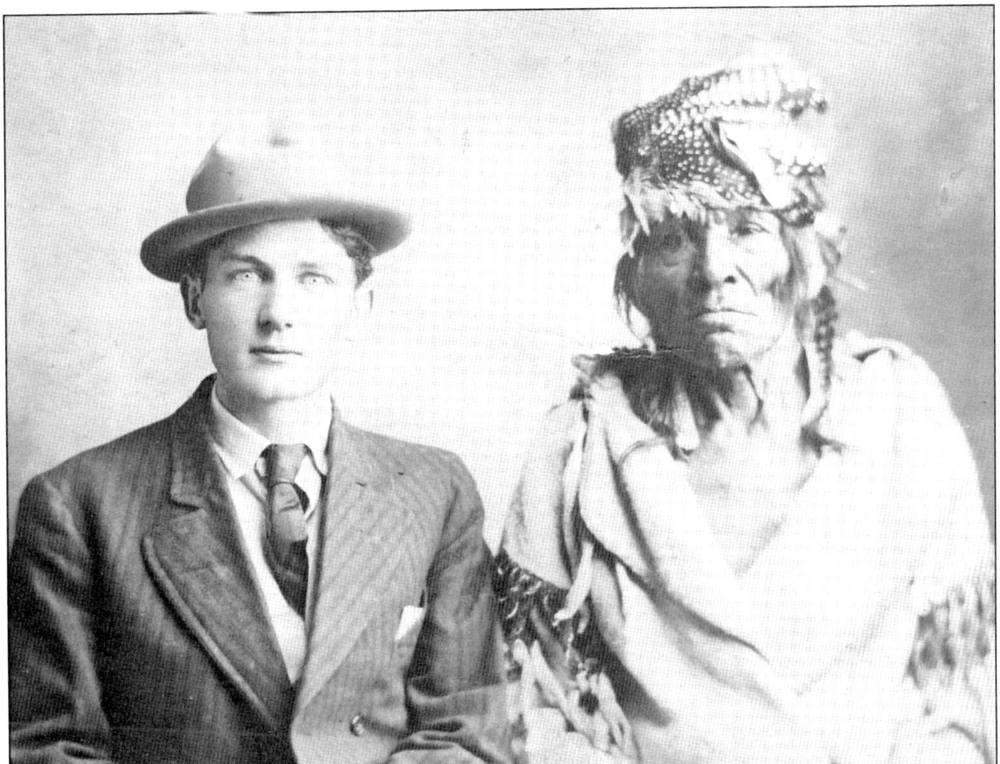

Pictured in 1908 are Clinton "C.J." Poe (left) of Medicine Lake and an unidentified friend, a tribal medicine man. The Assiniboine, along with members of the Sioux and Chippewa tribes, lived on the land that would become northeastern Montana. Today, their descendants share the Fort Peck Reservation; the Sioux tend to live on the east side and the Assiniboine on the west. (Courtesy of Virginia Carpenter.)

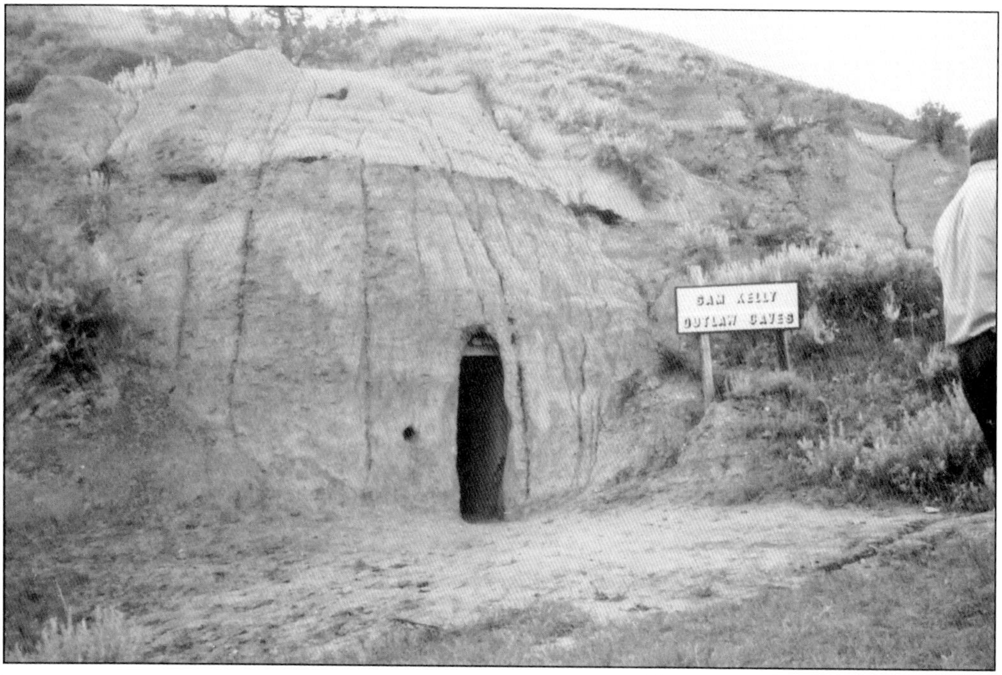

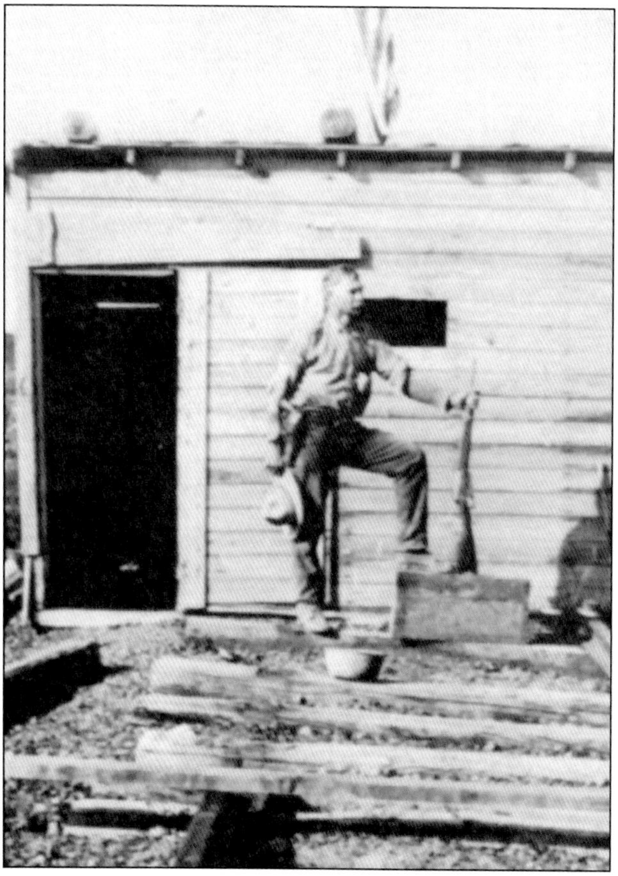

Shown above, the Sam Kelly Caves were named after one of the many horse thieves and cattle rustlers who roamed the Daleview area during the late 19th and early 20th centuries. According to *Outlaw Tales of Montana*, Kelly was a tall, red-headed Irishman and one of the most notorious outlaws of the region. A contemporary of the outlaws, Elmer "Hominy" Thompson, arrived in the Daleview area in 1894. Thompson clashed with the Minneapolis, St. Paul & Sault Ste. Marie Railroad, commonly known as the Soo Line, which crossed his property and allegedly interfered with his homemade irrigation system. In the left photograph, he is shown posing with a rifle in front of the shed that he moved onto the tracks to block the Soo. He was arrested and served time for interfering with the train's delivery of mail. (Above, courtesy of May Budke and Tammy Burgess; left, courtesy of *Sheridan's Daybreak*.)

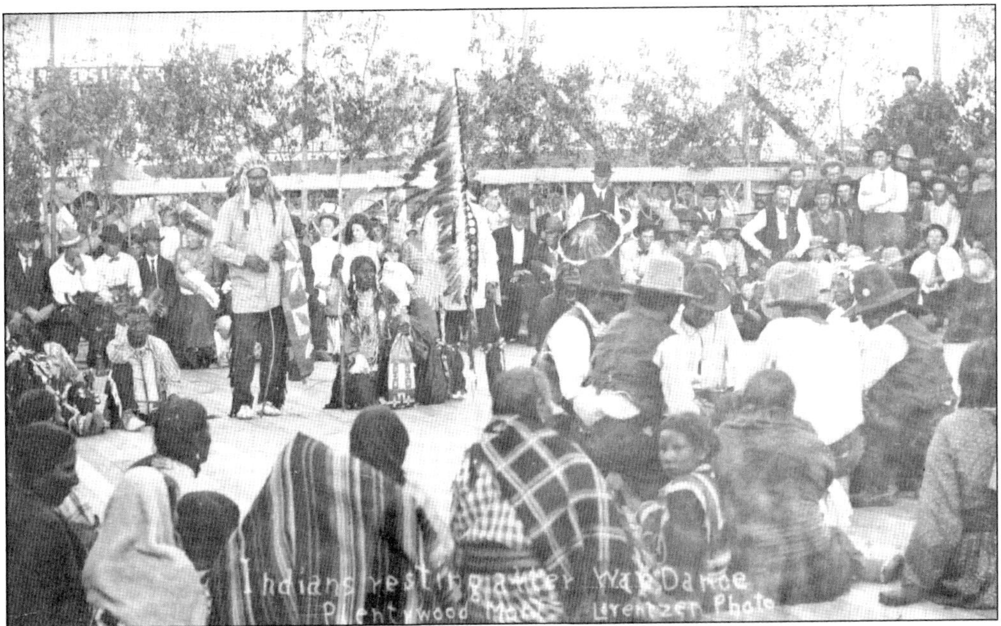

Plentywood's Independence Day celebration in 1911 was reportedly attended by a crowd of 4,000 people, including more than 300 members of the Sioux tribe. The above photograph shows Sioux after performing a traditional war dance. Shown below are Martha McCoy Nelson and Henry "Buster" Crohn, the first known white children born in what is now Sheridan County. Nelson made her first appearance in a tent southwest of present-day Raymond on the homestead of her parents, George and Annie Ator McCoy, in 1899. Crohn was born to Bill and Nellie Brown Crohn at the Bedford Halfway House, a lodge between Culbertson and what is now Plentywood, in 1902. (Above, photograph by Lorentzen Photography, courtesy of Maynard Johnson; below, courtesy of Helen Stoner).

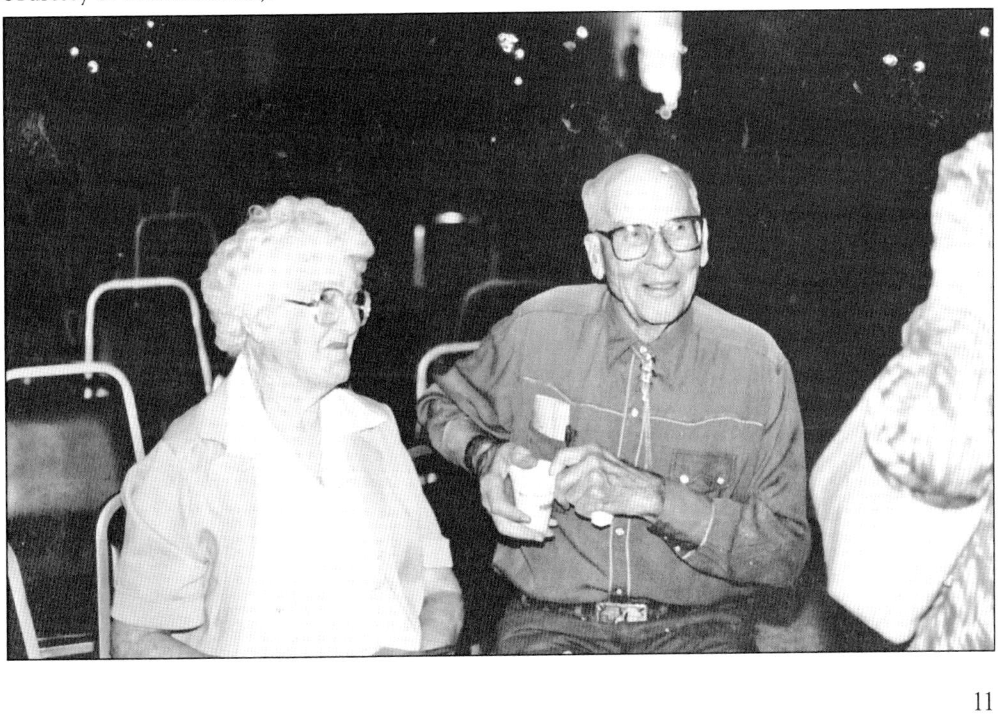

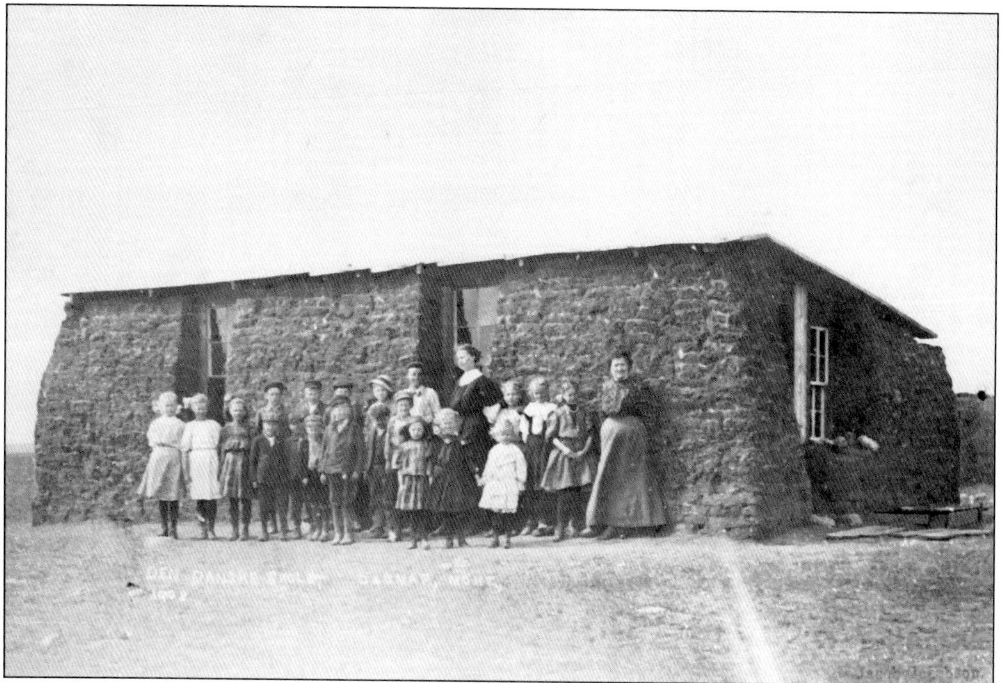

Dagmar was founded by Emil Ferdinand Madsen in 1906; a group of fellow Danes joined him in the "colony" the following year. Den Danske Skole, or the Dane School, was the first school in the area. The outer walls were prairie sod, with paper-covered boards on the interior. In the 1908 photograph above, Marie Hansen (right) poses with two unidentified teachers and the school's pupils. Below, John Egeland poses with his horse and plow. He homesteaded east of Reserve in the Eden Valley community in 1906 and lost much of his cattle herd during the harsh winter of 1907. He later wrote in his memoirs that he felt lucky to receive $1 each for the hides of the animals that had perished. (Above, courtesy of Jens Sundsted; below, courtesy of Gertrude Sundsted.)

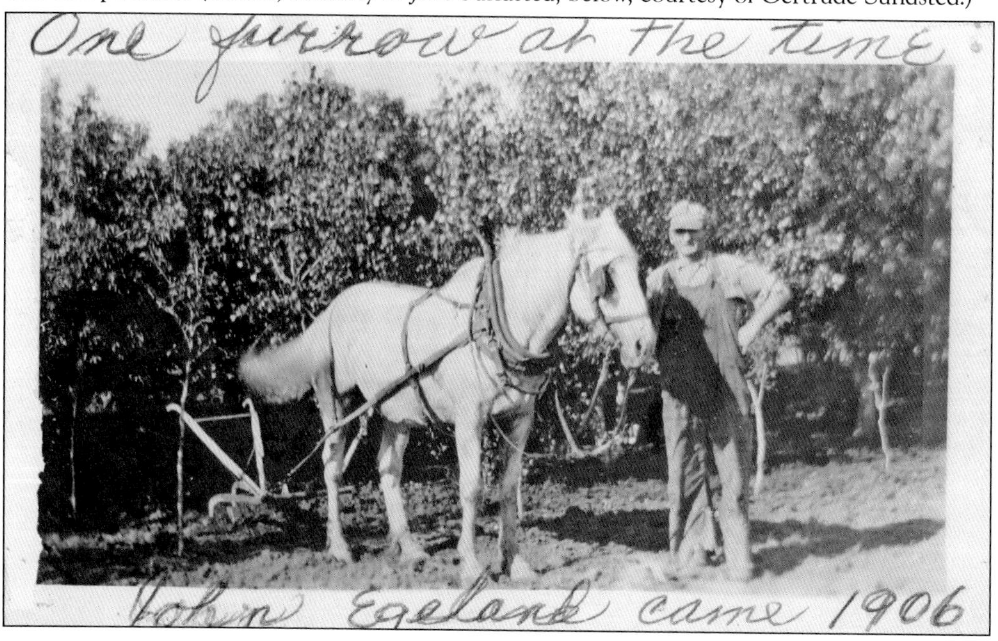

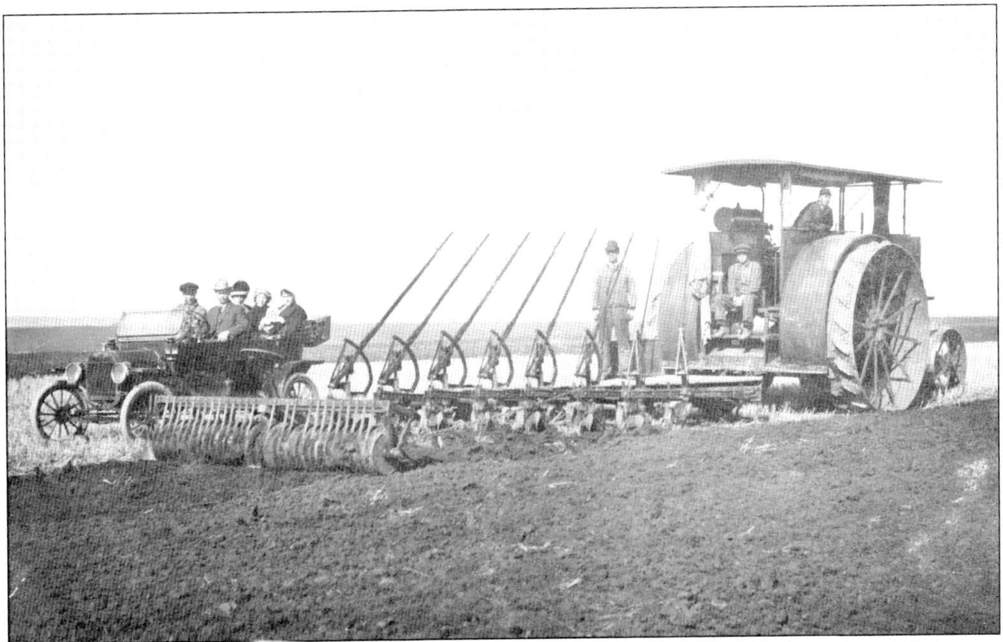

The above photograph was taken at the Martin Lundeen farm near Outlook in 1913. Steam engines were first used in the Outlook area in 1911 and could break roughly 15 acres per day, a significant improvement over horse-drawn plows. It was a complex operation, with an engineer manning the engine, a fireman shoveling coal and watching the steam pressure gauge, and a plowman adjusting the depth levers on the plow. Water and coal haulers were kept busy as well. After the soil had been broken, rocks emerged. Below, Westby pioneers Gunder Johnsboen (left), an unidentified hired man, and Ole Odegaard (right) are shown picking rocks in preparation for seeding. (Above, courtesy of Don McCrory; below, courtesy of Ken Keldsen.)

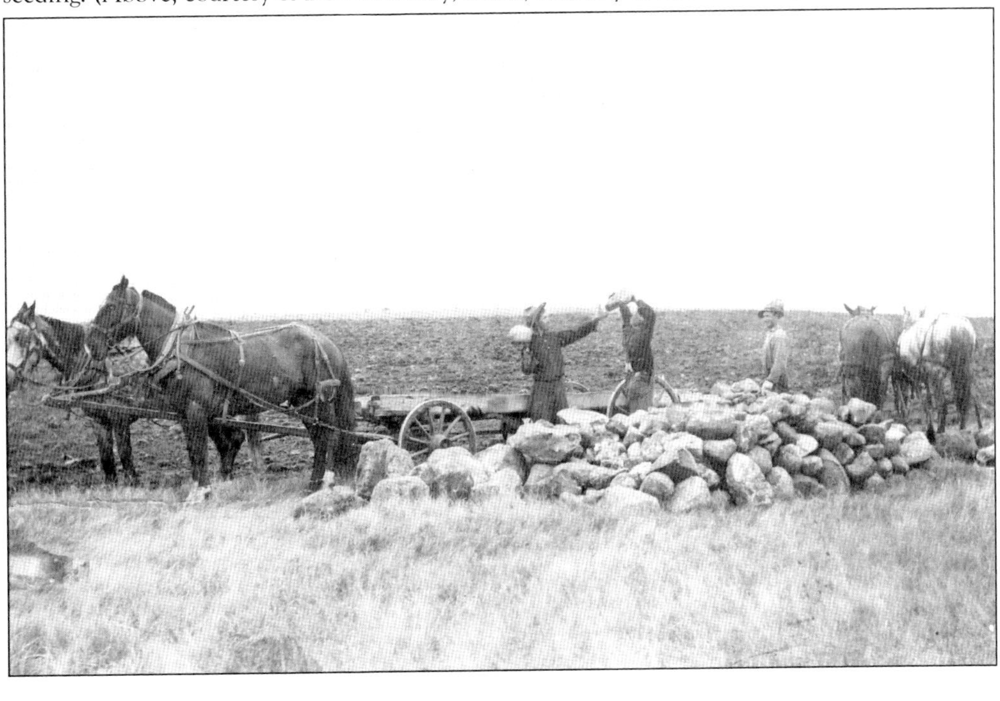

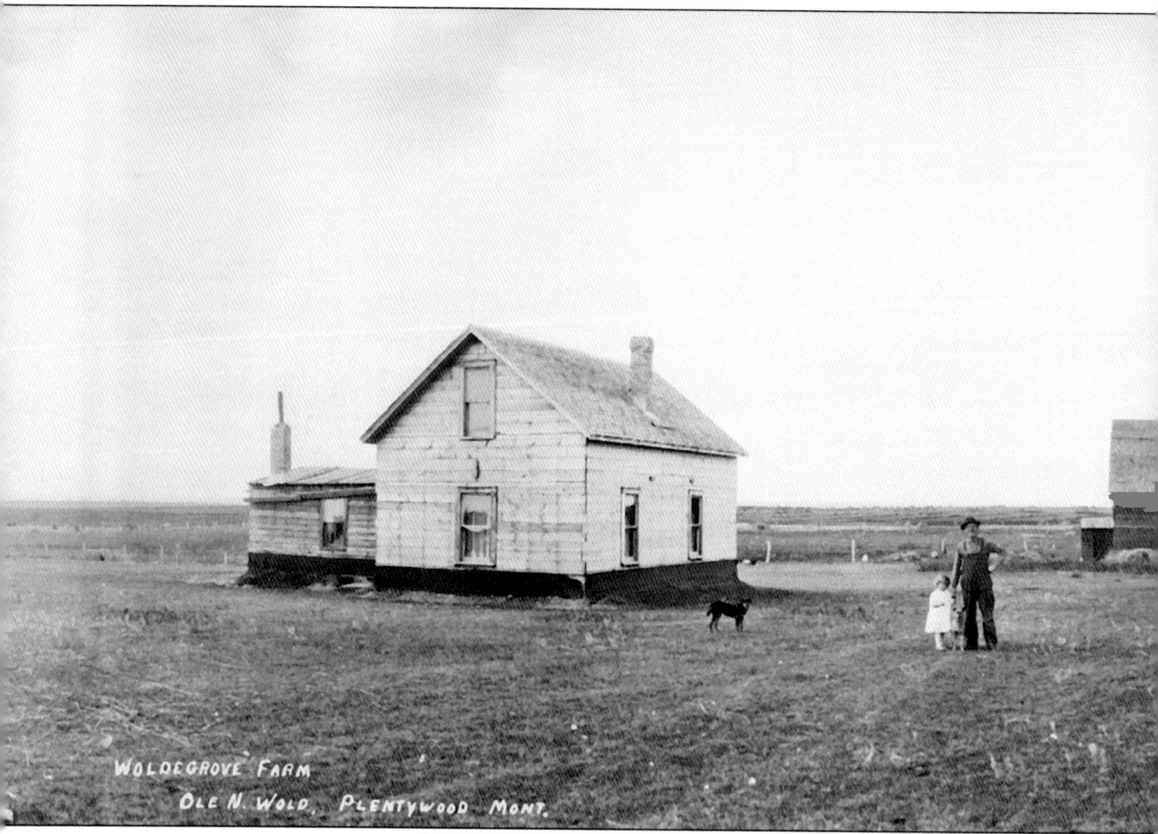

Ole Wold was 15 years old when he and his older brother emigrated from Norway in 1895. He married Martina "Tina" Wagnild of Wisconsin, and, in 1910, they went west with Tina's brother, Oscar Wagnild, selecting homesteads southeast of Outlook. Pictured in September 1915 are Wold and his daughter, Dagny, with family pets Teddy and Puppy. On the day the photograph was

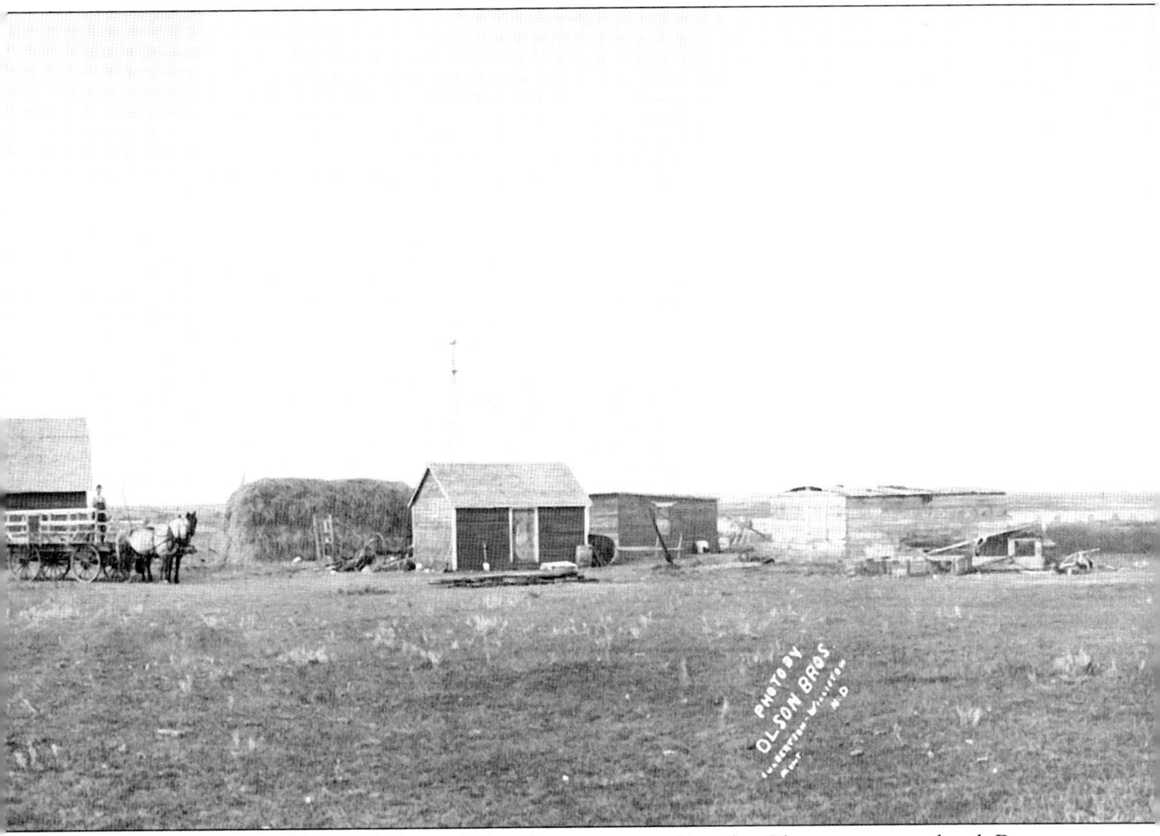

taken, the older children, Gladys and Orville, were attending the Olson country school. Because Tina Wold was expecting baby Myrtle later in the fall, she chose not to be in the photograph, as was the custom for pregnant women at the time. (Photograph by Olson Brothers, courtesy of Myrtle Waller.)

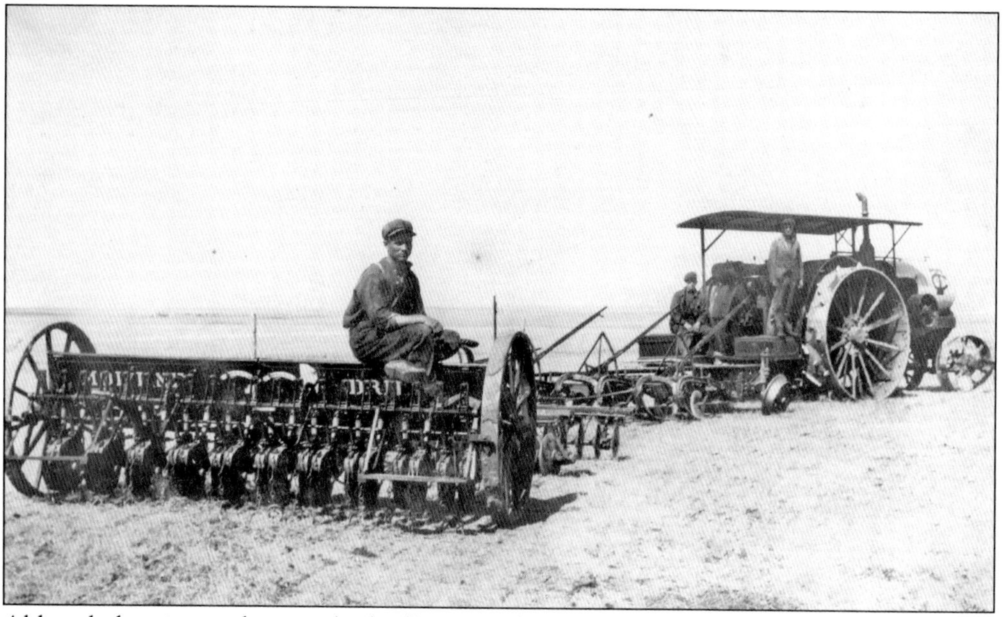

Although there is a tendency to think of homesteaders as having been single or married men, many women also staked their claims in Montana. Mildred Phelps and her sister, Elsie, homesteaded in the Wolf Creek community south of Redstone in 1910, sharing a small tarpaper shack. Mildred later married Hugh French, who had taken a claim in 1906 in the Flaxville area, and they chose to live on her homestead. Shown in the above photograph are Hugh French, standing in the steam engine, and sons Willard at his side and Glenn on the seed drill. Peter Keldsen, shown at right in the below photograph, arrived from Denmark in 1907 and staked his claim on 320 acres in the Westby area. He married Ellen Nielsen in 1922. She is seen here perched on her husband's knee. Their toddler, Elsie, stands next to them, and Ellen's uncle, Tido Madsen, is on the left. (Above, courtesy of Gordon French; below, courtesy of Ken Keldsen.)

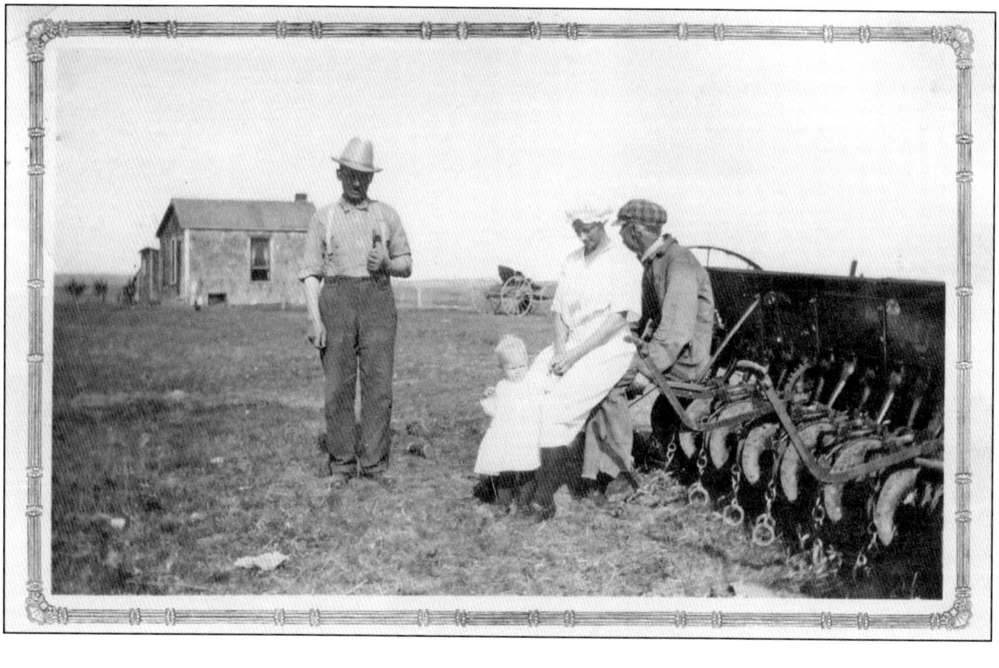

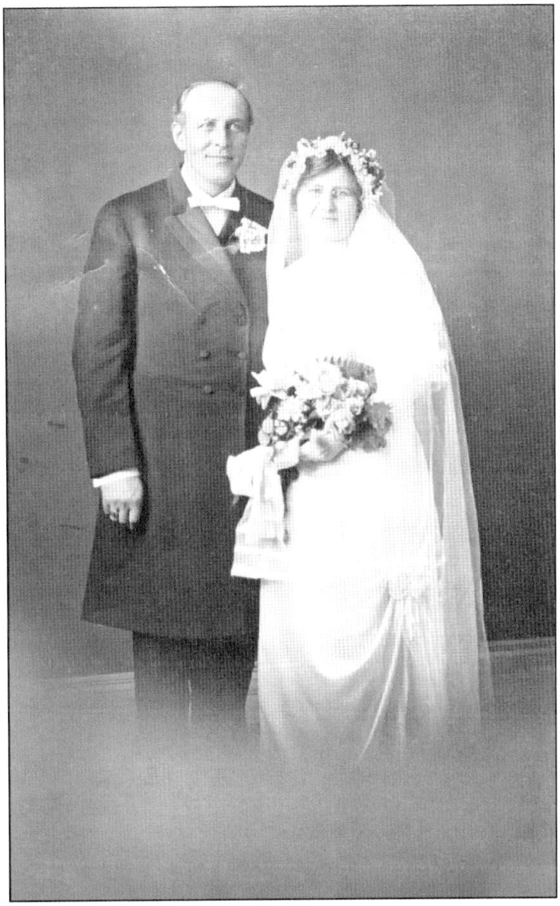

Reverend George and Lorense Dahl Tangvald, her sister, Adah, and the Tangvold's two children came to the Antelope area in 1909. He organized Lutheran Free Churches in rural Antelope, Homestead, northwest Plentywood, and Westby. Following the birth of a third child, Lorense Tangvald passed away and was the first person to be interred in the Antelope Creek Lutheran Cemetery. Her husband remarried, and he is shown at right in his wedding photograph with Emily Erickson Tangvald. They had one child, who was only an infant when Reverend Tangvald passed away at the age of 41. Following his funeral, pictured below, he was buried next to his first wife in Antelope. (Both, courtesy of Helen Stoner.)

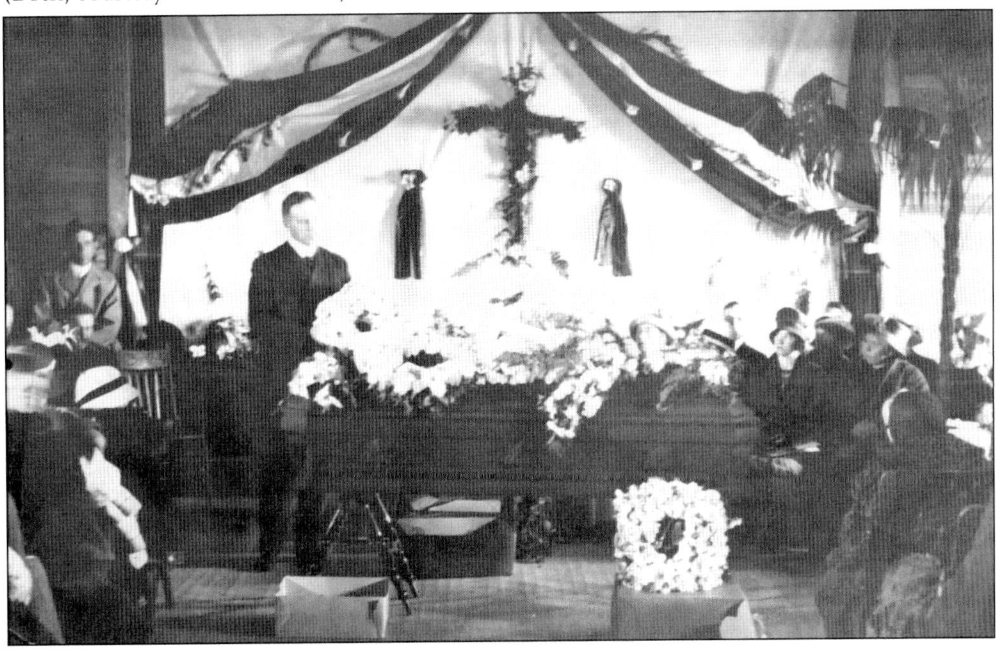

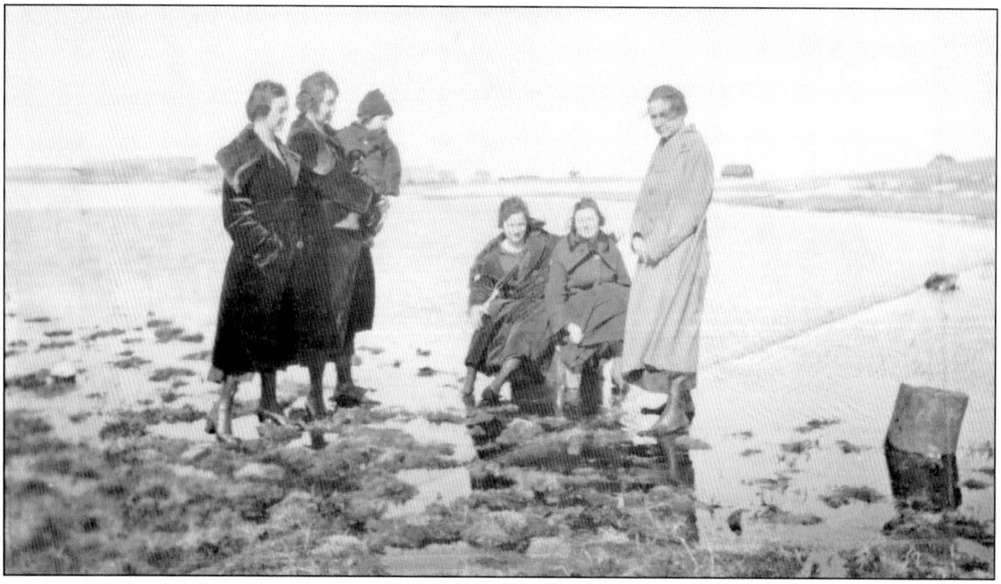

In the above photograph, some of the women of north Dooley explore the spring runoff. John Shoal's threshing crew is seen in the below photograph, an uncropped version of this book's cover image. Shoal is kneeling and pouring coffee for one of his crew members. Born in Michigan in 1894, he came to the Westby area around 1909 and farmed there for nearly 30 years. Tilda Sjaastad (far right) was born in North Dakota and later came to work for a family in Westby. Like many young women, she filed her own homestead claim. She worked her claim for several years before she and John set up housekeeping there after their marriage in 1921. In the 1930s, John Shoal helped organize and served on the board of the Agricultural Adjustment Administration's Plentywood office. He and his family moved to Plentywood in 1938, and he later served a term as mayor. (Above, courtesy of the Sheridan County Museum; below, courtesy of Heather and Mark Shoal.)

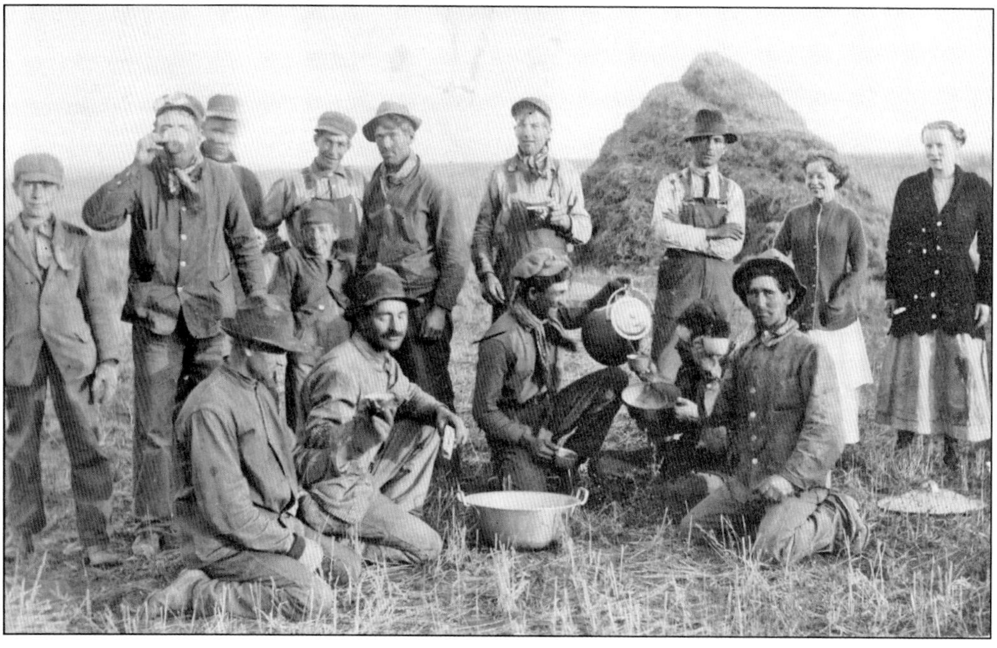

Two

Down on the Farm (and Ranch)

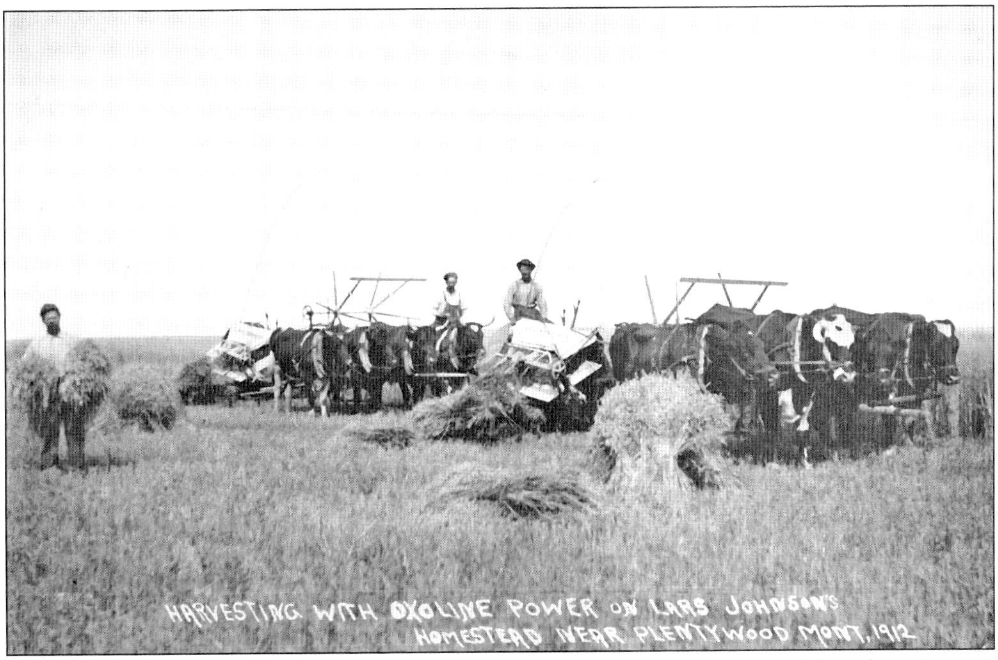

Raising livestock and coaxing crops from the soil has presented challenges to Sheridan County's farmers and ranchers for over 100 years. A binder cutting and shocking operation is shown at Lars Johnson's homestead north of Plentywood in 1912. The previous year, Johnson had brought his new bride, Guri Aarhus of North Dakota, on the first train to come into Plentywood when the spur line from Culbertson opened. (Courtesy of Gary Klofstad.)

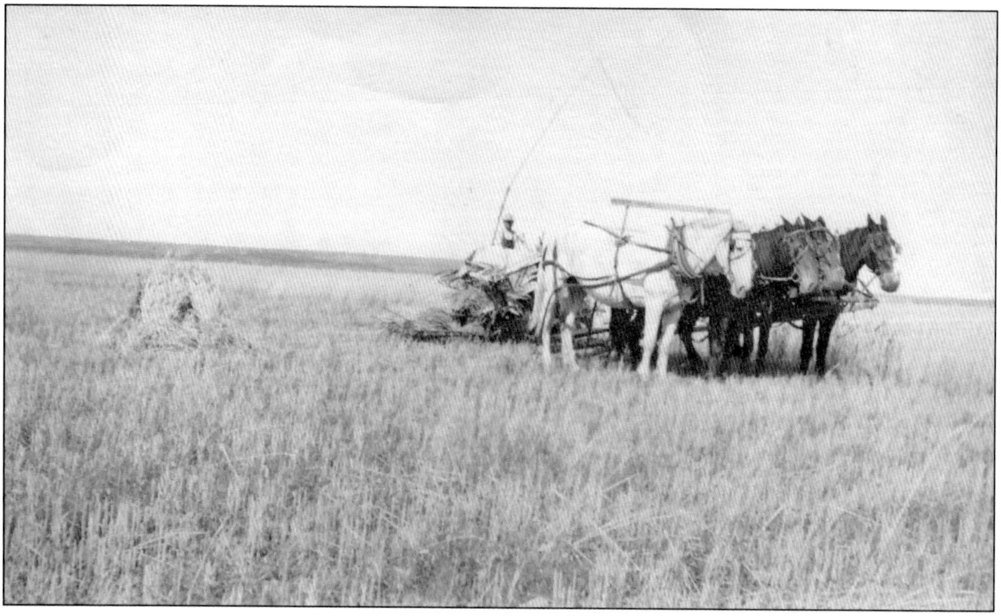

Above, Alvin Marsh cuts grain with a binder on his parents' farm south of Redstone. Binders cut the grain, bound it with twine into bundles, and then dropped the bundles on the ground in a row. Crews placed the bundles upright in shocks, which would shed water more efficiently if it rained during the two-week drying process. Threshers then moved through the community on a first-come, first-served basis, often working late into the fall. In the photograph below, Jacob Ereth is shown cutting wheat during the 1928 harvest season. Both he and his wife, Rosa Fenrich Ereth, had been born in Romania and later immigrated to Saskatchewan with their parents and siblings. The family lived for a time near present-day Minton, Saskatchewan, before coming to the Outlook community in 1923. (Above, courtesy of Gordon French; below, courtesy of Dorothy Melle.)

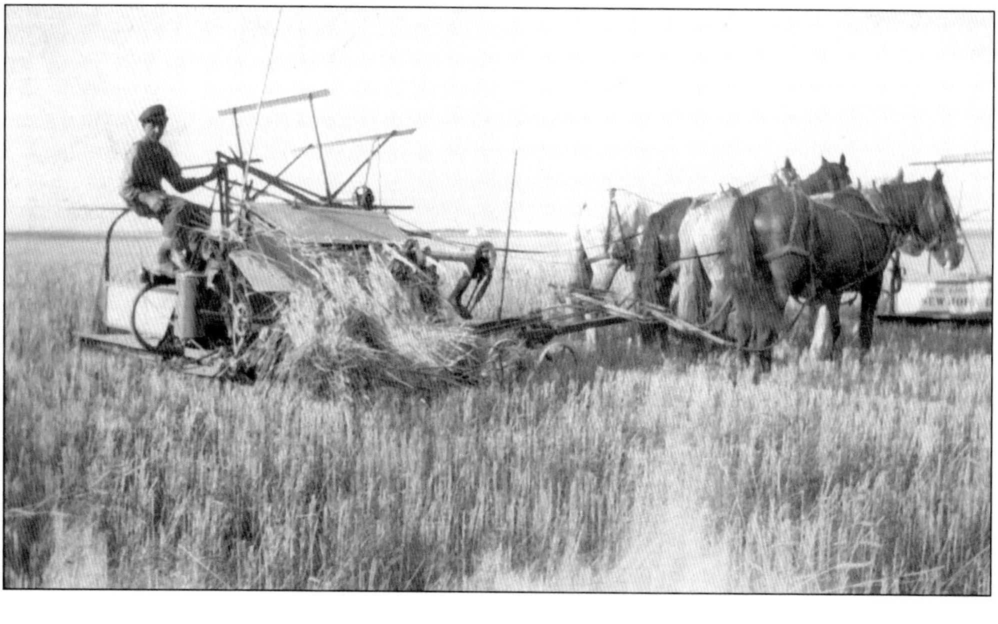

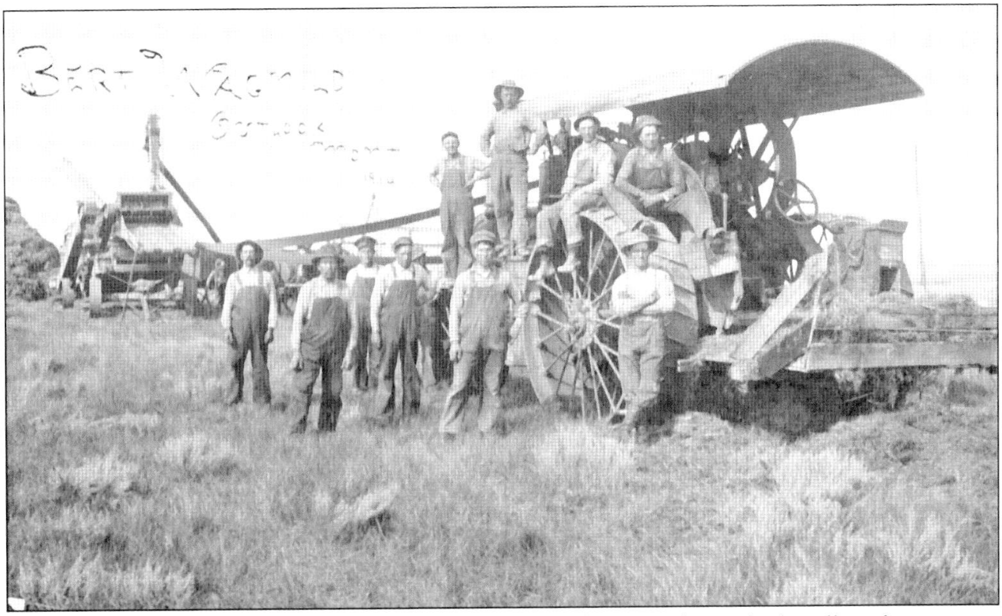

After shocks were dried, threshing began. Members of the crew threw the bundles of grain onto what was called a feeder chain, grain-end first. The twine around the bundles was cut by rotating knives, and the thresher separated the grain from the straw. The Bert Wagnild threshing crew of Outlook assembled for the above photograph in 1912. Shown here are, from left to right, (on the ground) John Hagstrom, John Stompro, unidentified, Pete Anderson, unidentified, and Christ Wagnild; (on the steam engine) Ole Wold, Bert Wagnild, Emil Stahlberg, and Oscar Wagnild. In the photograph below, the C.G. Bogeert threshing crew poses in 1914. The only identified crew member is Nels Thompson, who homesteaded south of Archer in 1914. He is standing between the two men seated together in the center. (Above, courtesy of Helen Stoner; below, courtesy of Millie Marsh.)

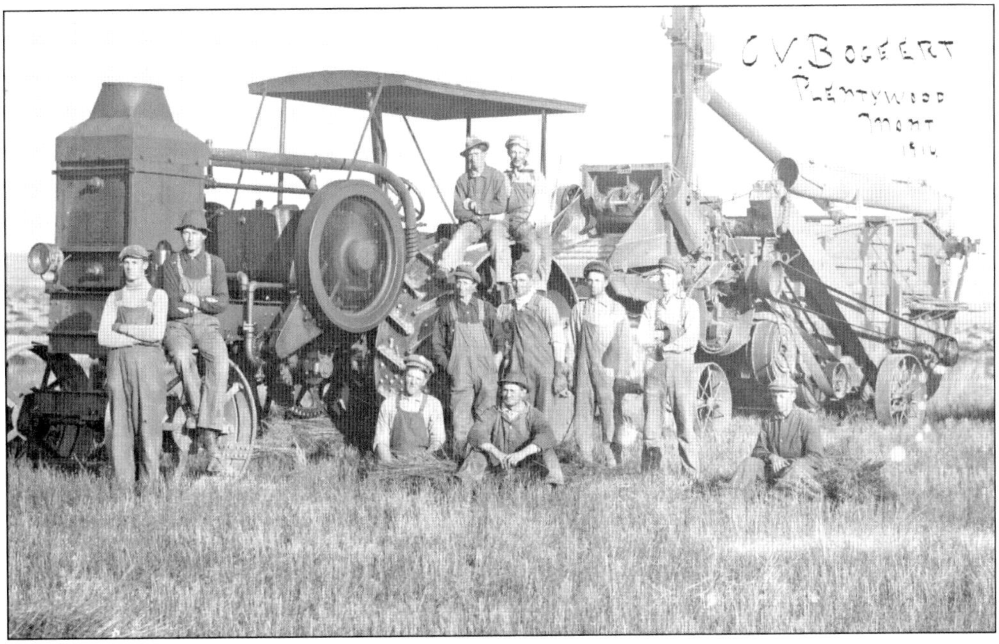

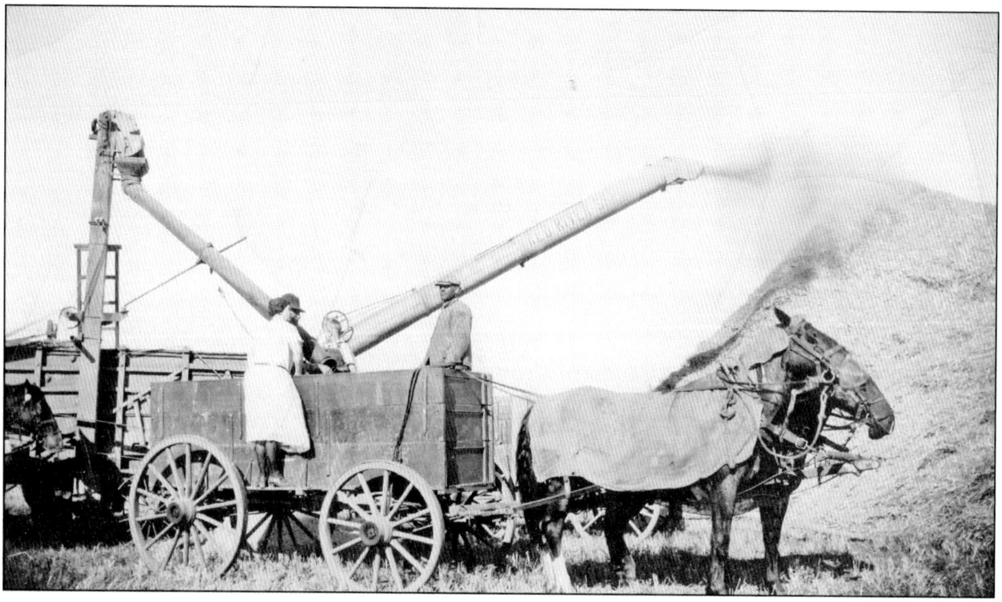

August Westphal, John Lindblom, and Jack Nelson organized the Pioneer Threshing Syndicate to thresh their own crops and those of their neighbors in the Raymond community. Shown in the above photograph are, from left to right, Hazel Madill Nelson, her husband, Jack (partially hidden) holding young Reuben Nelson, and Westphal, examining a wagonload of grain as the thresher expels chaff and straw into a pile. Below, Lindblom (left) shares a cup of coffee with Tony Melle during a busy threshing day. Lindblom, born in Sweden, homesteaded five miles northwest of Raymond. He married Agnes Bolander in 1920 and raised a family of four. Their descendants still farm on the original homestead. (Both, courtesy of Chester Lindblom.)

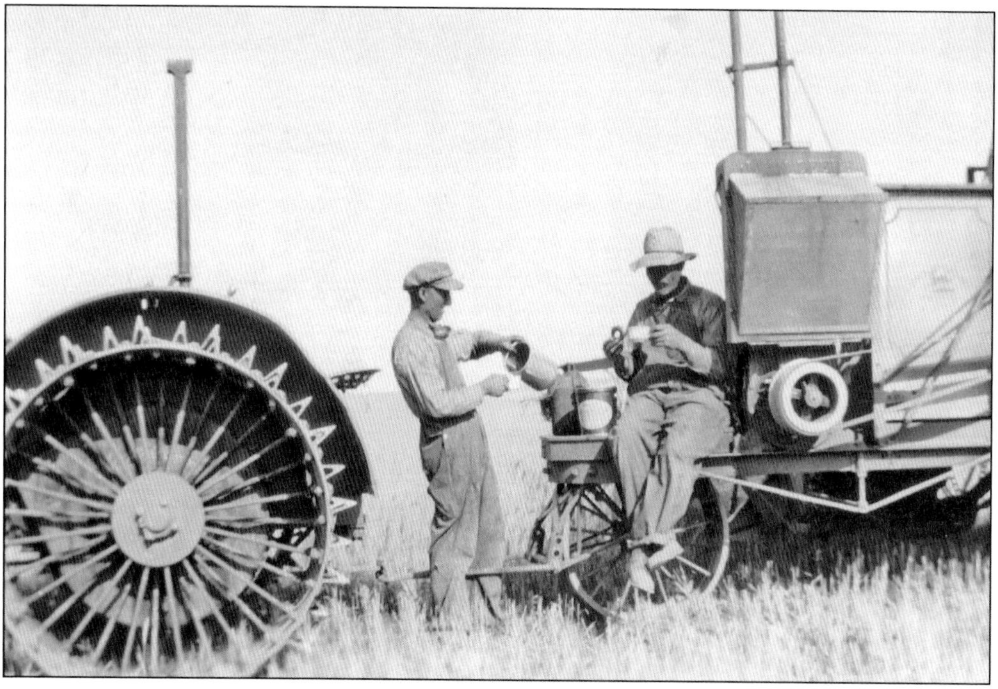

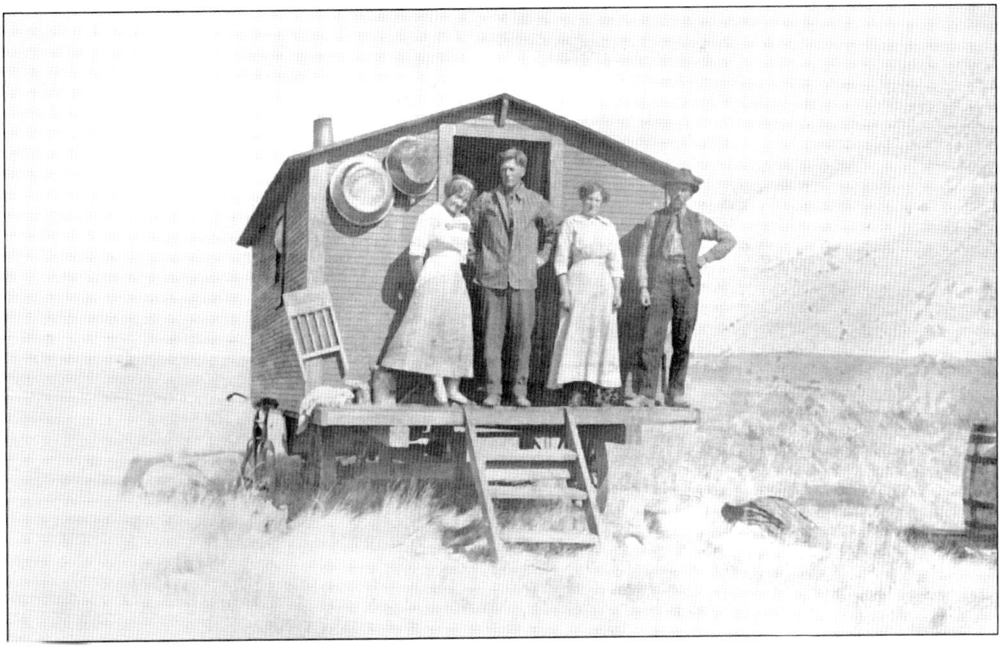

Threshing crews often included women, who usually staffed the mobile cook car, similar to a chuck wagon. Above, Ernest Olson and unidentified members of his crew pose in the doorway of their cook car, probably in the late 1910s. When the grain had been threshed, transporting it was the next chore. Charles Lundeen loaded up his 1910 crop and headed for the Plentywood grain elevator, roughly a 50-mile, four-day round-trip from his homestead in the "old" Outlook area, as shown below. The Soo Line extended to Outlook in 1913 and the town moved to its present location. Soon, four elevators were in operation, easing the burden of hauling crops. (Above, courtesy of Marlys Vogt; below, courtesy of Helen Stoner.)

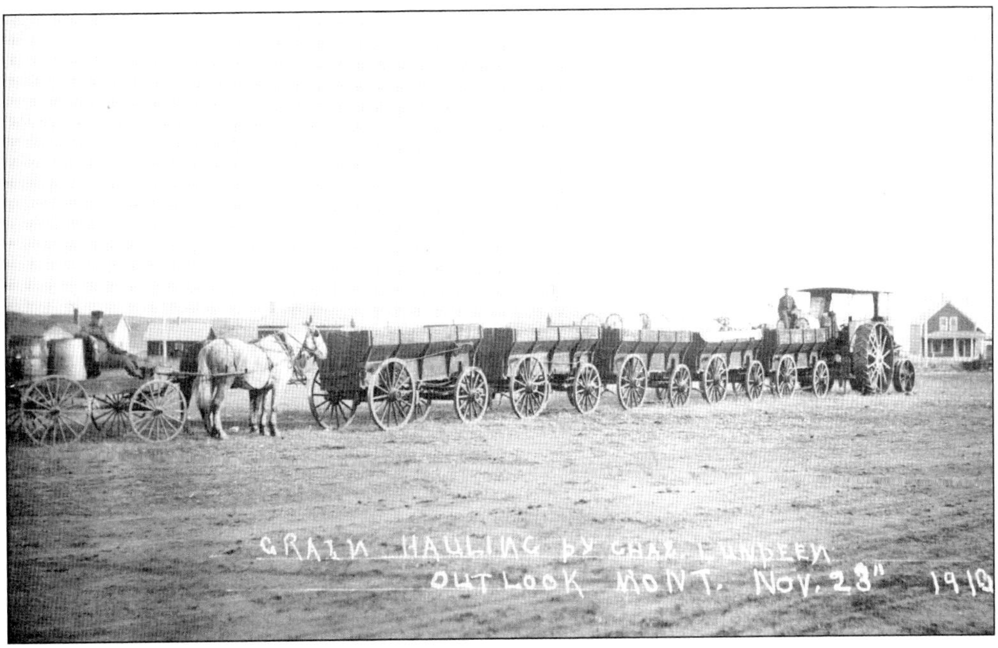

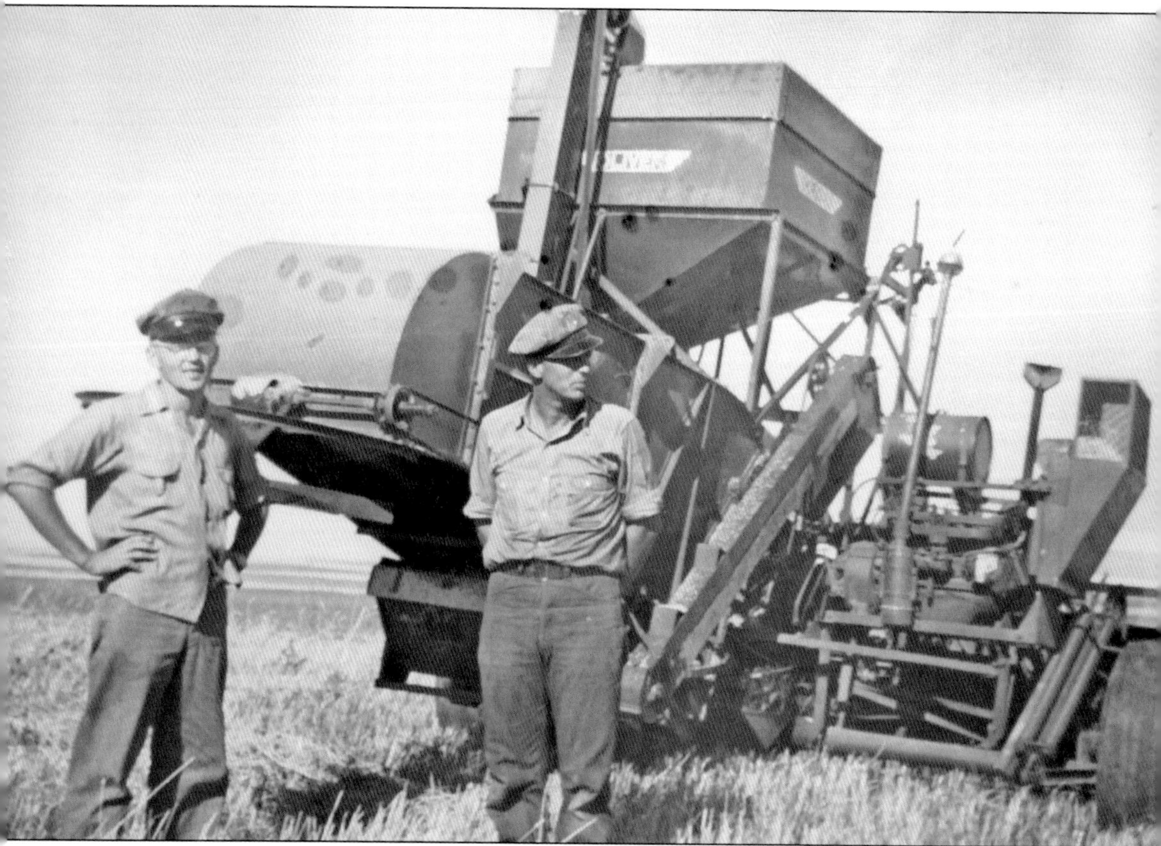

The evolution of grain farming in Sheridan County can be traced by observing the developments in harvesting equipment over the years. Threshing, as the previous images illustrate, was a complex, multistep operation that required a crew of 15 or more. Individual farmers rarely owned their own threshers, but hired traveling crews, not unlike contemporary custom combining operations. By the 1930s, tractor-drawn combines had been developed, allowing farmers who could afford them to buy their own implements. Harvesting crews became smaller and the processes were simplified, although the work remained intense. Shown here during the harvest of 1946 with their 12-foot Oliver pull-type combine are Leonard Urdahl (left), who drove the tractor, and Stanley Urdahl, who ran the combine. The Urdahls had come to Sheridan County with their parents from North Dakota in 1928, first living west of Medicine Lake, and later moving to a farm in the Homestead community. (Courtesy of Janis Bakken.)

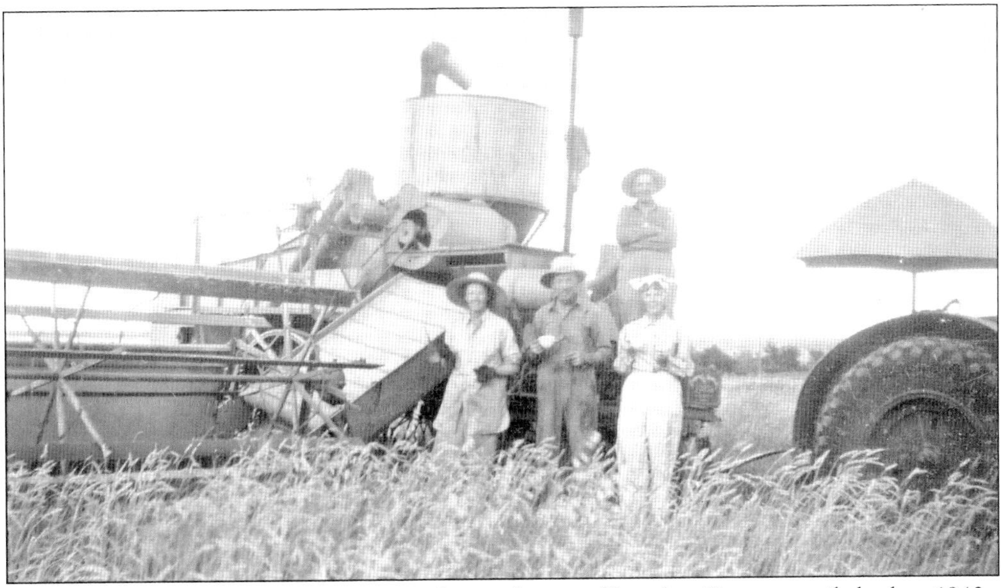

Self-propelled combines did not enter widespread use in Sheridan County until the late 1940s. In the photograph above, taken during a harvest season in the 1940s, Ole Wold stands on his tractor-pulled combine. Standing on the ground are, from left to right, his daughters and son: Myrtle Wold Waller, Orville Wold, and Dagny Wold. Below, Max Rasmussen of northeast Antelope sits on his Massey Harris combine in 1953. The British company had revolutionized harvesting with its self-propelled combines in the 1940s and gained a foothold in the American implement market even before the merger that made it the well-known Massey Ferguson Company. (Above, courtesy of Myrtle Waller; below, courtesy of Max Rasmussen.)

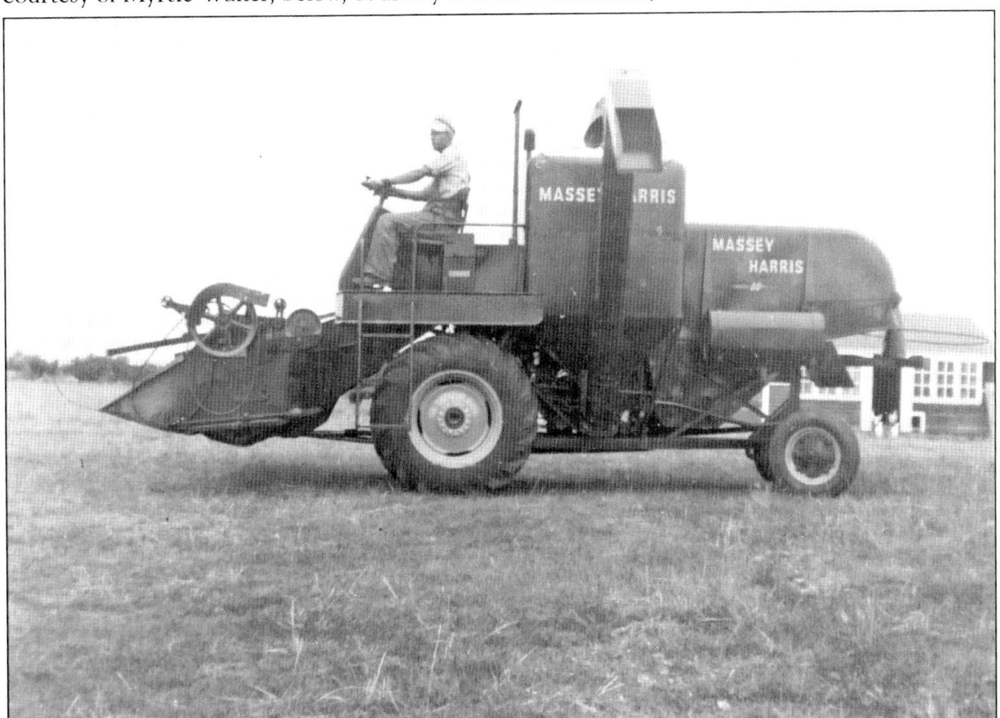

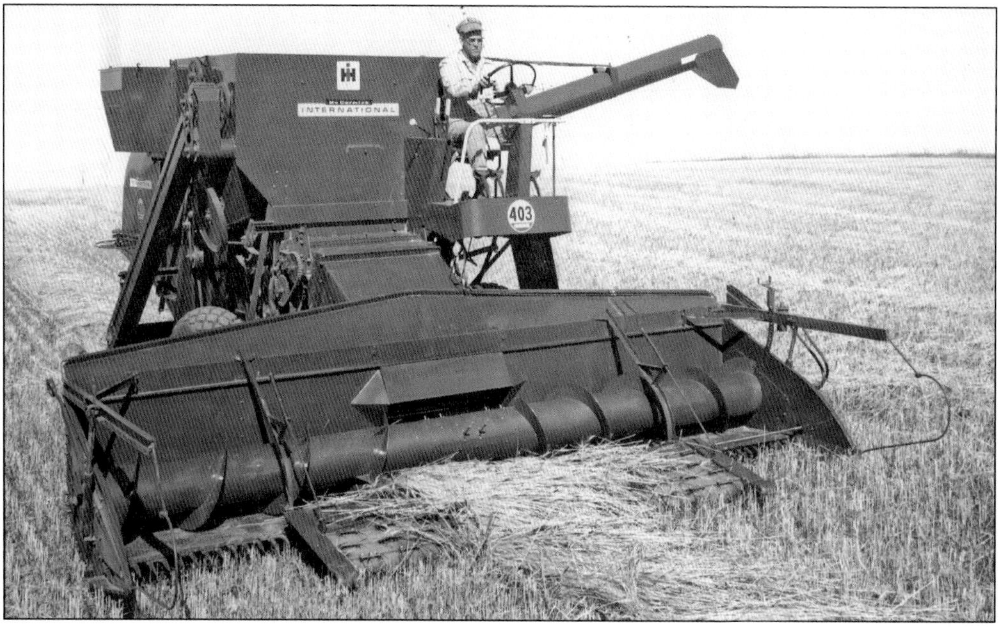

Marvin Wagnild of Outlook is shown in the above photograph field-testing his brand-new International Harvester Model 403, probably in the fall of 1962. The Model 403 was IH's most popular combine of the 1960s, but still did not offer what has today become standard equipment: an air-conditioned cab. Seen below are members of a harvest crew at the Gordon Hovet farm in 1972. Shown are, from left to right, Pete Scully, Max Rasmussen, Harold Hovet, Don Hovet, Bob Spoklie, Jack Rasmussen, and Jon Rasmussen. The Oliver 430 combine behind them debuted on the market in 1963 and boasted 93 horsepower, according to the book *Oliver Hart-Parr.* Nearly 50 years later, John Deere combines claim 400 to 600 horsepower. (Above, courtesy of Marvin Wagnild; below, courtesy of Jack Rasmussen.)

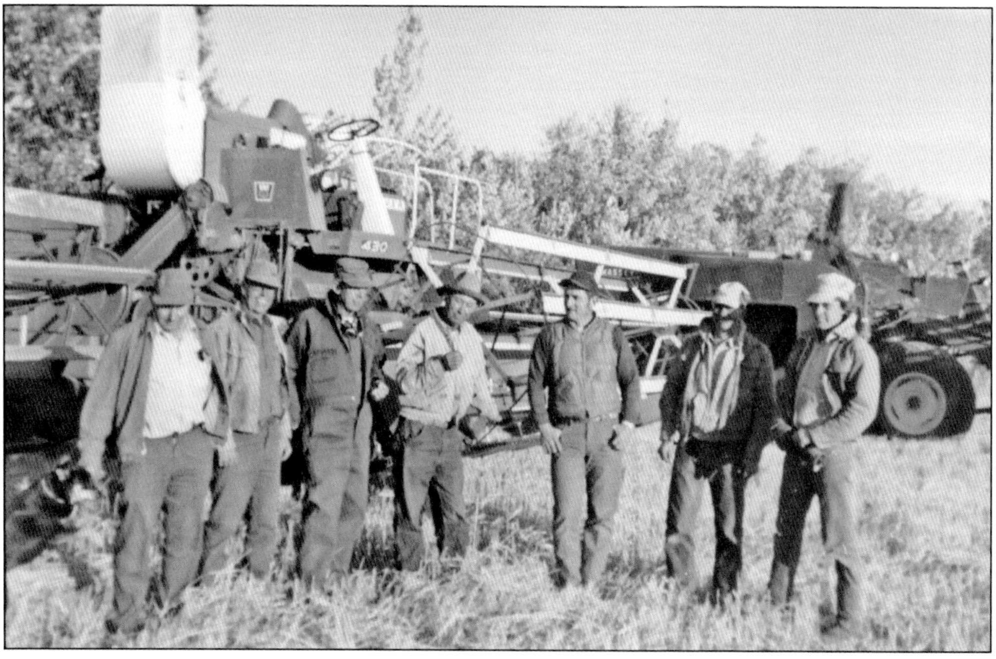

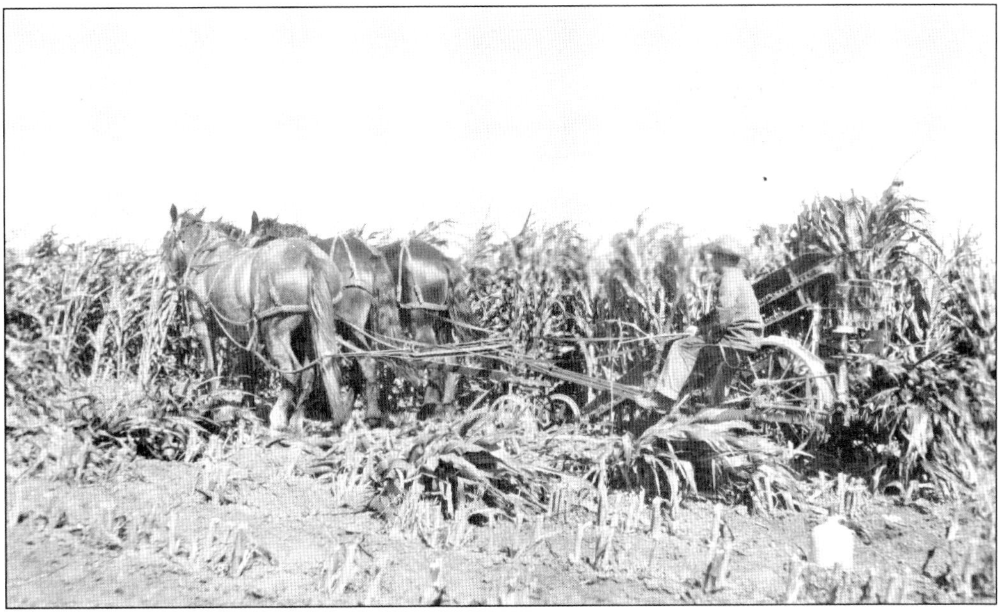

With a long growing season, corn was the last crop to be harvested before winter. In the photograph above, Art Hagan of the Wolf Creek area harvests corn that will be shocked and transported to the homestead to serve as fodder for his cattle and pigs. In the area of Plentywood now known as the Woodland Addition, corn once grew. Below, children play among the shocks south of the Riba house, built by Adolph and Mae Rue Riba in 1913. The water tower, filled from wells in the valley, served the town of Plentywood. (Above, courtesy of Eugene Hagan; below, courtesy of the Sheridan County Museum.)

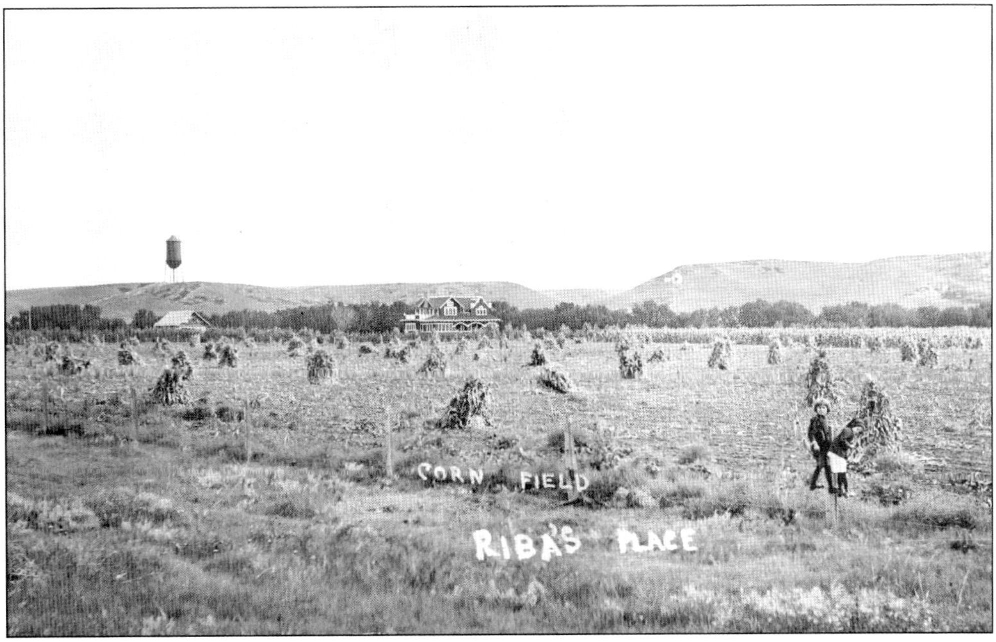

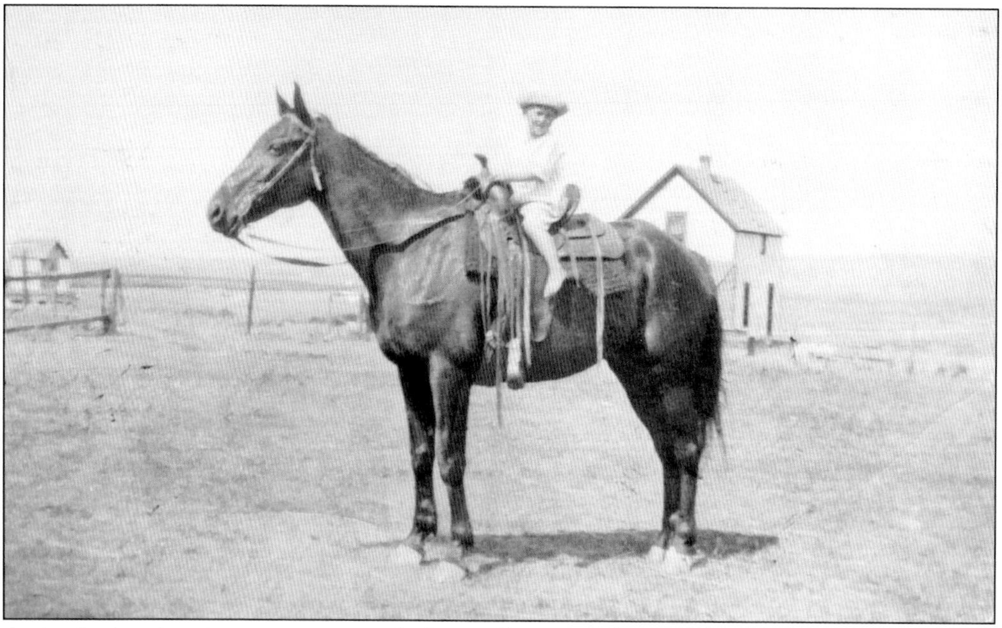

Animals played an important part in the lives of homesteaders and their children. A beloved pet of Harvey French, Nick the horse, had been left in the care of the Hugh French family south of Redstone by their bachelor neighbor, Bill McDougal. They owned Nick for 20 years until he died in 1936. Below, Joe Becker goes for a ride with the guidance of his oldest sister, Agnes. They were two of Joseph and Appolonia Schmidt Becker's six children. The Becker parents were born in Romania and married in 1907 before immigrating to Saskatchewan in 1914. Later, they settled in the Raymond area. (Above, courtesy of Ardelle French; below, courtesy of Marlene Bummer.)

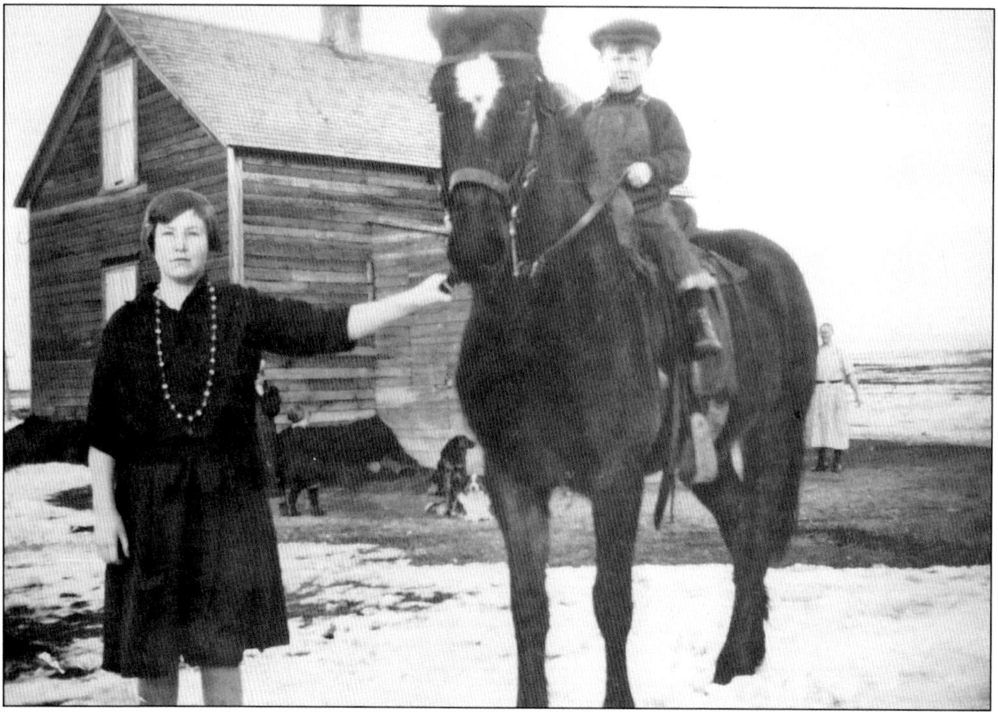

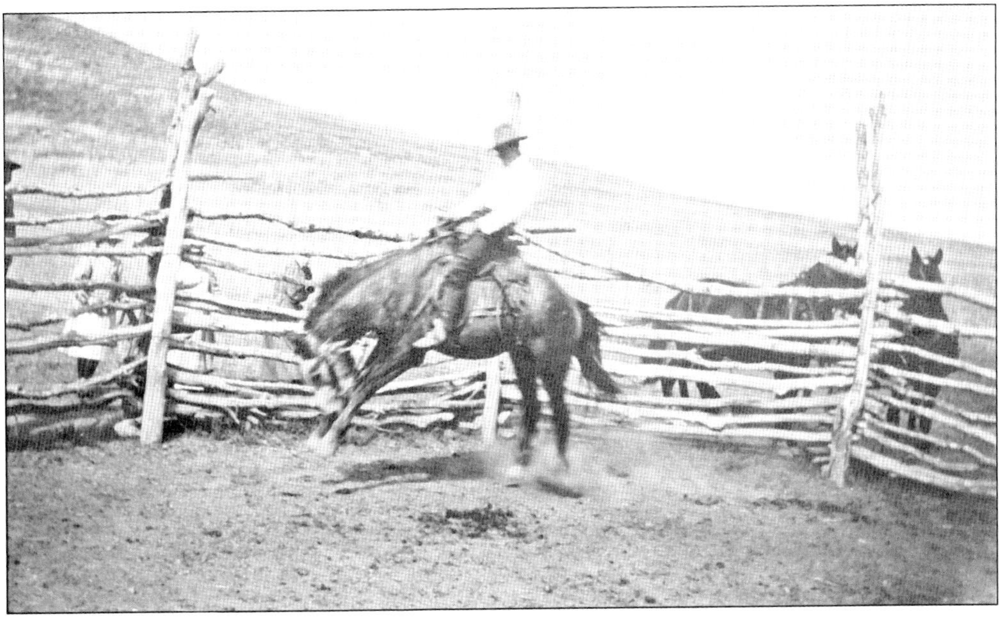

Dick Savage is shown above breaking one of the many horses on Frank Nichols's homestead southwest of Plentywood. His parents, Henry and Emma Fough Savage, homesteaded in 1905. Just five years later, Henry fell from a loaded wagon, was run over, and died, leaving behind his wife and two young children. Albert Walikonis (below) was born to Lithuanian immigrants Joe and Mary Walikonis, who came to the Reserve area in 1919. Walikonis raises sheep on his parents' homestead, noting that "their love is genuine for their caregiver and they are suspicious of strangers." (Above, courtesy of May Budke; below, courtesy of Albert Walikonis.)

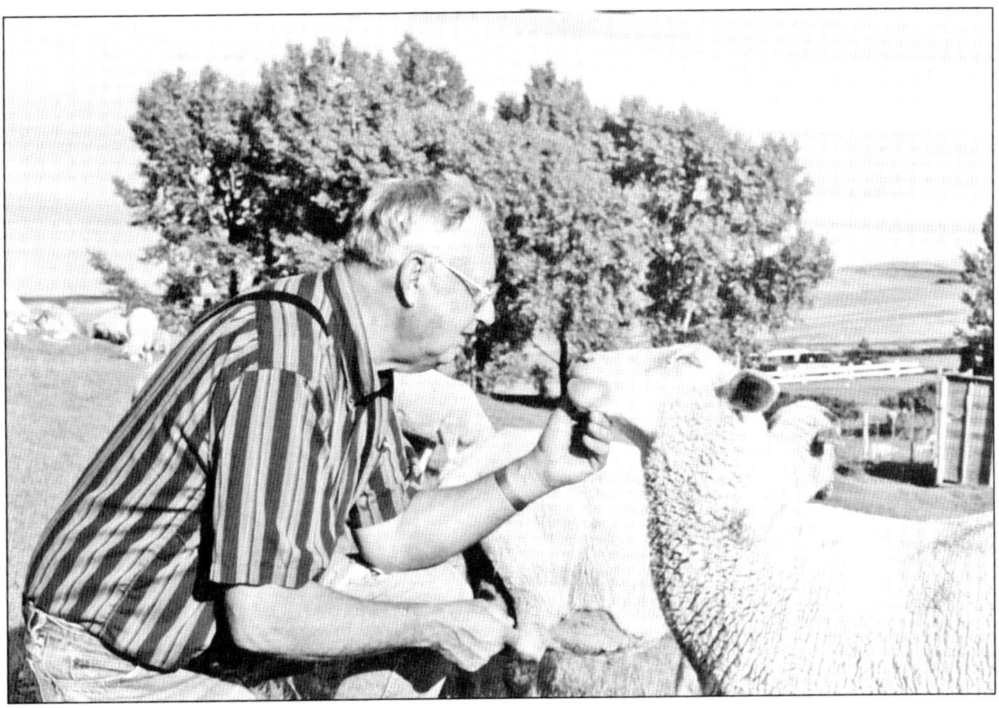

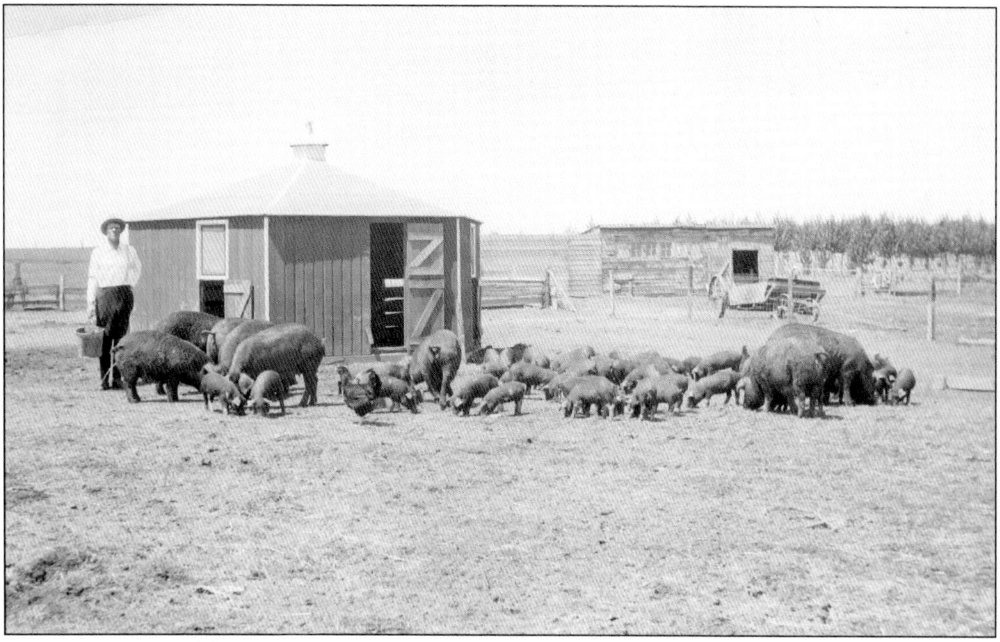

John Norbo arrived from North Dakota in 1907, settling three miles south of present-day Medicine Lake and marrying Nellie McElwain. Norbo is shown above feeding his pigs in 1925. When his health failed in the 1930s, Norbo's only child, Walt, took over the farm. He and his wife, Julia, raised three children on the farm. It was not uncommon for farm families to care for orphaned animals, including fawns, which could be easily tamed. In the photograph below, taken in the early 1950s, Patsy Norbo perches on a truck bumper and her pet deer looks on as her father, Walt, unloads grain. (Both, courtesy of Patsy Morstad.)

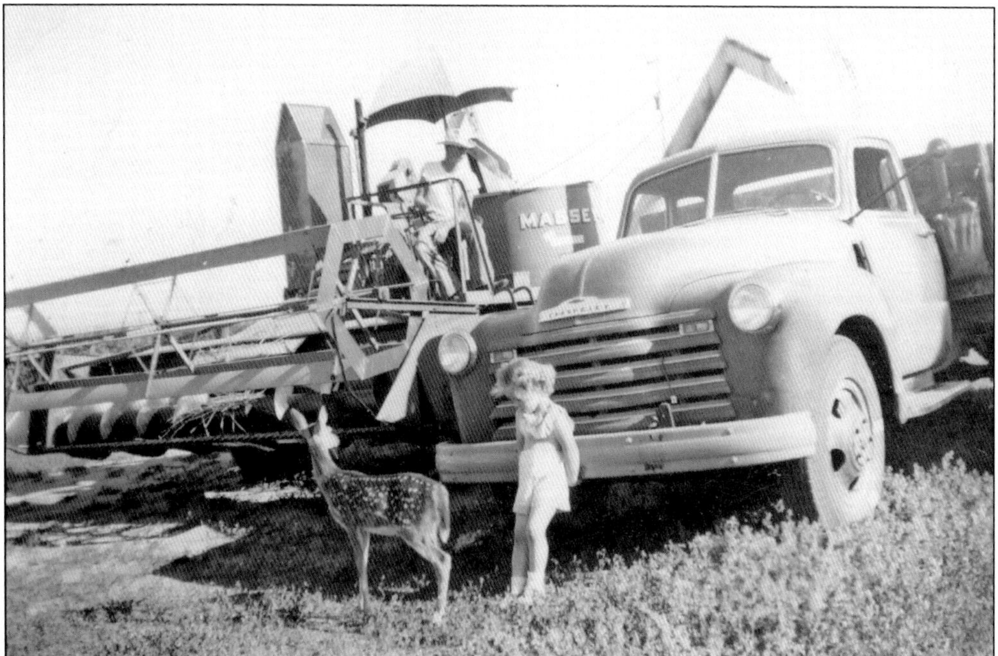

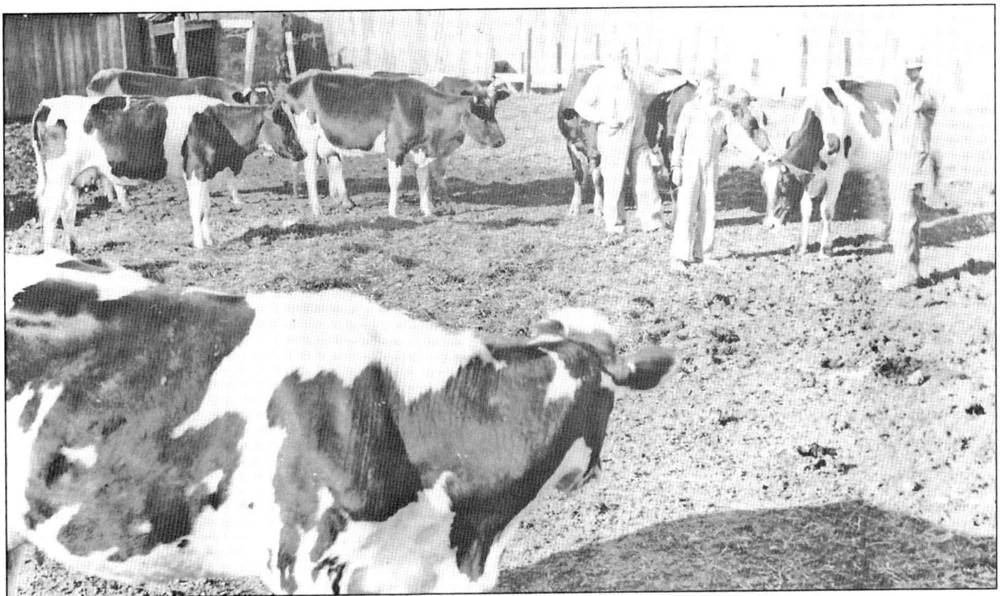

In the above photograph, Lars Angvick (left) is shown with his son, John (center), and the county agent checking cows in 1934, as Agnes the cow observes from the foreground. Angvick came from Wisconsin in 1918 and married Beatrice Vincentsen, also of Wisconsin, the following year. They bought the former Romine homestead southeast of Reserve and raised five children. Angvick was civic-minded and took part in community, county, and state affairs. Shown below in a 1952 photograph are Jack Rasmussen and his daughters Vicki (center) and Wanda feeding chickens on their farm northeast of Antelope. (Above, courtesy of Marbea Lane; below, courtesy of Jack Rasmussen.)

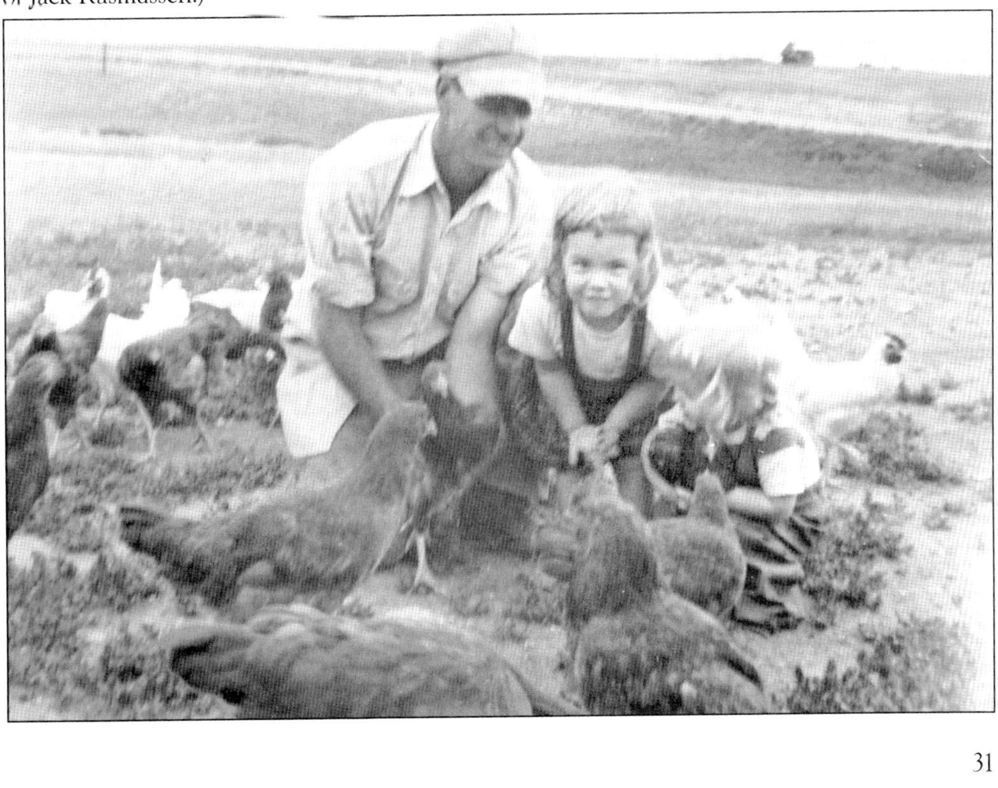

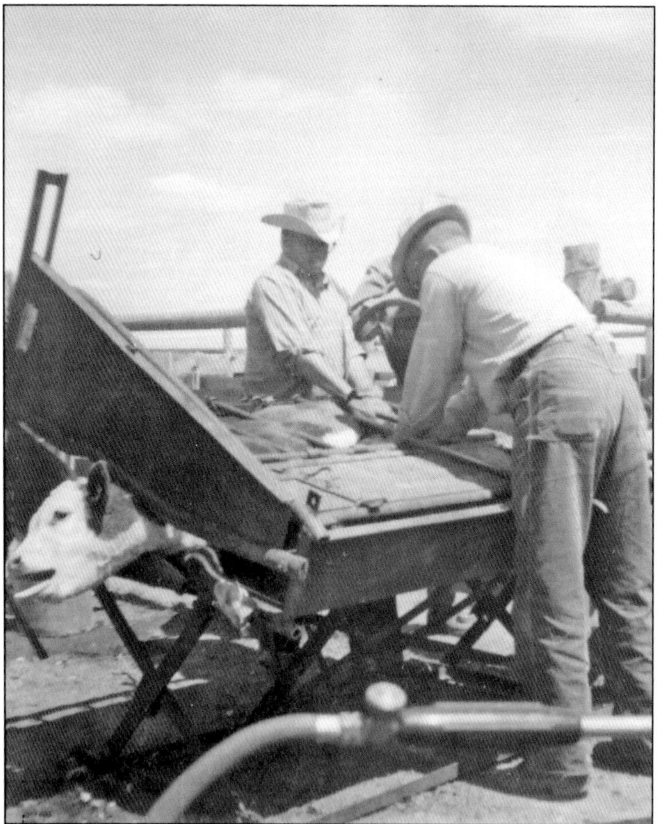

Branding day is under way at the Frank French ranch (left). French came from Ohio in 1906 to stake his claim southeast of what is now Medicine Lake, returning to Ohio to court and then marry Susan Fry, who accompanied him to Montana as his bride in 1909. They farmed and later expanded into ranching; at one point, they owned 200 cattle, 50 horses, and 3,500 sheep. Shown below are some of the participants in the 1963 Big Muddy Bull Sale, held at the fairgrounds in Plentywood. Posing here are, from left to right, Art Haugen and Arnold Joyes of Comertown, Waldo Morstad of Raymond, Charlie Johnson of Savage, and Joe Eggen of Archer. (Left, courtesy of Jeanne French; below, photograph by Glyn Deem, courtesy of Patsy Morstad.)

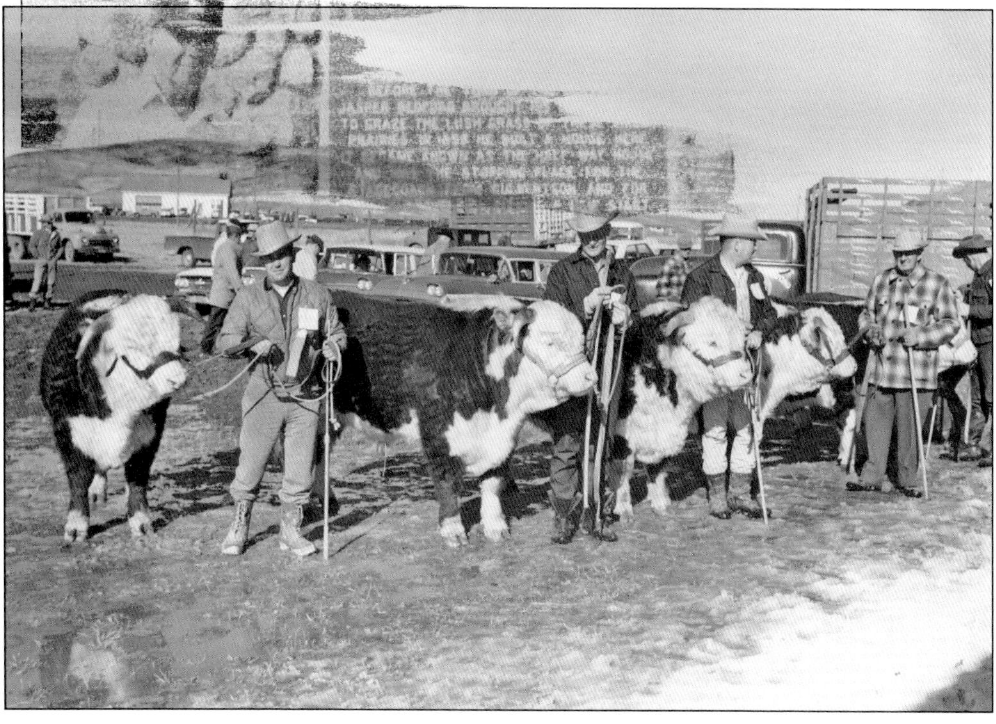

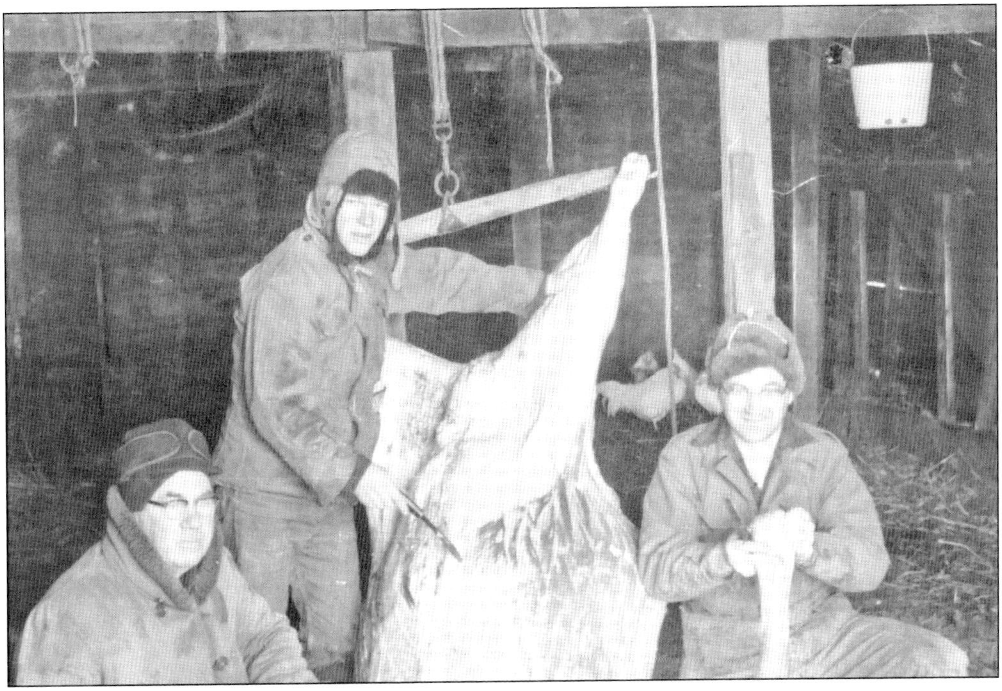

Butchering is the logical but not always pleasant outcome of raising livestock. Above, Selmer Espeland (left) and his sons Dennis (center) and Richard do the winter's butchering in McElroy. Before electric refrigeration, families relied on icehouses, pits dug roughly four to six feet deep and topped by a shack. Ice blocks about three feet square were cut from ponds or creeks and stacked in the pit before being covered with straw. Butchered meat and other perishables were stored on the ice, which did not melt until well into the summer months. Homesteaders also canned meat, rendered lard, and put up all types of fruits and vegetables, allowing them to enjoy the bounty of the season's hard work throughout the year, as did the Joe and Elda Kowski family of Outlook, seen in the stereograph below. (Above, courtesy of Richard Espeland; below, courtesy of Don McCrory).

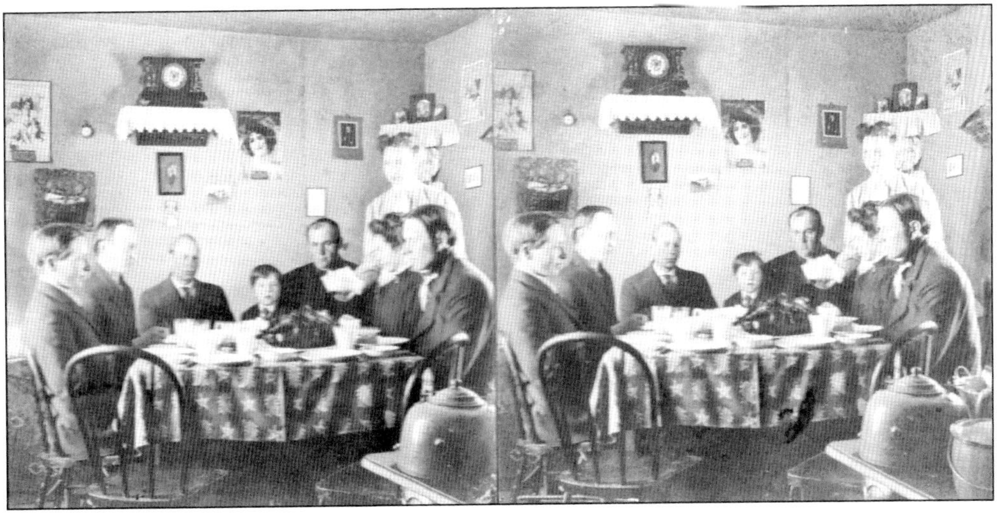

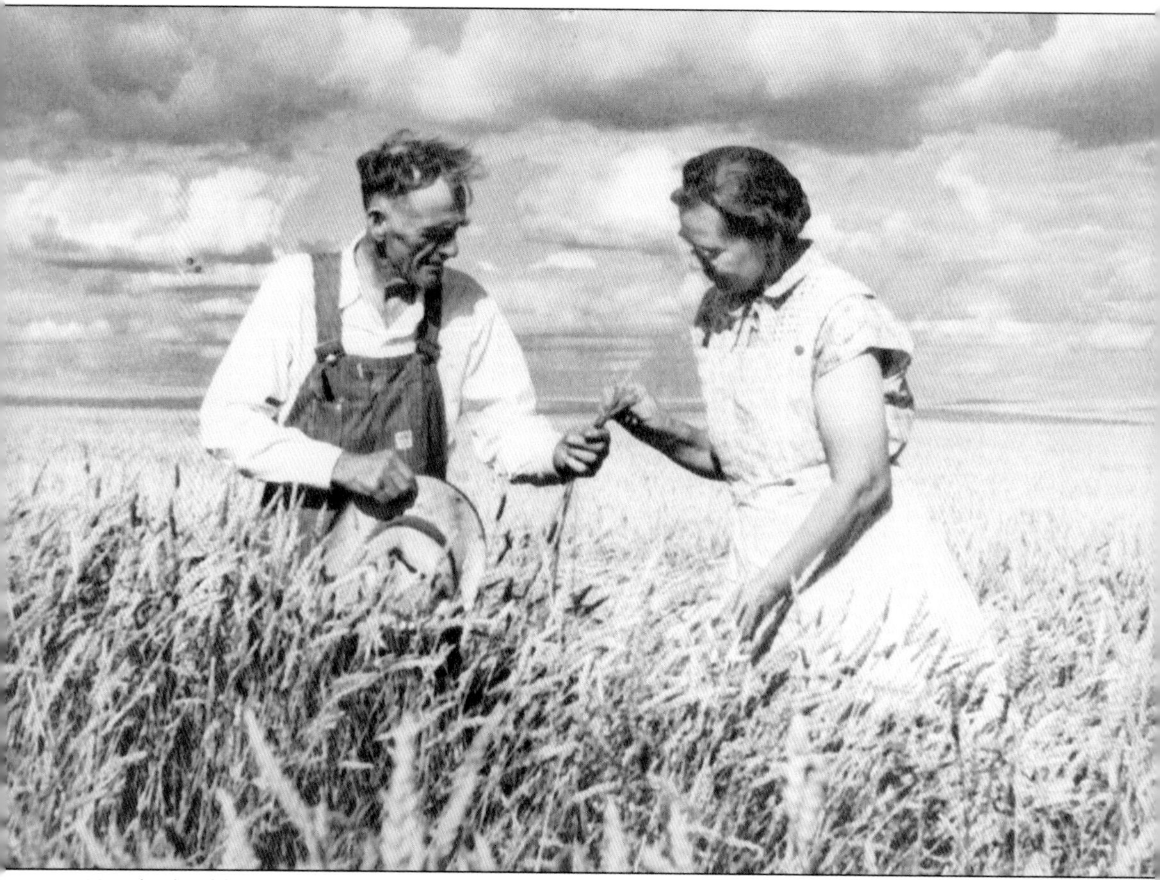

Hundreds of families who homesteaded in Sheridan County during the first two decades of the 20th century probably shared a common dream, captured in this photograph: standing in a field they owned, surveying what promised to be a bountiful harvest. The dream was often elusive. However, 1952 did produce just such a harvest for many, including Bert and Lina Selvig of Outlook. In 1908, he had homesteaded one mile from his brother Alfred; later, their parents, Harry and Else, took up a claim as well. The brothers later married Norwegian immigrant sisters, Dagmar and Lina Anderson. In this award-winning 1952 photograph by their son-in-law Eustace Hill, entitled *The Reward of Toil*, Bert and Lina examine their wheat crop. Today, a member of the seventh generation of Selvig descendants, Briahnna Ordahl, is growing up on the farm homesteaded by Harry and Else Selvig more than 100 years ago. (Courtesy of Roald Selvig.)

Three

HOMETOWNS

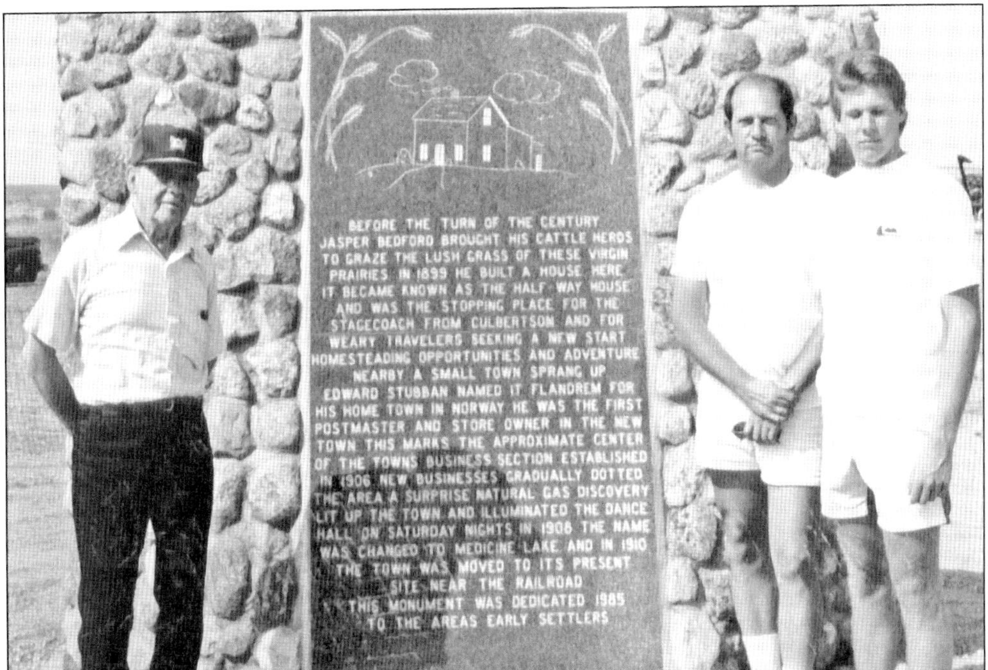

Medicine Lake, which was originally called Flandrem, dates to 1899, with the arrival of Jasper Bedford. The town moved one mile south when the Great Northern railroad extended northward in 1910. Flandrem's first postmaster was Edward Stubban. Three generations of his descendants, John Arnt (left), John Howard (second from left), and John Phillip Stubban, are shown by a monument dedicated in 1985 at the site of "old" Medicine Lake. (Courtesy of Lorraine Johnson.)

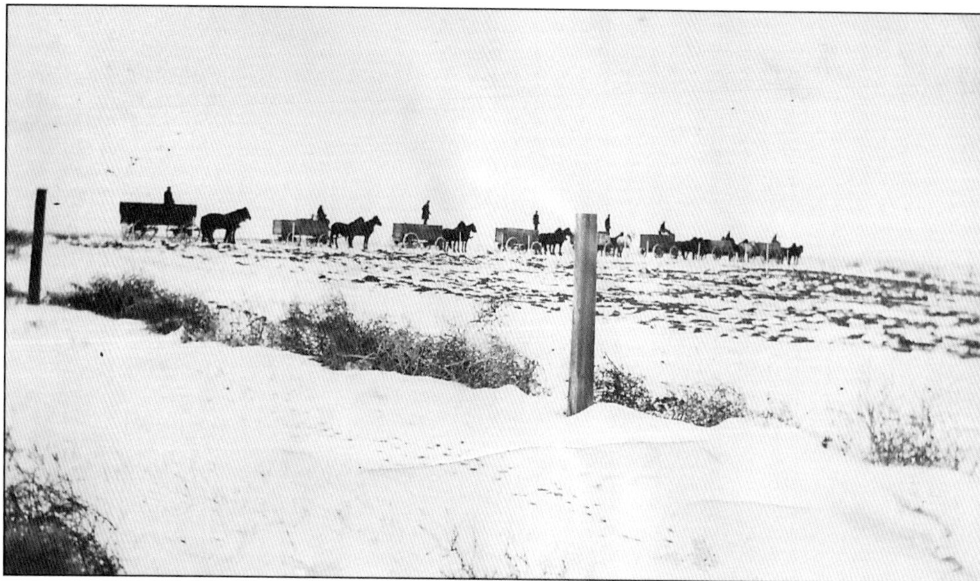

As the Great Northern and Soo Line railroads extended their reach, towns grew up roughly every seven miles or, like Medicine Lake, moved to the railroad. When the Great Northern arrived in 1910, the town of Reserve gained a depot and a post office. Its name referred to the Fort Peck Indian Reservation; before that, the Sioux had called the area Wakea, meaning "shelter." Above, the men of Reserve are shown in 1912 making the 14-mile trip to Coalridge for coal. Further up the road was Antelope, which began as a post office and store in a homesteader's house. Antelope was chosen in 1966 as the namesake for a United States naval gunboat. In the below photograph, 20 Antelope residents attend the 1967 commissioning ceremony of the USS *Antelope* in Tacoma, Washington. (Above, courtesy of Marbea Lane; below, courtesy of Don Hedges.)

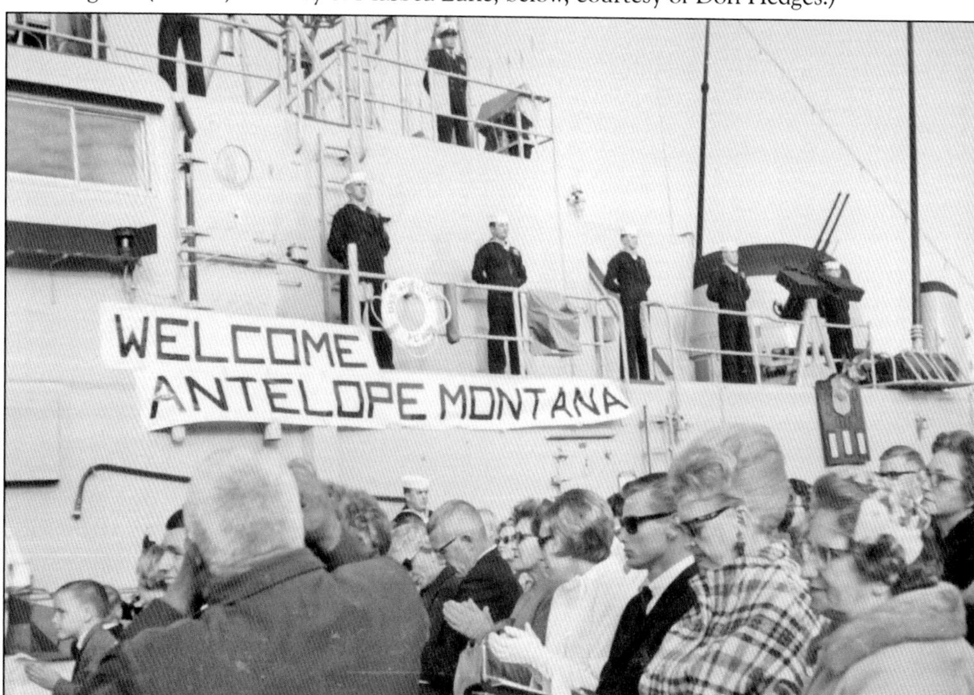

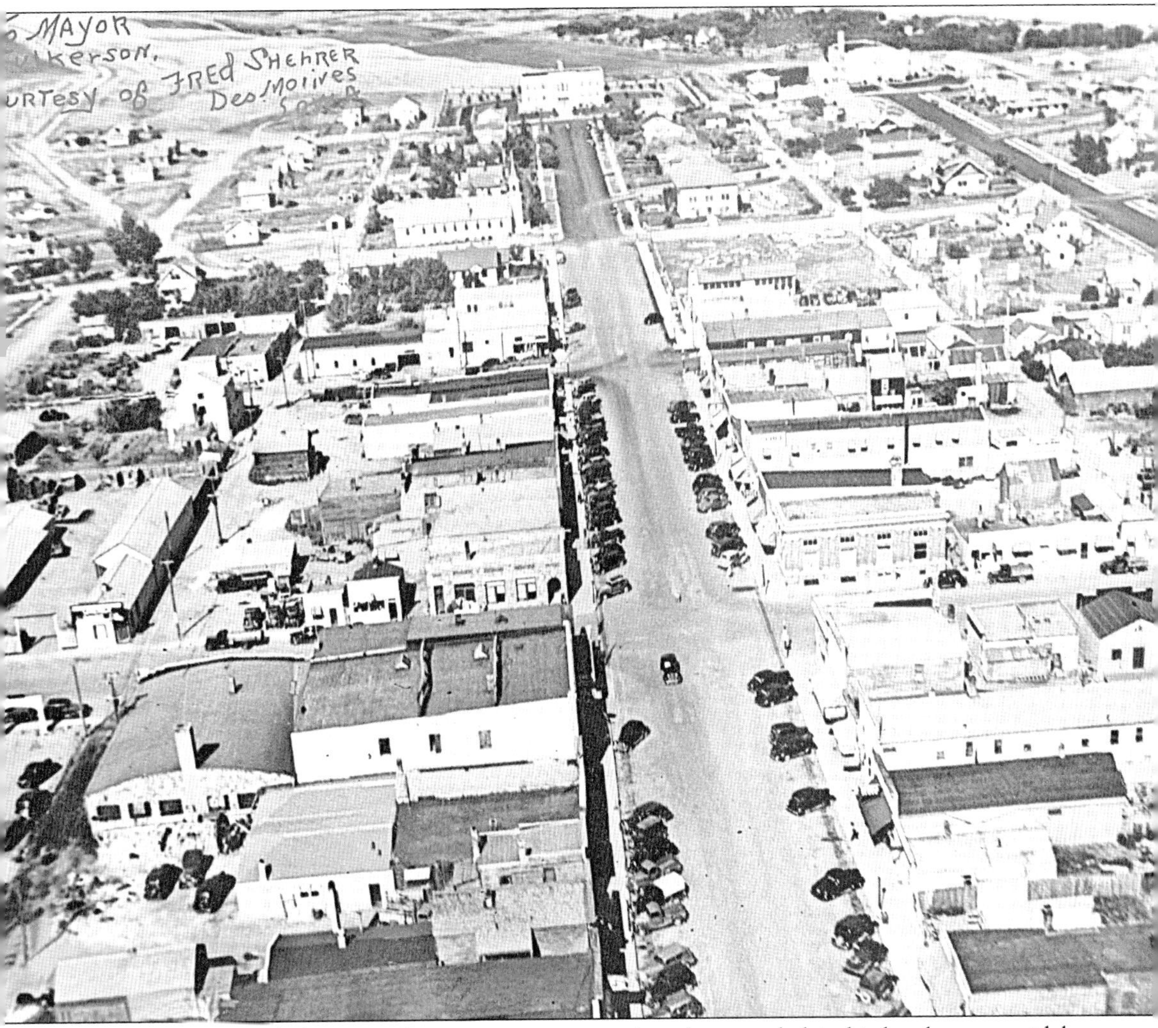

The true origin of Plentywood's name is uncertain, but the story behind it has become widely accepted. Legend has it that notorious cattle rustler "Dutch" Henry Ieuch advised a group of cowboys that, if they followed the creek, they would find "plenty wood." When Bill and Martha Stewart homesteaded a few miles west of present-day Plentywood in 1902, they chose this name for the post office they set up in their home. The homestead was later purchased by Forrest and Alice Goodman, who maintained the post office. In the meantime, George and Gertie Bolster, who had homesteaded a few miles to the east along Box Elder Creek, established a store, restaurant, and rooming house known as Bolster House. Bolster would be known as the father of Plentywood, and the post office moved to town from the Goodman ranch in 1905. This aerial photograph of Plentywood was taken in the late 1930s, following the construction of the county courthouse, a Work Projects Administration project. (Photograph by Fred Scherer, courtesy of Dave Fulkerson.)

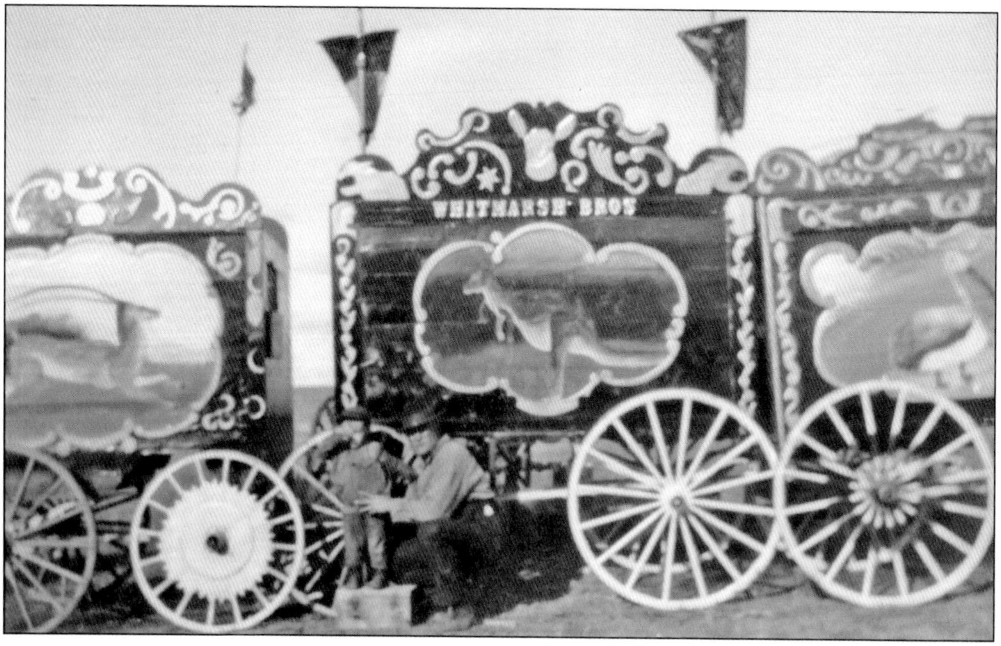

As the Great Northern made its way west from Plentywood, it stopped in Archer, which had been named for the homesteader William Archer. Local resident William Whitmarsh designed, carved, and painted circus wagons in the late 1920s and early 1930s, as shown above. Further west, the train stopped at Redstone. It had been settled in 1900 by Olaf and Mary Bergh, who moved their store and post office twice in anticipation of the railroad's arrival. Local residents considered naming their community Red Rock, Coal Creek, and Beaver Creek before finally settling on Redstone. Pictured below are members of the Redstone band in 1915. (Above, courtesy of Millie Marsh; below, courtesy of Florence Rasmussen.)

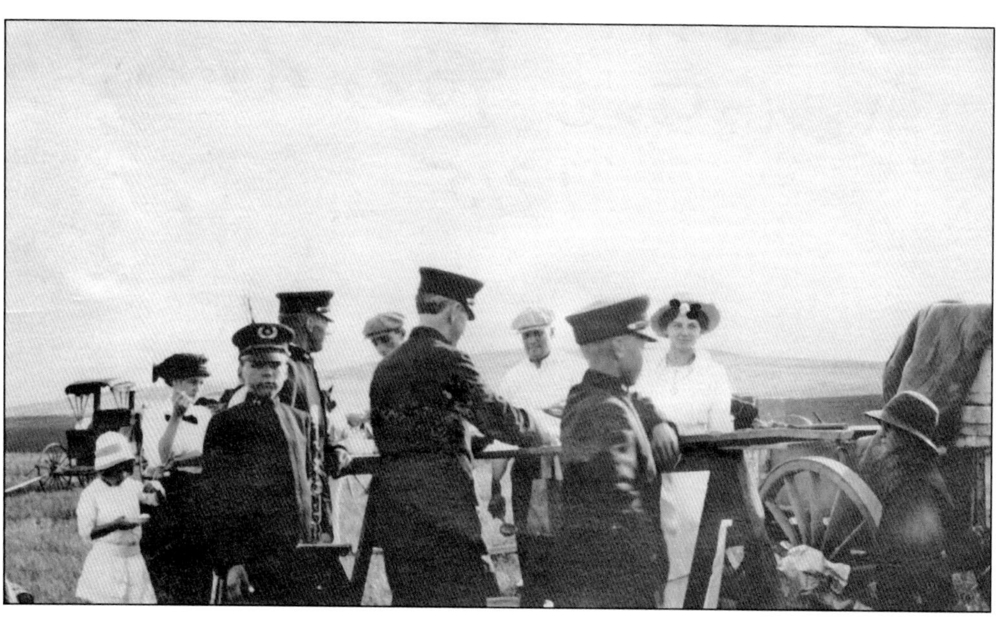

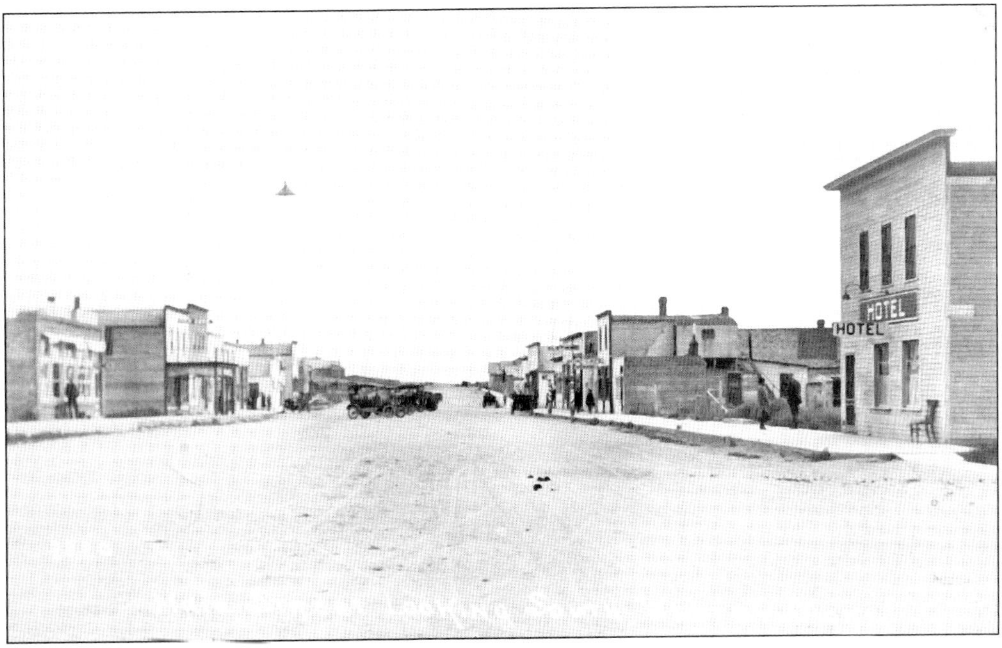

Like Redstone, the town of Westby was moved from its first location, in North Dakota. Settled by Danish immigrants who added the Danish word *by*, meaning town, to "west," the town was originally about three miles southeast of its present site. When the Soo Line was set to extend west in 1913, the comparatively higher freight rates in Montana apparently influenced the decision to move Westby over the border. The above photograph of a Westby street scene was taken in the mid-1920s. The next stop on the Soo was McElroy, named after local brothers John, William, and Bernard McElroy. The town had a grain elevator and grade school until 1948. Its last teacher before closure was Richard Espeland of the McElroy community. Members of his family are shown below during the harvest of 1942. (Above, courtesy of Ken Keldsen; below, courtesy of Richard Espeland.)

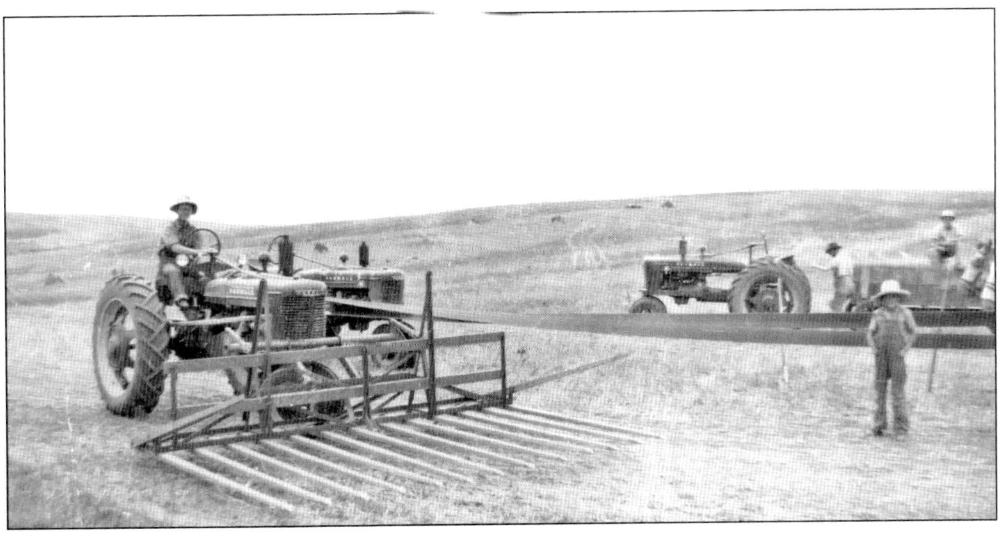

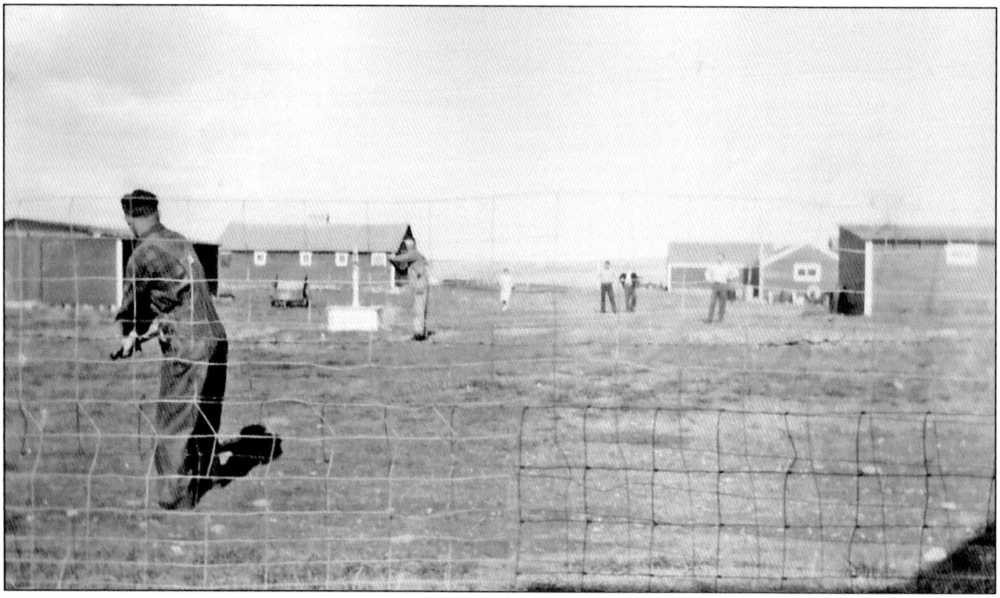

From McElroy, the Soo Line continued on to Comertown, named after the landowner on whose property the town was established, W.W. Comer. Above, Waldemar Lane is at bat in a 1948 family baseball game on his Comertown farm. West of Comertown was the Dooley community, named for homesteader W.D. Dooley. Some of the community's children are shown below in 1945. Posing outside are, from left to right, (first row) Leslie Anderson, Ronald Johnson, Virginia Ruggles, Lovina Johnson, Sharon Grendahl, and Roger Nelson; (second row) Lloyd Anderson, Marilyn Goetzinger, Trudy Grendahl, Bertha Falk, Chester Goetzinger, Olaf Johnson, and Mari Laverdure; (third row) Calvin Nelson, Ruth Griffin, Genevieve Ruggles, Gertrude Laverdure, Nora Laverdure, and Duane Falk. (Above, courtesy of Marbea Lane; below, courtesy of Bertha Anderson.)

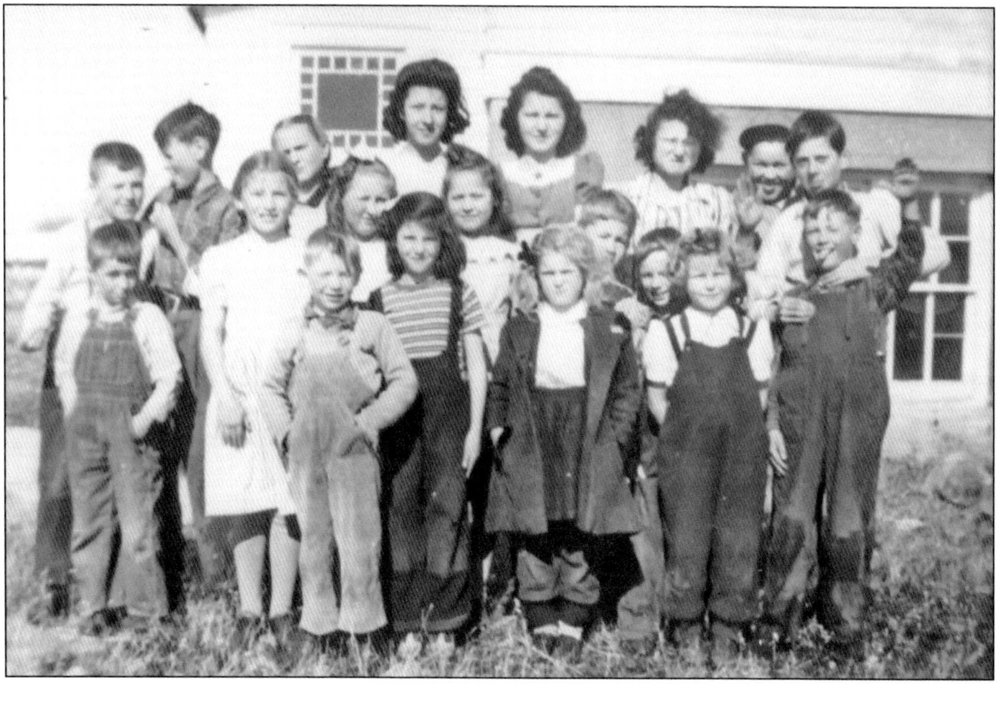

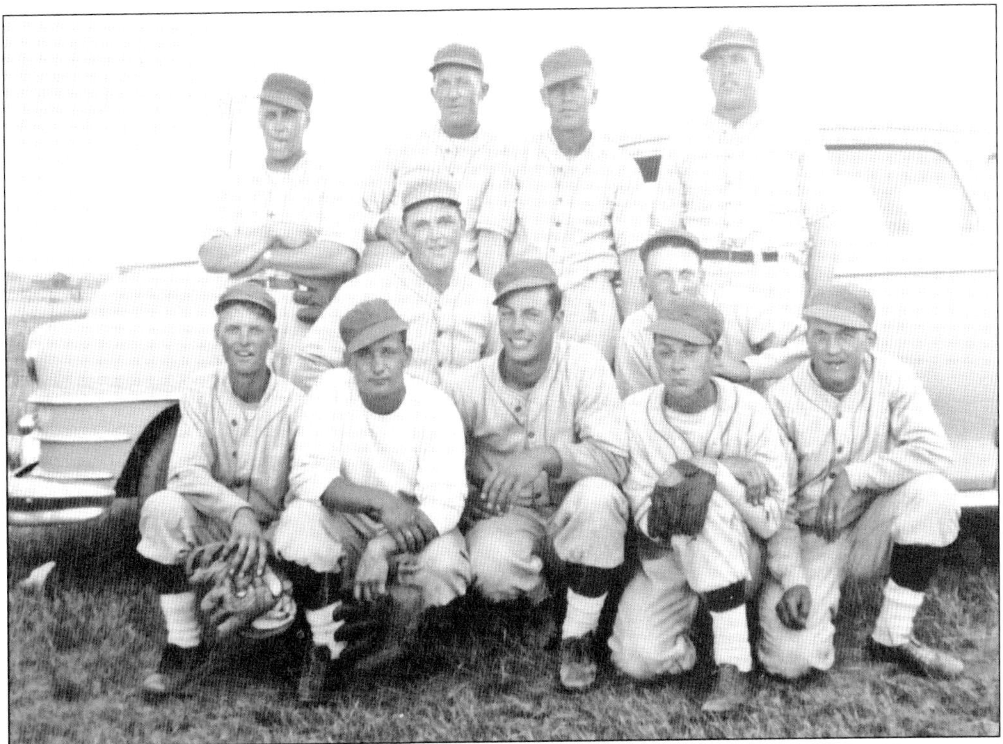

The fifth Soo Line town in Montana was named after landowner Joe Raymond, despite Plentywood businessman Adolph Riba's lobbying to give it his name. The 1950 Raymond baseball team members shown above are, from left to right, (first row) Ed Heisler, Griff Collins, Howard Syme, Calvin Syme, and Gene Paulson; (second row) Jack Westphal and Delmar Stadstad; (third row) Bob Wankel, Merrill Wankel, Neil Huffman, and Don Blair. A plateau northwest of Plentywood was called the Outlook Bench because of its scenic view of the valley where Highway 5 now runs. Like other towns, Outlook pulled up stakes when the Soo Line arrived in 1913, moving roughly two and a half miles southeast of its original site. Below, members of the 1912 Bench Browns pose for a photograph. Shown here are, from left to right, George "Shorty" Bantz, Ed Hill, Earl Nickerson, Harry Willard, and Elmer Nickerson. (Above, courtesy of Roxy Westphal; below, courtesy of Jack Nickerson.)

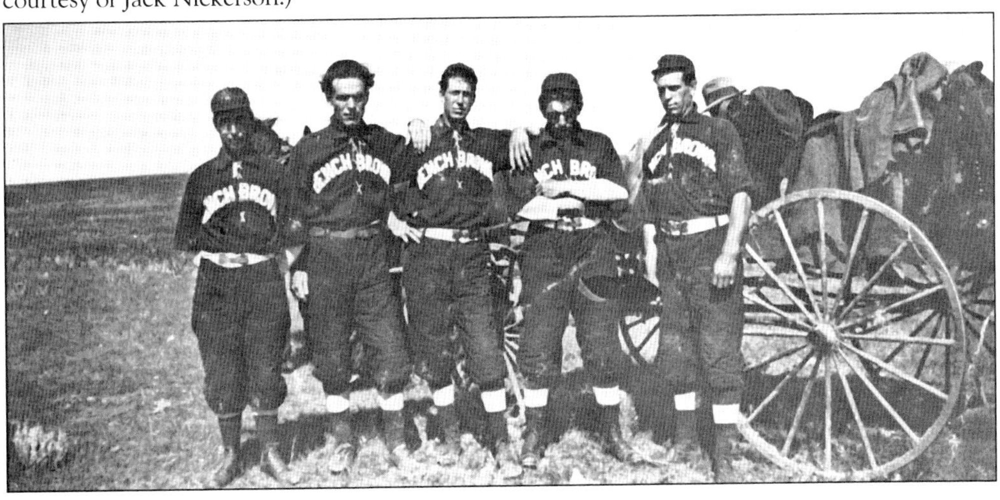

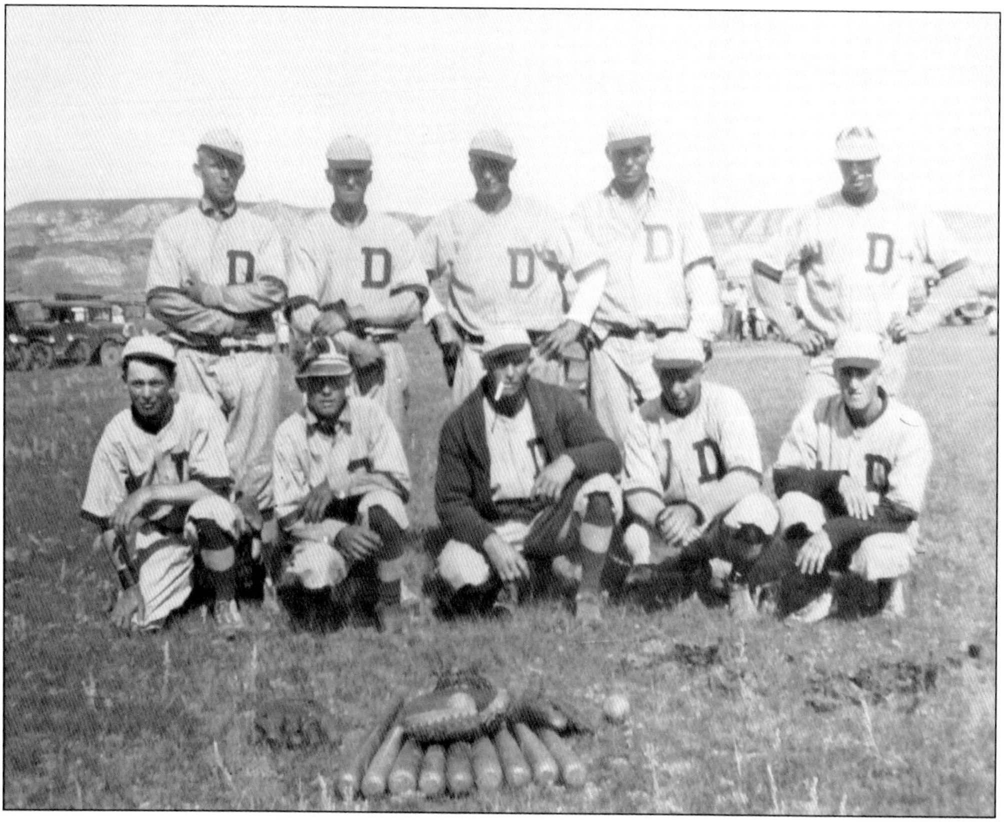

Daleview was the last stop on the Soo Line before its terminus in Whitetail. Its name dates to the early 1900s, when it was the postal delivery address for mail brought by stagecoach to the Cartwright Wager ranch. The community baseball team, shown in 1929, includes, from left to right, (first row) Karl Bantz, Fred Christenson, Elmer Chaffee, Ralph Chaffee, and John Desonia; (second row) Hargo Christenson, Frank Desonia, Earl Chaffee, Walt Lee, and Norman Chaffee. Across the county to the east was the town of Dagmar. Its band members are shown below in 1912. (Above, courtesy of Gary Lee; below, courtesy of Norman Jensen.)

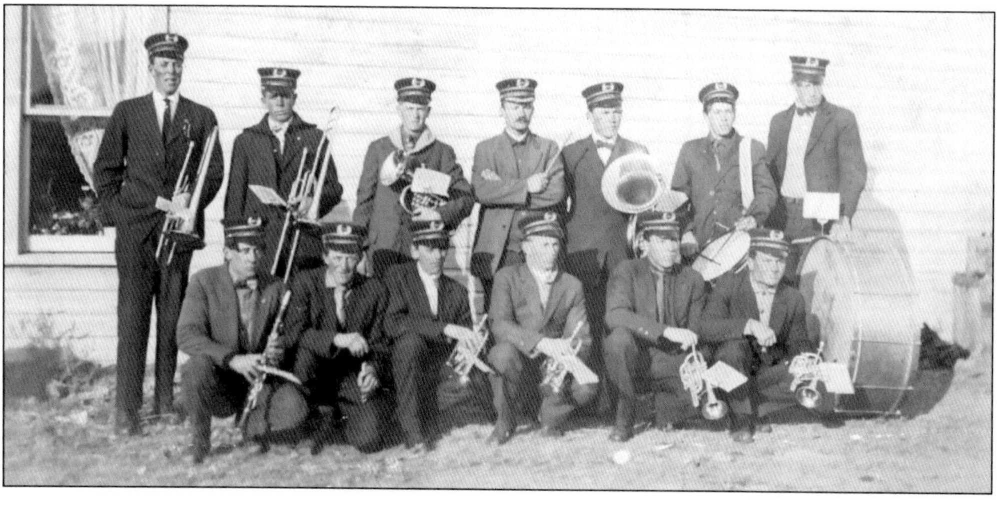

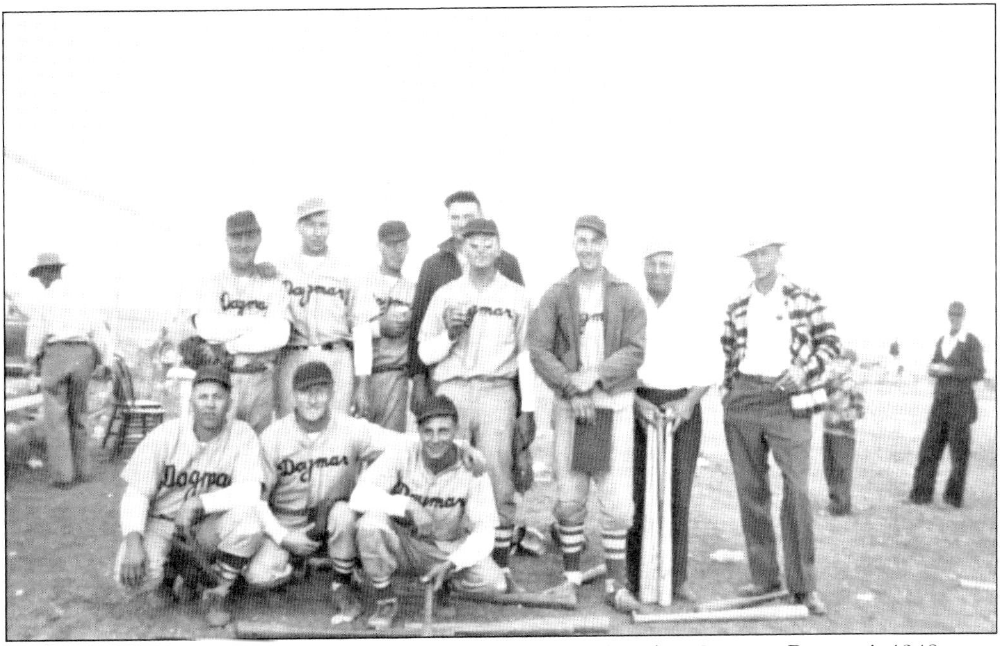

For many years, baseball was the most popular sport in Sheridan County. Dagmar's 1948 team includes, from left to right, (first row) Art Torgerson, Chris Rasmussen, and Otto Jensen; (second row): Buck Andersen, Ove Nielsen, Vic Torgerson, Ed Smith, Norman Jensen, Ken Nyby, Bill Andersen, and Art Jonasen. During his years as a pitcher, Smith came to be known as "Big Ed," a nickname he retained for life. North of Dagmar was "Old Coalridge," which was originally located nearly two miles northeast of the present site. In the 1939 photograph below, Acme Coal miners hold their carbide lamps. The men are, from left to right, (first row) Bert Eckanger, Hans Elmer Nielsen, Vernon Brenteson, Clarence Tommerup, and Raymond Brentesen; (second row) George Nielsen, Melvin "Fritz" Brenteson, Henry Mathisen, and Clifford "Buster" Brenteson. (Above, courtesy of Doug Smith; below, courtesy of Bernice Jacobsen.)

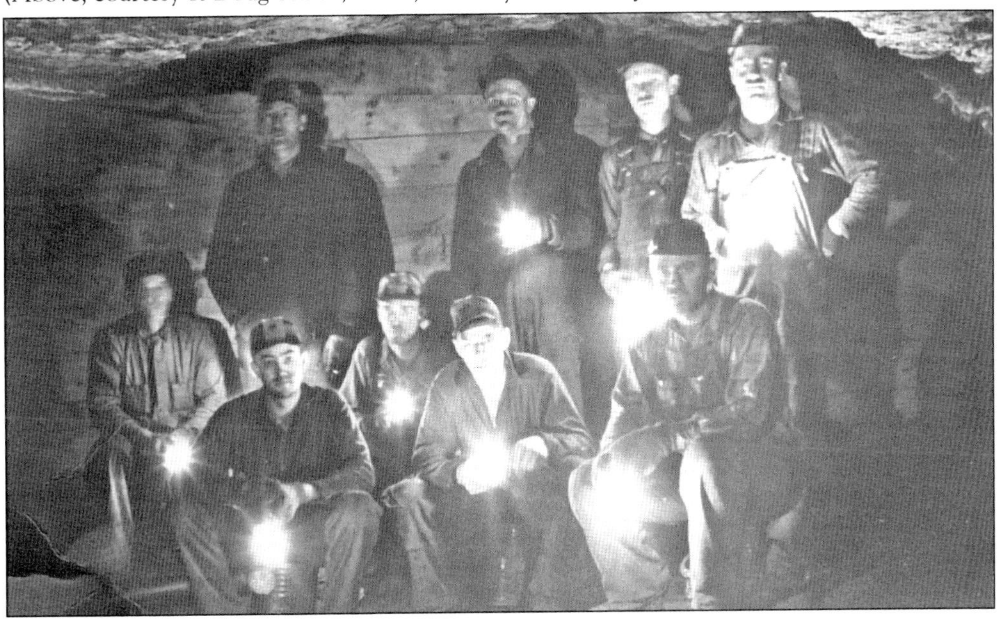

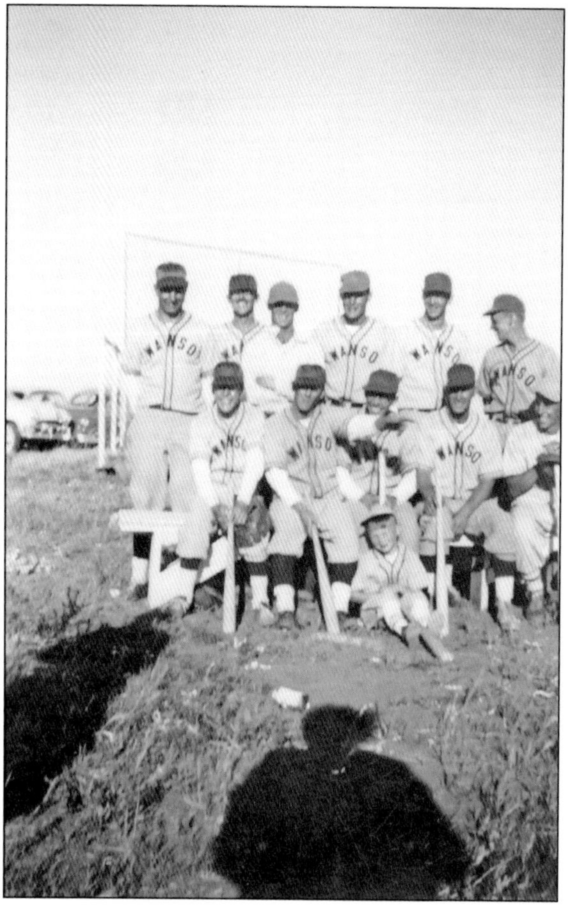

Even communities like Wanso, west of Reserve, that did not have a railroad station or post office fielded baseball teams. This 1950s group includes players such as Royal Granning, Glenn Jacobsen, Elmer Nielsen, Ivan Sebastian, Olaf Vik, and Alfred White. Although most of the towns and communities in Sheridan County were established by homesteaders, only one can claim that name: Homestead. The village went through three names—Barford, Pederson (the surname of its first postmaster and store owner), and Fort Peck—before settling on its present name in 1910. Below, harvest is in progress on the A.J. Olson homestead. (Left, courtesy of Marlene Bummer; below, courtesy of Virginia Carpenter.)

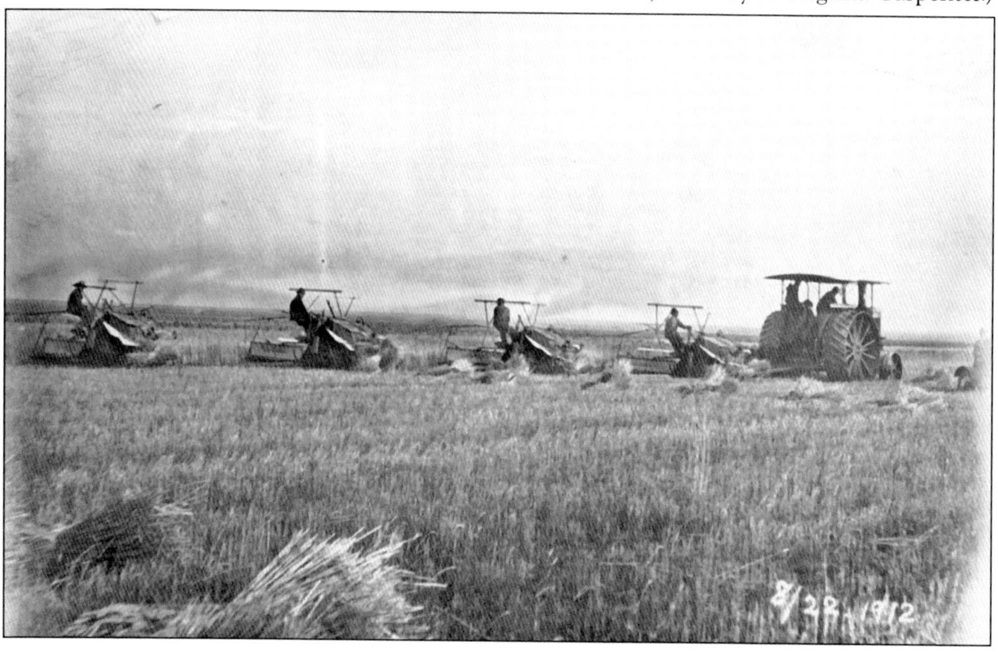

Four

Street Scenes and Businesses

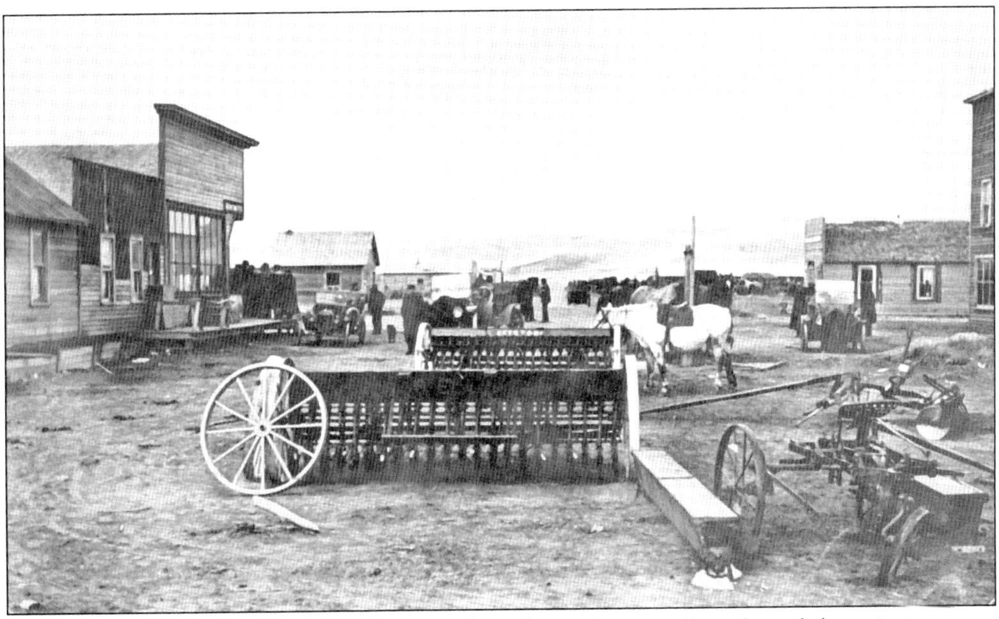

The Redstone area was home to a number of ranchers who grazed cattle and sheep in its grassy hills extending as far north as the Daleview community. The arrival of the Great Northern railroad spurred the town's growth. In 1917, Rudolph and Louella Palutzke arrived from Wisconsin, eventually building a hardware store and lumberyard, shown here, in Redstone. (Courtesy of Eugene Hagan.)

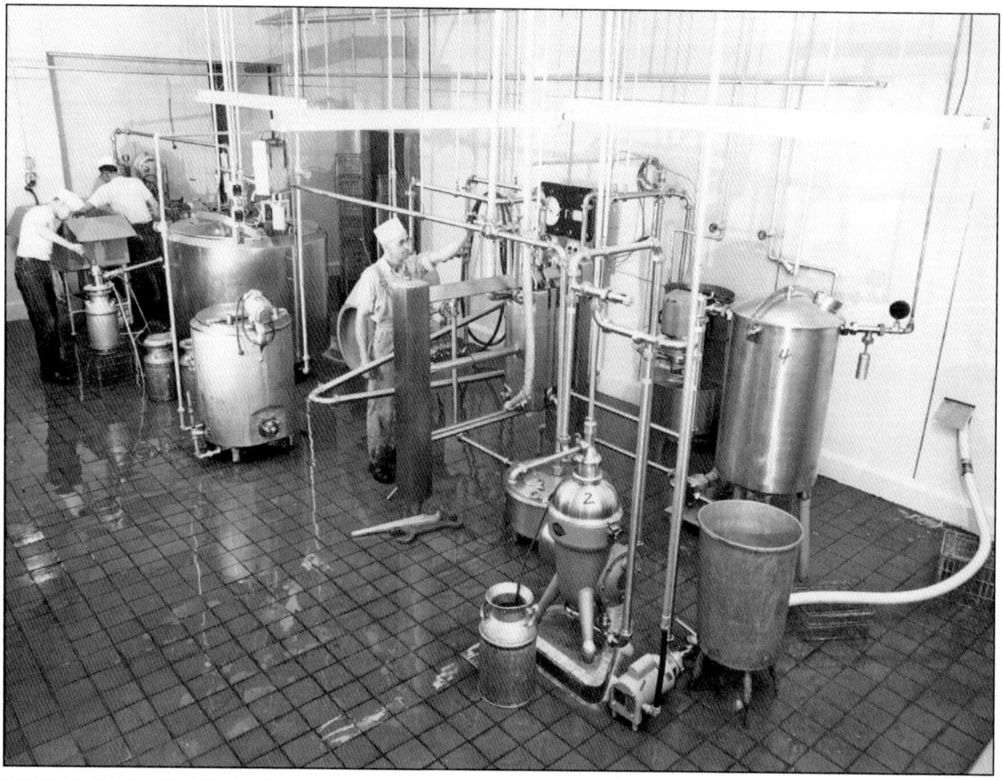

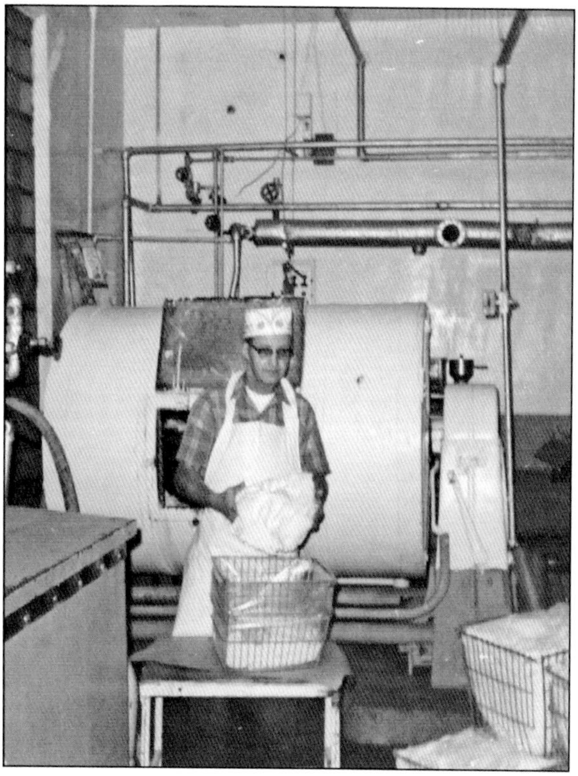

Grocery stores and restaurants in the early days depended upon local farmers for cream and home-churned butter and upon a few dairy farms that could provide larger quantities of milk. Town residents often arranged for dairy deliveries from local farmers; this weekly "cream check" was a lifesaver for many rural families in difficult times. In 1943, the Frank Power family moved to Plentywood from Crosby and built a creamery on the site of the present-day liquor store. Dairy farmers who supplied milk to the creamery included Selmer and Roy Johnson of Plentywood, Eldon Hanson, Bill Herman, and Lloyd Kittleson of Westby, and Lawrence Loupe of Raymond. Pictured above are, from left to right, creamery employees Russell Ness, Don Larson, and Tony Larson. At left, Tony Larson makes butter. (Above, photograph by Glyn Deem; both, courtesy of Don and Ginny Larson.)

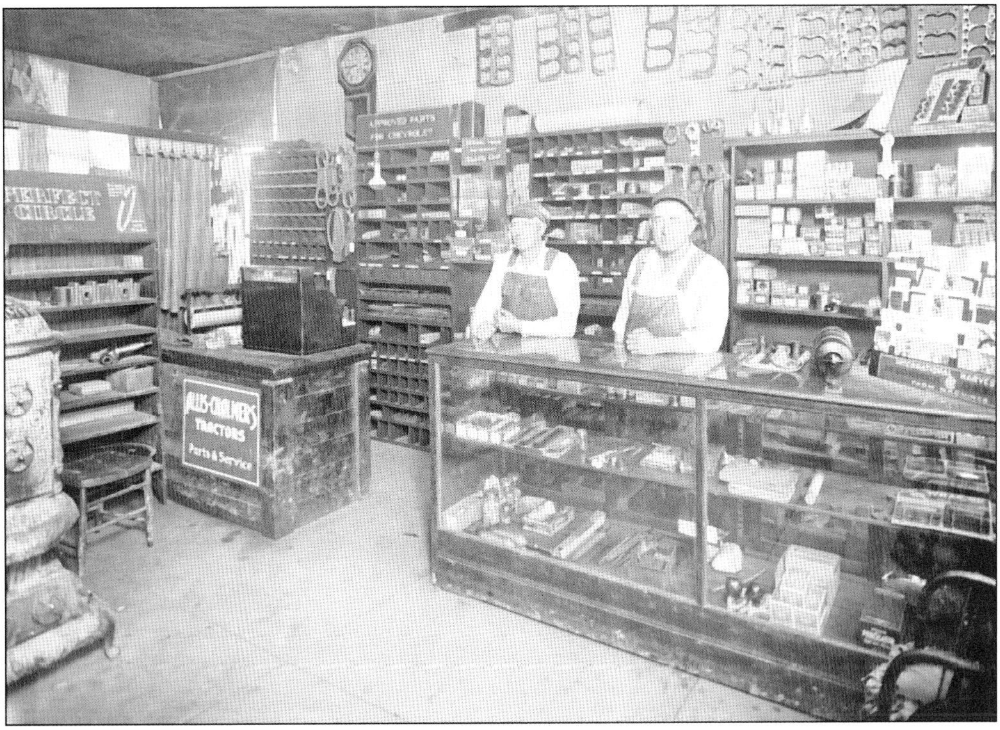

Louis Rippley Sr. came from Illinois in 1913 to his brother's homestead in the Whitetail area. Rippley worked for many farmers in the Outlook community before serving in World War I. Upon his return, he and Henry Walder became partners in farming and in the Outlook Implement Company. In the above photograph, Rippley (right) and Bob Fitzgerald are shown at the counter of the store. The third generation of Rippley's descendants continues the farming operation at the time of this publication. Below, members of the Reserve community gather for an equipment demonstration in the 1940s. (Above, courtesy of Gordon Garrick; below, courtesy of Marbea Lane.)

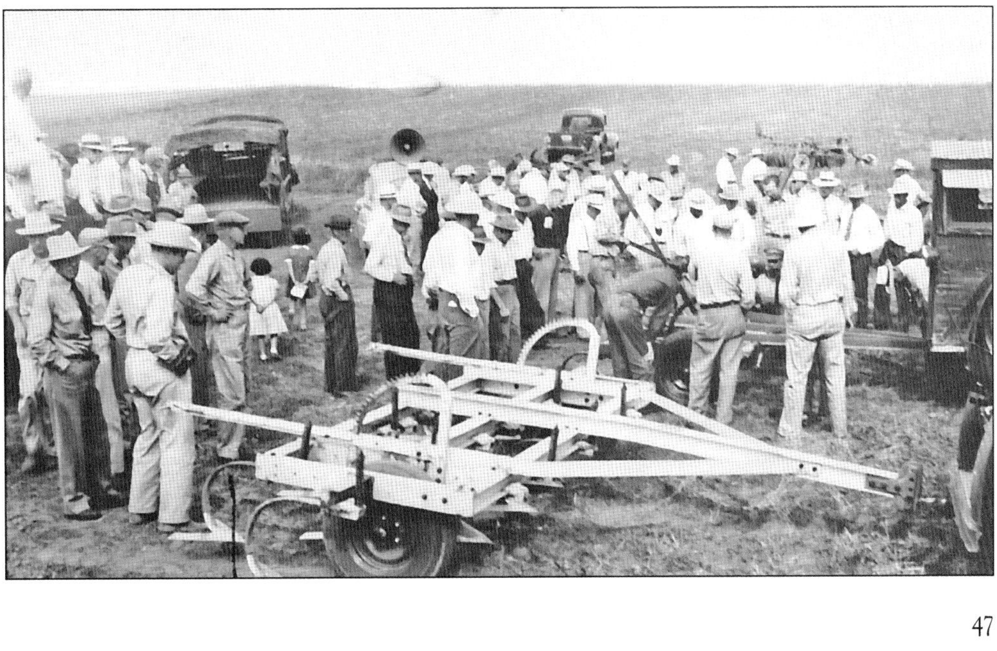

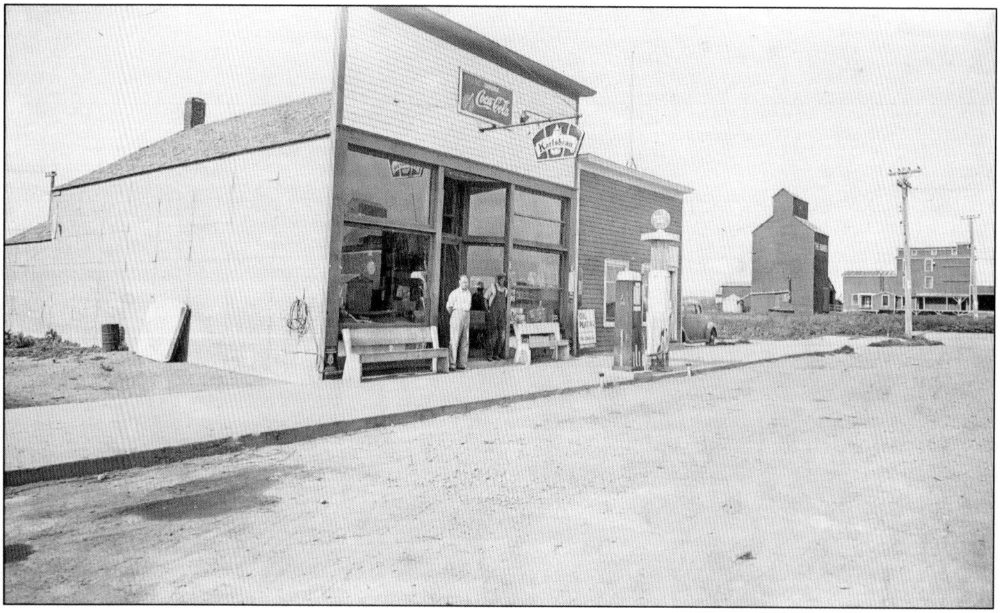

Robert and Kate Clark came to Antelope in 1915, buying the farm of Christian Island, located six miles northeast of town. Their son, Bob, worked at the Antelope Bar and is pictured above at left. At the building to the right of the elevator shown in the background, farmers could have wheat milled into flour and packed in white sacks for home use. When the flour was gone, families often halved and hemmed the sacks for use as dish towels or made them into aprons. Below, Clark is shown at work, where a photograph of Pres. Franklin D. Roosevelt hangs above the bar. (Above, courtesy of Jens Sundsted; below, courtesy of Jack Rasmussen.)

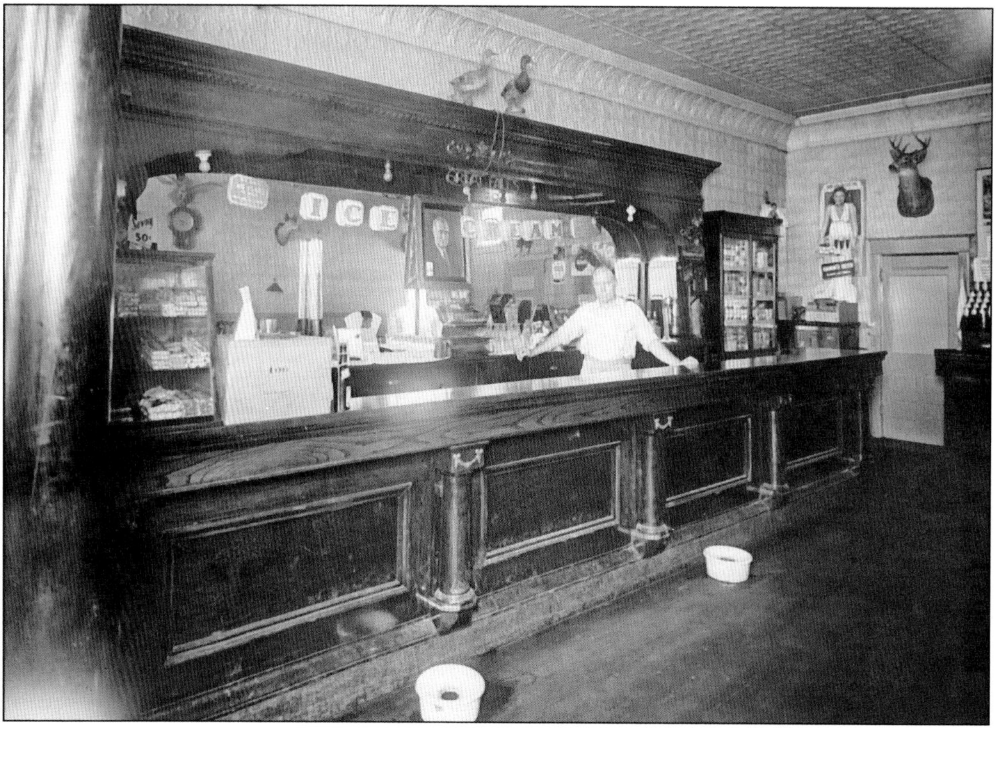

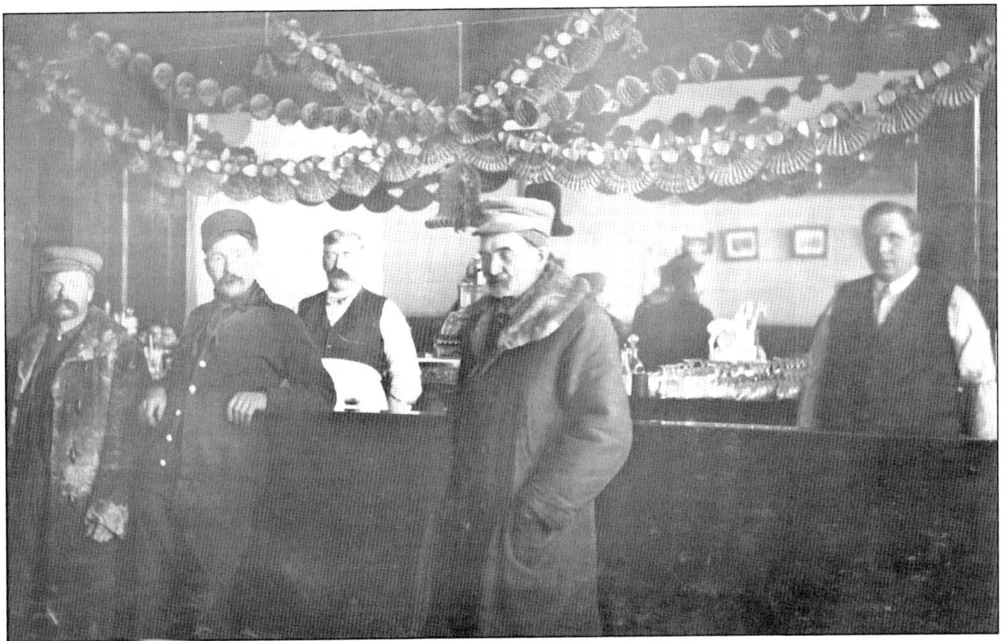

John Wolter homesteaded five miles southeast of Outlook in 1910, marrying Elvina Thorstvedt eight years later. She had homesteaded with family members in 1908 in the Raymond area. Later, Wolter sold his land to Morten Norager and moved to Plentywood, where he owned and operated John's Place, a pool hall and beer parlor. "Big John" is pictured above on the right along with some unidentified patrons. The former John's Place, at 111 North Main Street, is now known as the One Eleven Casino. The photograph below shows some of the establishments in Westby prior to Prohibition, which began in late 1919. Slocum & Simpkins Liquor saloon is on the left. Also shown are the Kelly-Gordon saloon, a billiards room, and a bowling alley. Other Westby businesses during the early years were the Planter's Hotel, Otto Enger Shoe Store, and the C.N. Rostad Drug Store, among many others. (Above, courtesy of Linda Nelson; below, courtesy of Ken Keldsen.)

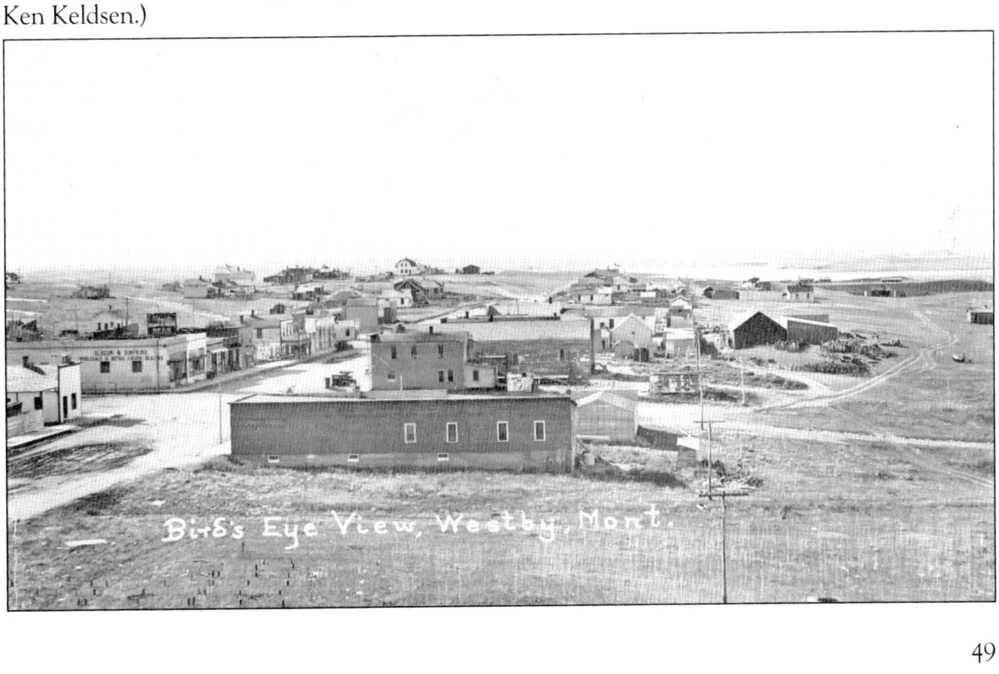

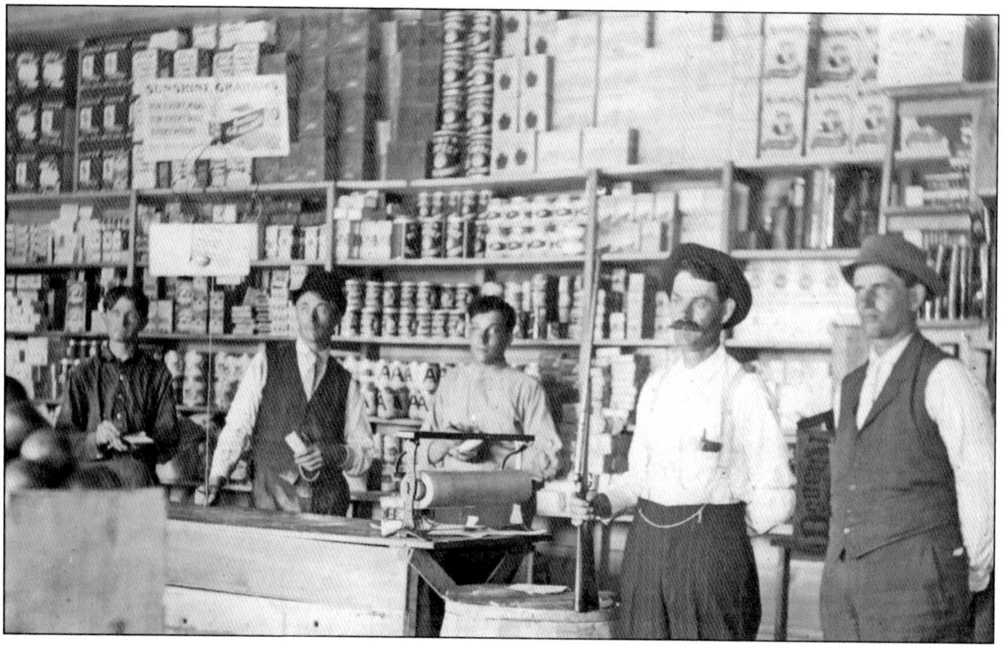

Above, a group of men is gathered at the Dagmar store, including Alfred Jensen (right). He was raised in Kearney, Nebraska, where he read about a Danish settlement, the future Dagmar, being planned in Montana. He arrived in Culbertson in 1907 and staked his claim one and a half miles southwest of the present town of Dagmar. To supplement his income on the farm, Jensen worked as a clerk at the store and, in 1918, he became manager of the newly formed Farmers Cooperative store. A Medicine Lake barbershop owned by William Dilly is shown below, probably in the 1910s or early 1920s. A sign between the mirrors reads, "Patronizing us is like making love to a widow. You can't overdo it." (Above, courtesy of Norman Jensen; below, courtesy of Virginia Carpenter.)

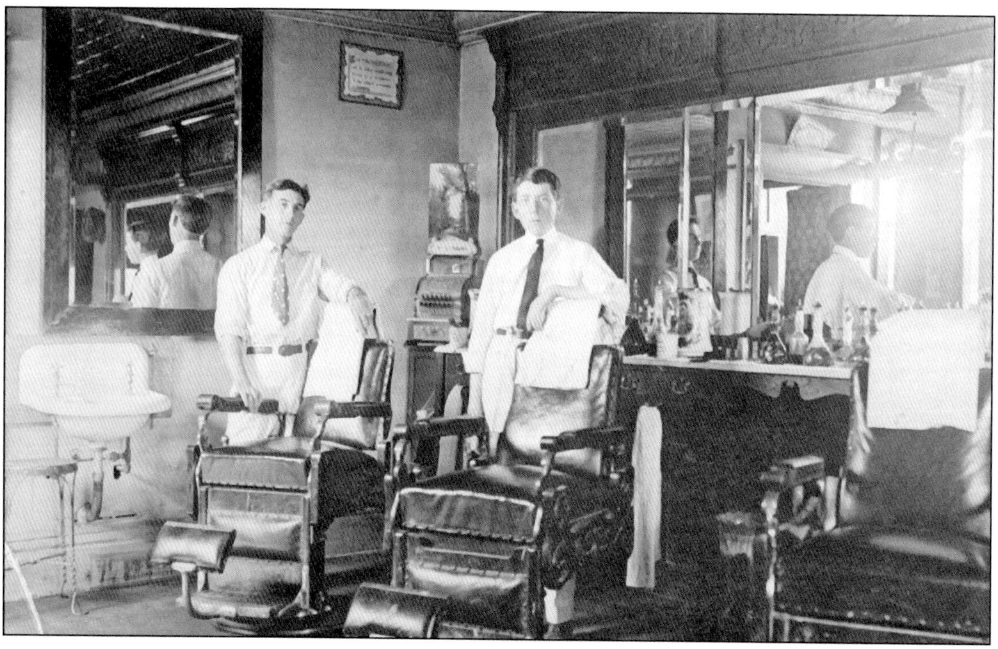

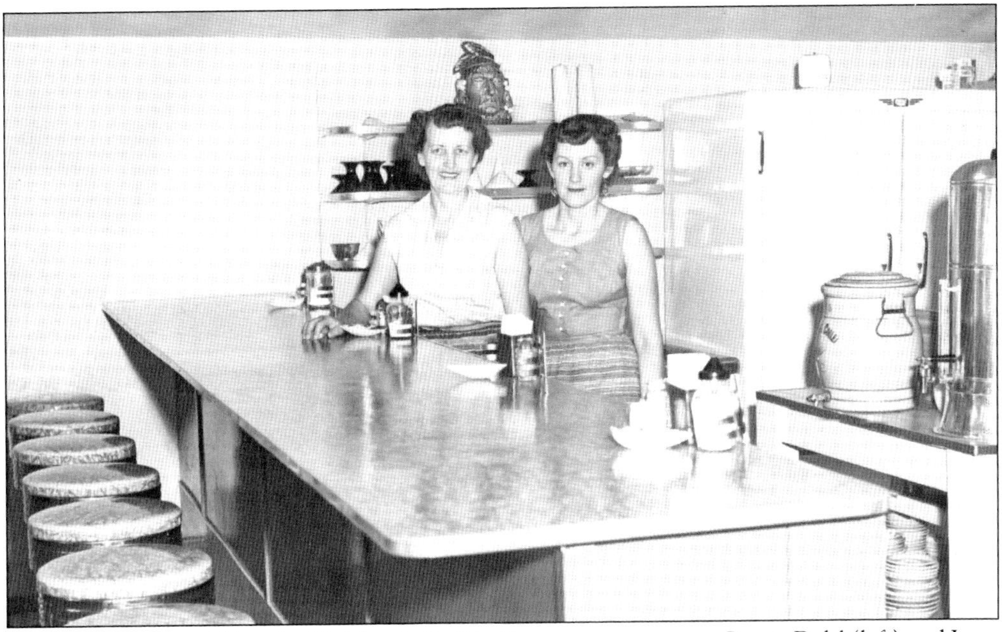

Pictured above in 1956 at the Walikonis Café in Reserve are manager Carrie Dahl (left) and Jerry Olson. Dahl arrived in Sheridan County at the age of six weeks when her parents, Christian and Severina Ibsen, came to the East Coalridge area. Members of the community helped them finish the roof of their homestead shack, and Severina baked and washed laundry for some of the local bachelors who furnished the family with ducks, geese, and rabbits they had hunted. The family had eight children and moved west of Reserve in 1931. Below, members of the Medicine Lake community enjoy refreshments outside the old Imperial Elevator. Among those gathered are George Wesner, Frank J. French, Emmett Gormley, Mike Eckley, John Jensen, John Miller, and Bud Stephens. (Above, courtesy of Sheridan County Museum; below, courtesy of Virginia Carpenter.)

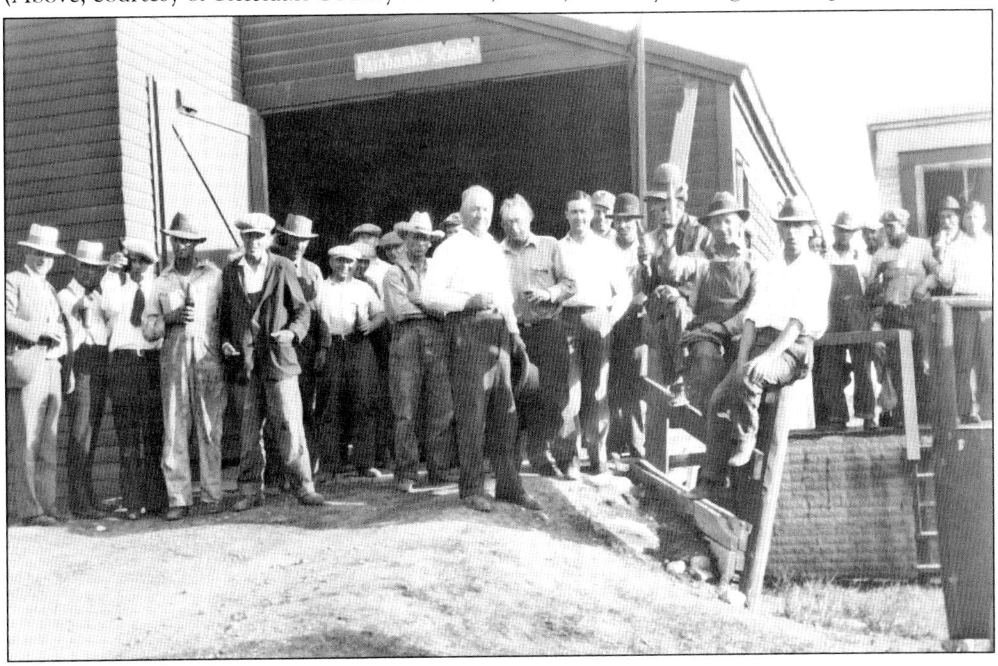

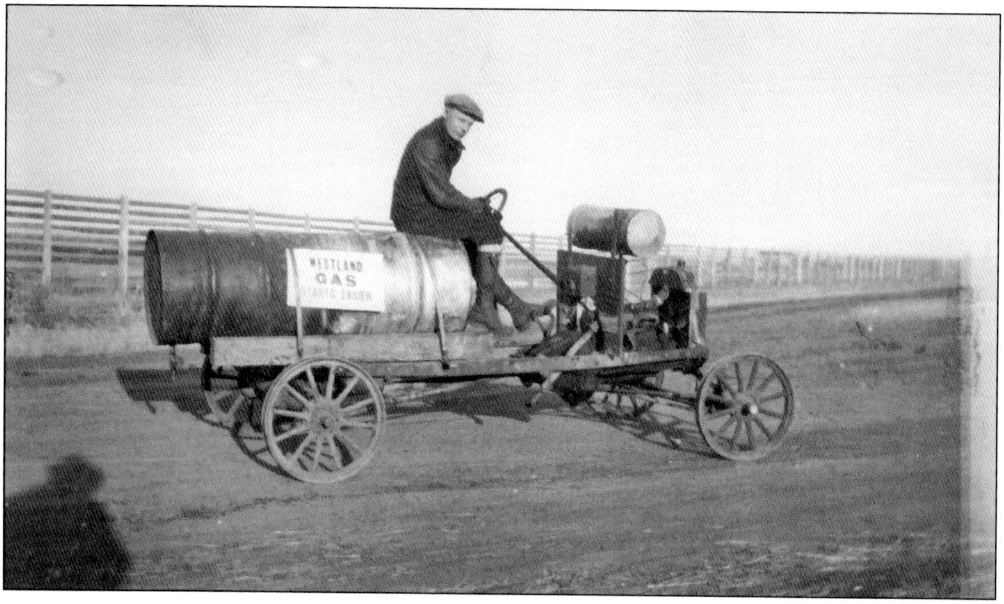

Following their marriage in 1925, Roland and Gertrude Cook Wilson moved from North Dakota to Medicine Lake. Roland Wilson worked for the Markuson & Epler Ford Company, where he served as a bookkeeper and parts man. He is shown above delivering gas in 1925. The Wilsons later moved to Plentywood, where, for 52 years, he was affiliated with the Ford dealership that became known as Plentywood Motor Sales. Pictured below is Soren Rungborg in 1926. Born in Denmark, he was raised in Dagmar and then worked at the Ford Company in Medicine Lake until 1929, when he became manager of the International Harvester dealership in Reserve. Rungborg later became manager of the Community Oil Company. He and Myrtle Andersen Rungborg raised four children. (Both, courtesy of Jean West.)

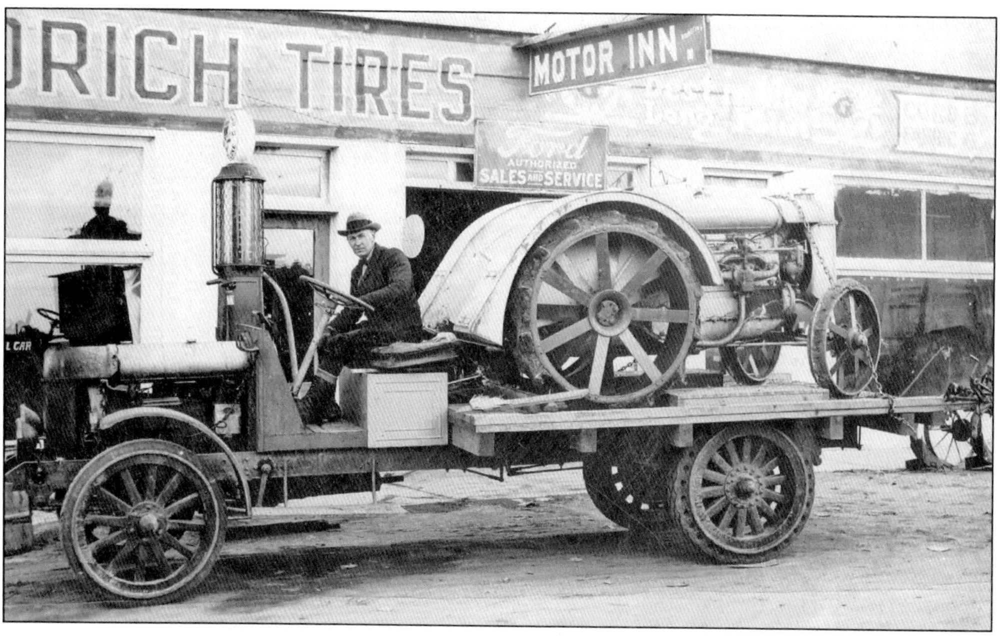

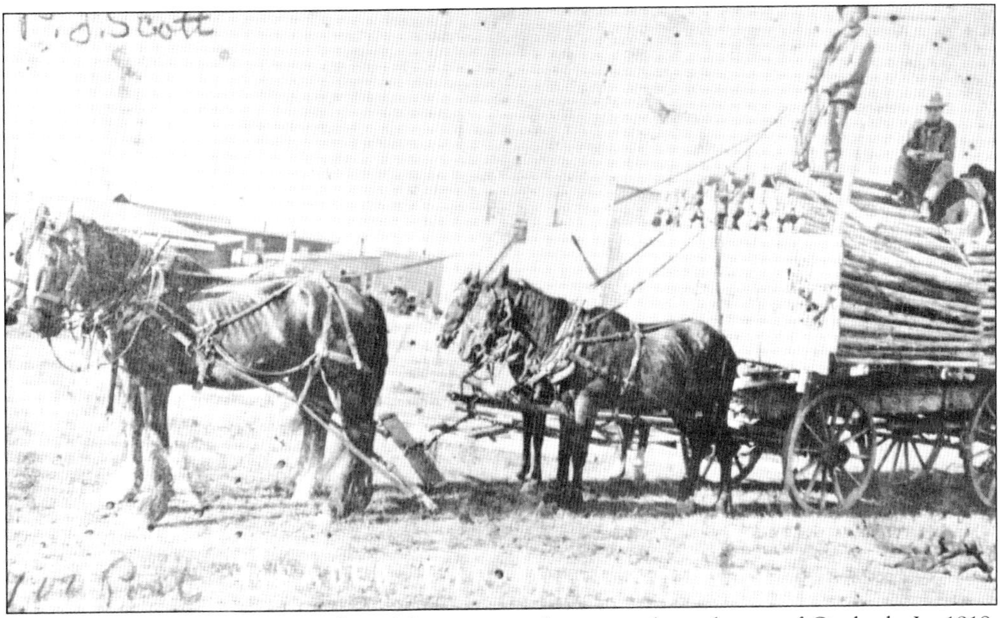

Palmer John "P.J." Scott came from Minnesota to homestead northwest of Outlook. In 1918, Scott, a widower, married Beulah Bjornethun, who had also lost a spouse. The couple later had two sons, George and Robert. Scott is pictured above hauling a load of poles and lumber behind two teams of slender horses. Prior to the Soo Line's extension into Montana, he hauled freight for Outlook merchants from as far away as Ambrose, North Dakota. He also delivered groceries from Plentywood to be stocked in Outlook's N.J. Nelson store. Below, spectators observe the 1952 fire at the McCabe Elevator Company in Medicine Lake. (Above, courtesy of Janet Strand; below, courtesy of Virginia Carpenter.)

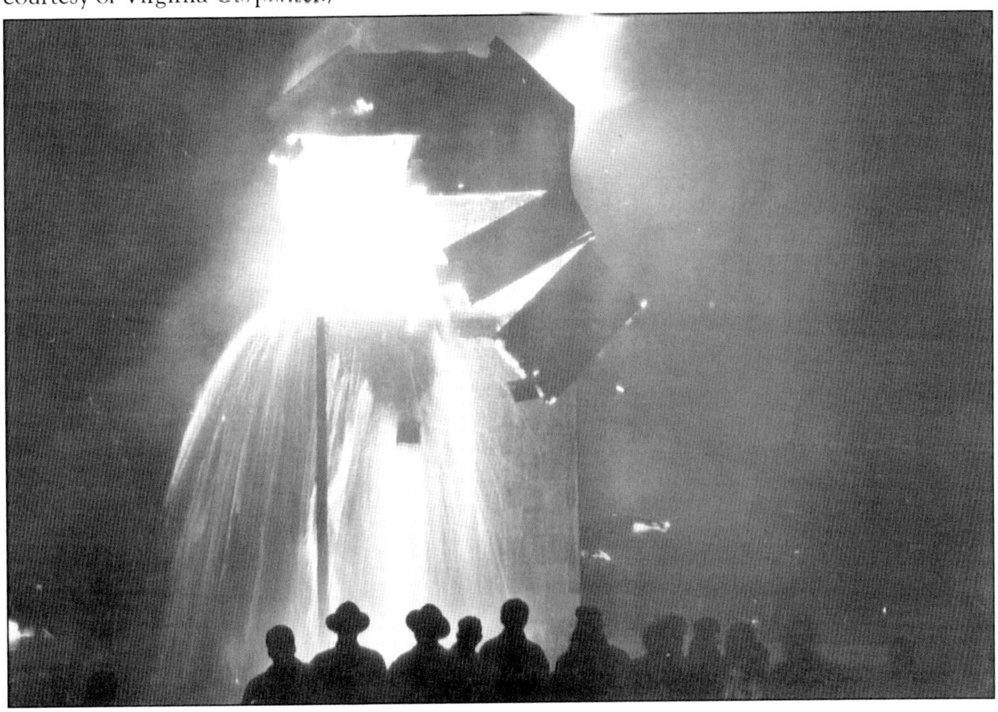

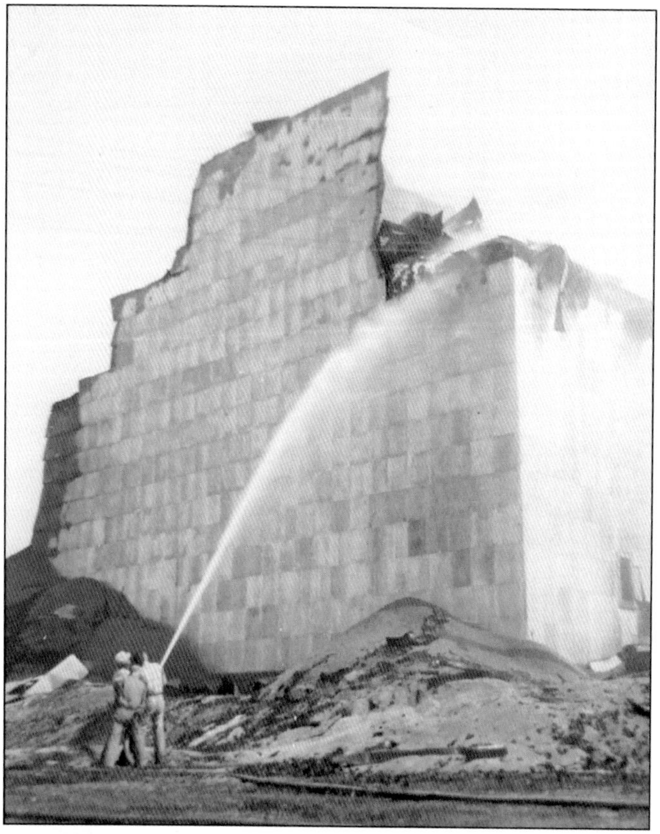

When the McCabe Elevator caught fire, it was full of grain, which smoldered for days while local residents continued to douse it with water, as shown in the 1952 photograph at left. Below is the Rostad store in Comertown. In 1908, Martin Rostad and his mother came to the Coalridge area, where he later married Hannah Benrud. The couple lived in a tent as their first home. After returning for a time to Minnesota, the Rostads moved to Comertown, where Rostad bought a half-interest, along with George Onstad, in a hardware store. It burned down in 1922, and Rostad rebuilt the store. Martin is pictured, below, in 1954. The establishment sold gas, merchandise, and bulk oil. (Left, courtesy of Virginia Carpenter; below, courtesy of Merlin Rostad.)

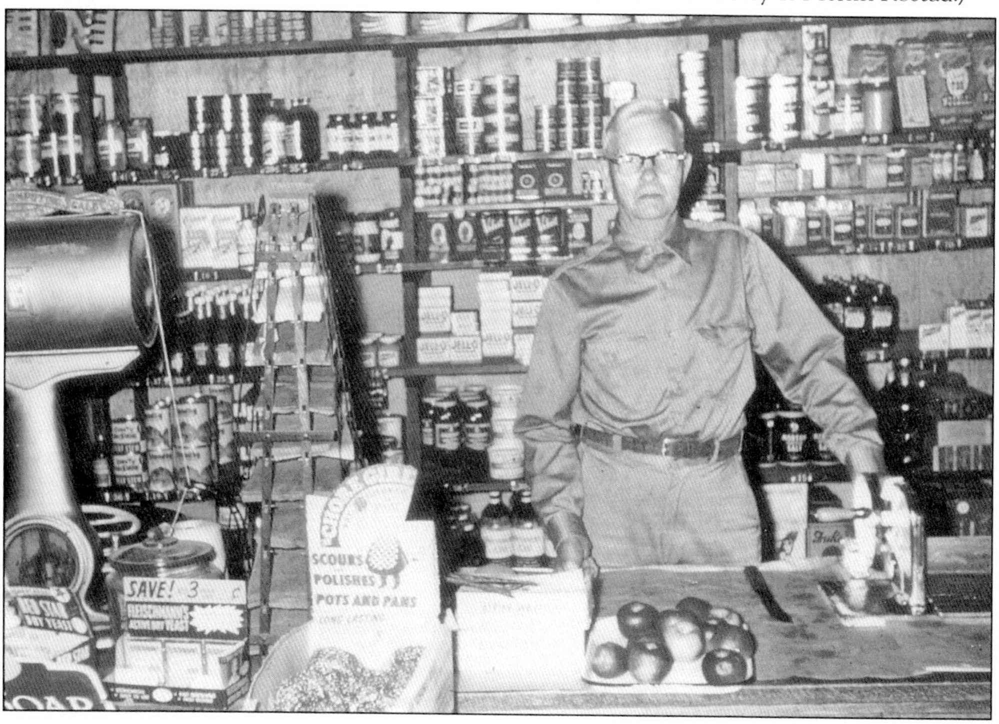

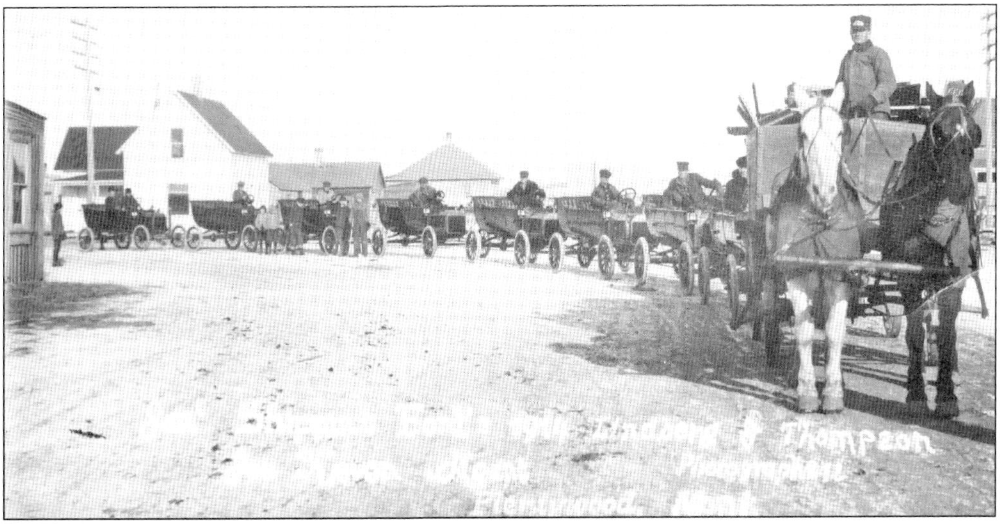

Pictured above in 1914 is Plentywood's first shipment of Model Ts. The local Ford agent, Joe Kavon, was born in Bohemia and immigrated with his parents when he was two. After arriving in Sheridan County, he owned a harness and horseshoeing business in what is now Plentywood's town square area. His Ford dealership was near the present-day post office and later moved to what is now the Rocky Mountain Bank lot. Kavon was married to Louise Looman Kavon, who became the first woman in Plentywood to drive a car. She worked in the car dealership as the "parts man." Below, posing in front of the Kavon garage in 1927 are, from left to right, Claude Wineland, Emmet Turner, Arthur "Spike" Knutson, Louis Mehl, Joe Kavon, Frank Gunther, C.G. Christianson, and unidentified. (Above, photograph by Lindberg and Thompson, courtesy of Sheridan County Museum; below, courtesy of Karla Kavon.)

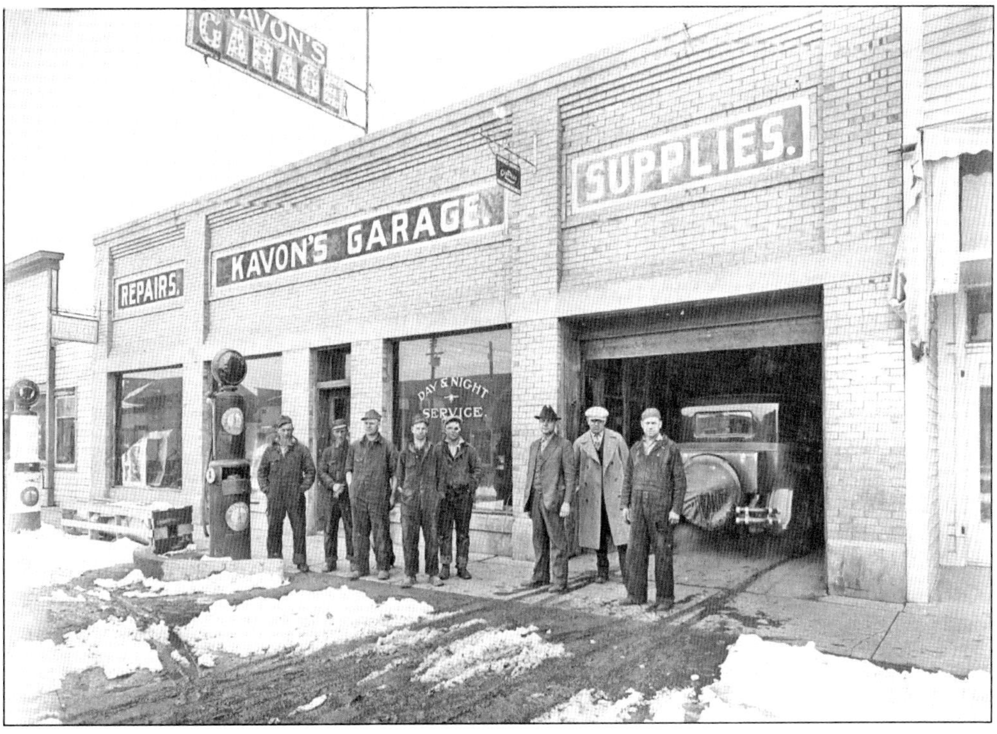

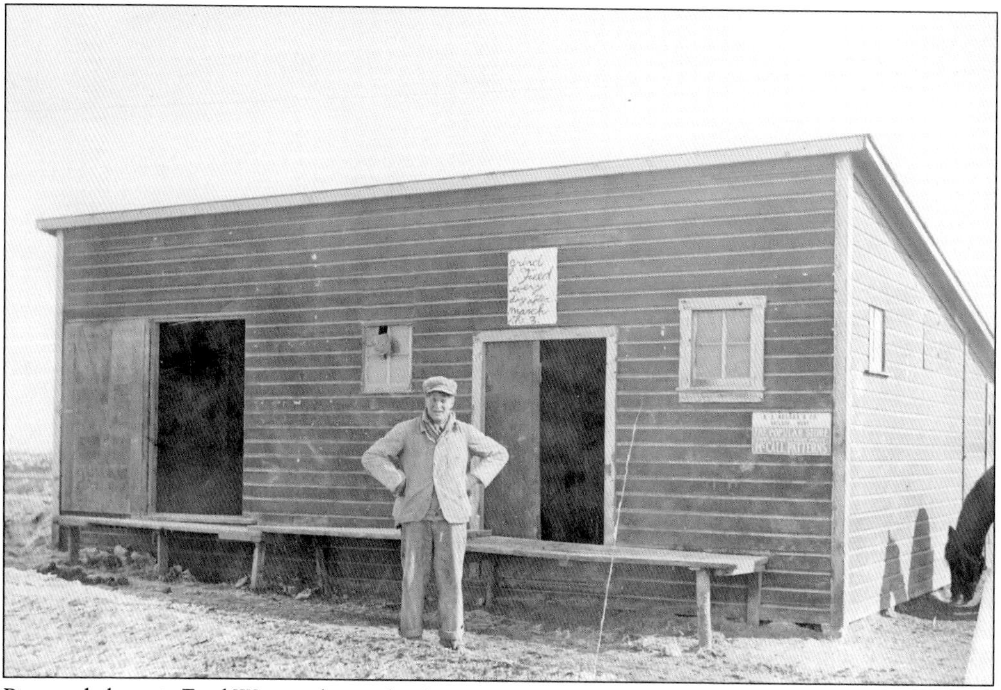

Pictured above is Fred Wirtz, who took a homestead in the Outlook area before he was drafted in World War I. After the war, he set up a feed-mill business in 1919 with a homemade sign, "Grind Feed Every Day after March the 3." Wirtz also advertised another local business, "N.J. Nelson and Company . . . The Popular Store." Wirtz married Anna Yung, whose parents had emigrated from Austria-Hungary, and they raised seven children on the family farm. The Wirtzes' son Chester and grandson Greg carry on the farming operation today. The below photograph shows a wreck on the Great Northern line near Plentywood. (Above, courtesy of Grace Wirtz; below, photograph by Lorentzen, courtesy of Millie Marsh.)

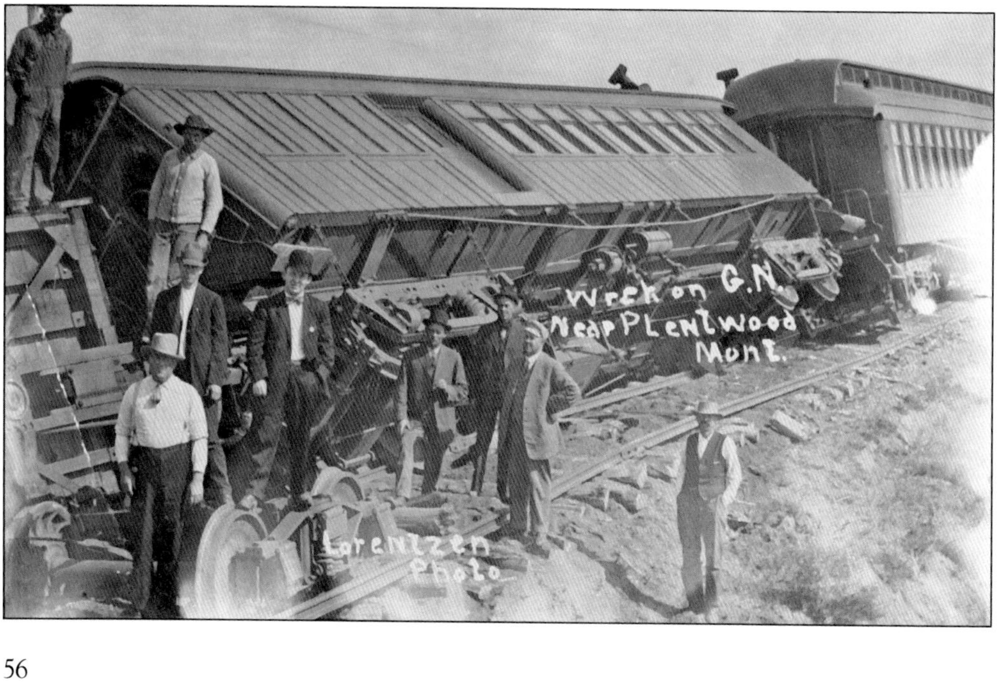

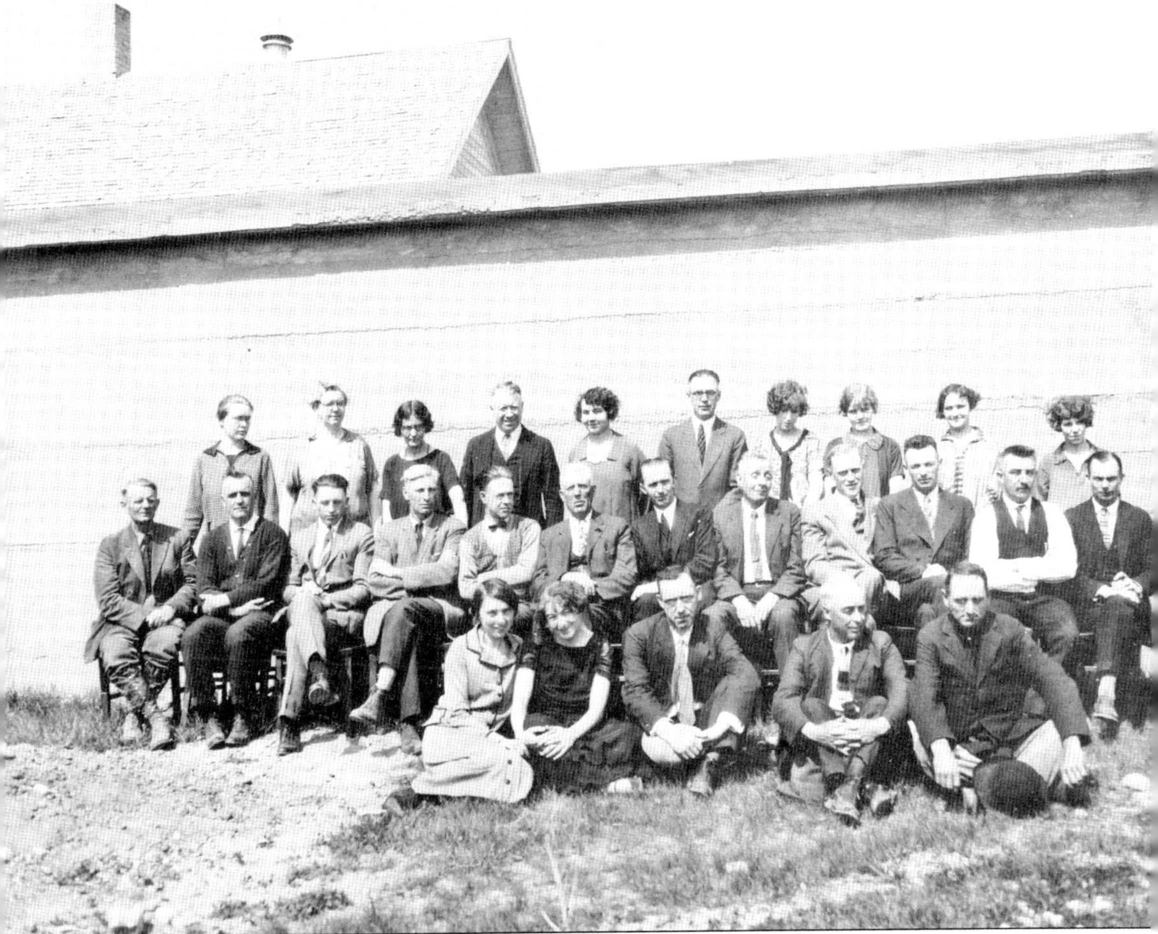

Much has been written about Sheridan County's Communist era. Posing in this 1926 photograph of the courthouse staff are, from left to right, (first row) Alice Redmond, Emma Braden, Pete Gallagher, George Bantz, and George Wheeler; (second row) Hans Rasmussen, M.P. Ostby, C.F. Christensen, Clair Stoner, Ralph Hare, Ole Aspeland, Nicolar Stenbak, Dan Olson, Ed Koser, Rodney Salisbury, Niels Madsen, and Eng Thorstensen; (third row) Nora Thompson, Linda Hall, Lillian Paske, A.C. Erickson, Ann Hanson, S.E. Paul, Helga Hanisch, Anna Hovet, Erna Timmerman, and Ellen Pierce. Certainly not all of the staff were Communists, but several, including Salisbury and Rasmussen, were. Others had been elected with the local Reds' endorsement. A few months after this photograph was taken, Thorstensen and Hovet were accosted by armed robbers, who stole over $100,000 from the county treasury and were never apprehended. (Courtesy of Myrtle Waller.)

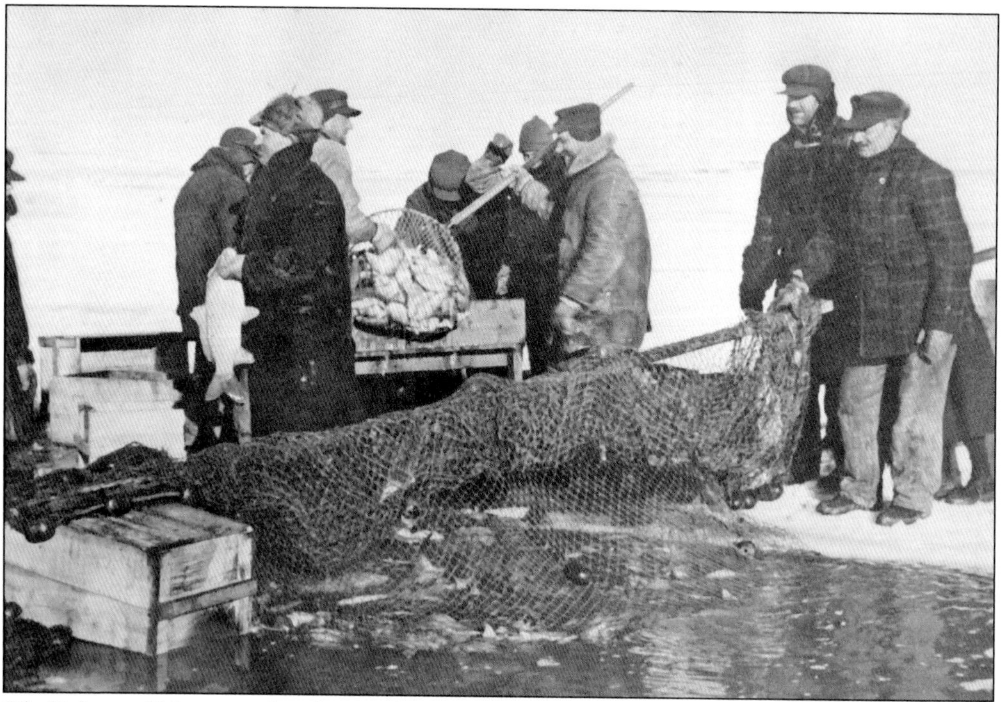

Ole Nelson of Homestead is shown above (center, in profile) displaying his catch at Medicine Lake. The Medicine Lake National Wildlife Refuge was created in 1935 through an executive order signed by Franklin D. Roosevelt, whose Civilian Conservation Corps set up a camp to improve the refuge. Located on the west side of present-day Highway 16, south of Medicine Lake, the camp brought together 180 young men to build dikes and ditches, and to fence the area that today is home to over 200 species of birds. Roosevelt's Works Progress Administration (WPA) also brought important projects and employment to Sheridan County, including a dam, pictured below, that was built on the Swen Soderquist farm between Comertown and Dooley in 1936. (Above, courtesy of Orvis Nelson; below, courtesy of Evedine Lane.)

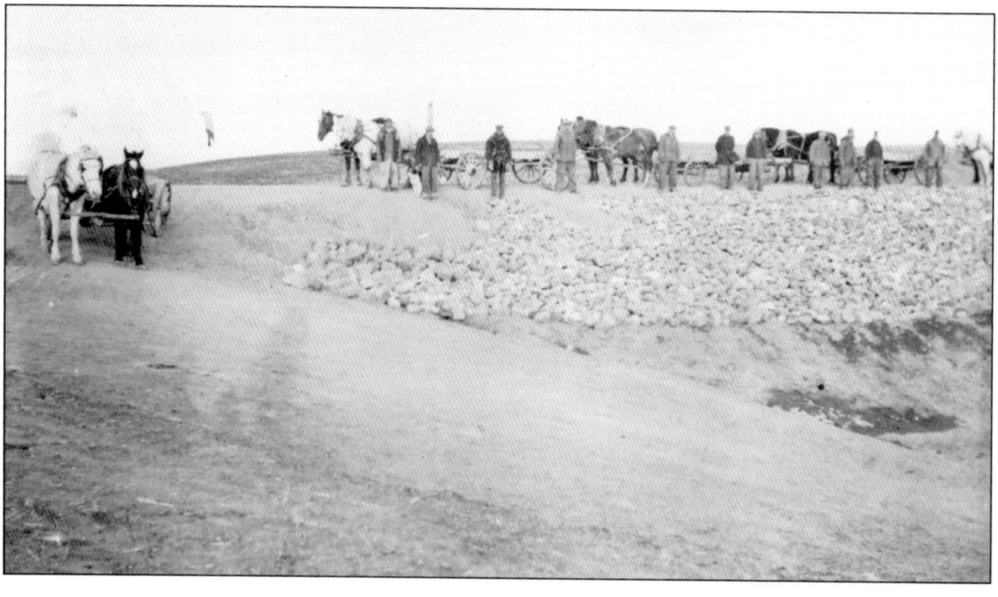

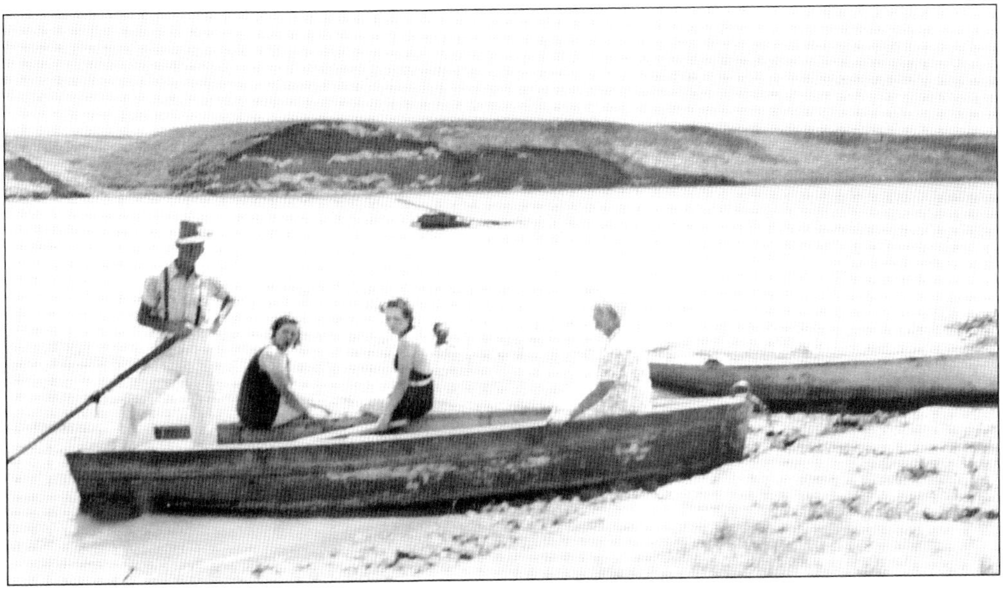

Another WPA project was Carroll Dam. Above, the Eggen family is seen boating at the dam in 1940. The family members shown here are, from left to right, Gene, Dorothy, Lillian, and Tillie. The dam was named for John and Vera Carroll, who came to Sheridan County in 1915 and bought the Astrup homestead, eight miles northwest of Plentywood. The hilly area was an ideal location for the planned dam, and the Carrolls were offered land north of Plentywood in exchange for their property. The dam was completed in 1936. The below photograph depicts Dooley's Main Street. An accompanying caption reads, "Joe Redmond foreman of the crew." Redmond served in World War I, opened a tire shop in Plentywood following his discharge, and married Alice Melquist, with whom he had three children. (Above, courtesy of Lillian and Lyla Frasier; below, courtesy of Sheridan County Museum.)

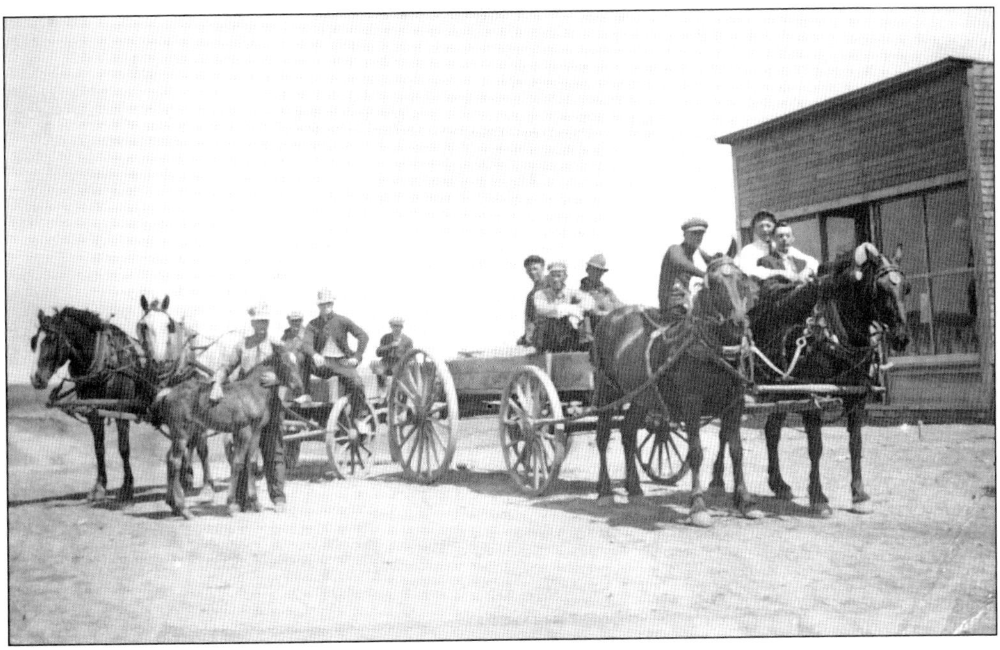

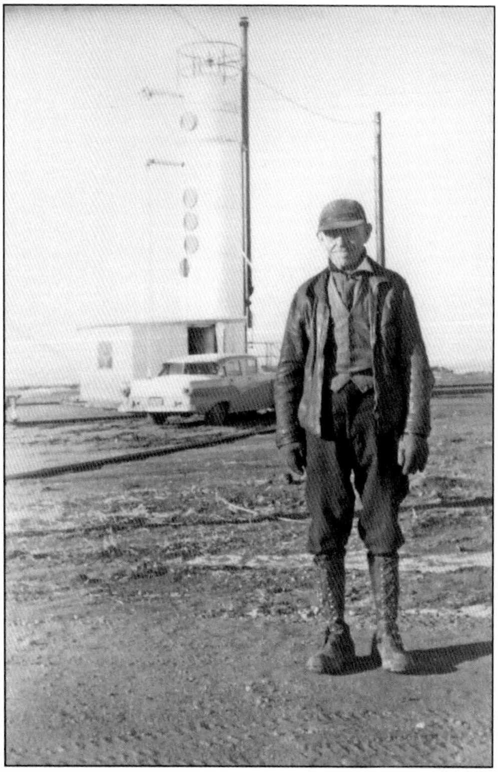

Sheridan County's first oil exploration dates back to at least 1928, with a drilling attempt on the Martin Olson homestead near Archer. Left, Jens Tange is shown in 1956 by his Outlook oil well. The well was drilled to nearly 10,000 feet and produced over 2,700 barrels on its first day, a record in the Williston Basin at that time. Just as oil is again bringing business to Sheridan County, the Canadian port of entry north of Raymond is busy with its Department of Homeland Security staff. Pictured below on either side of Congressman Orvin Fjare in 1956 are Plentywood businessmen Robert Johnston (left) and Fay Chandler, who met to discuss extending the port's hours during the summer season. Only in 1974 did the port begin staying open around the clock. (Left, courtesy of Rita Werdal; below, courtesy of Karla Kavon.)

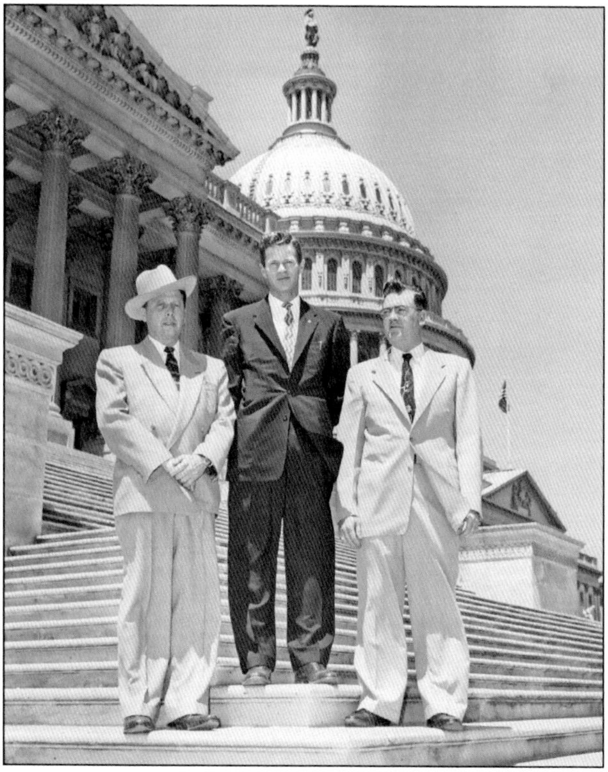

Five

Modes of Transportation

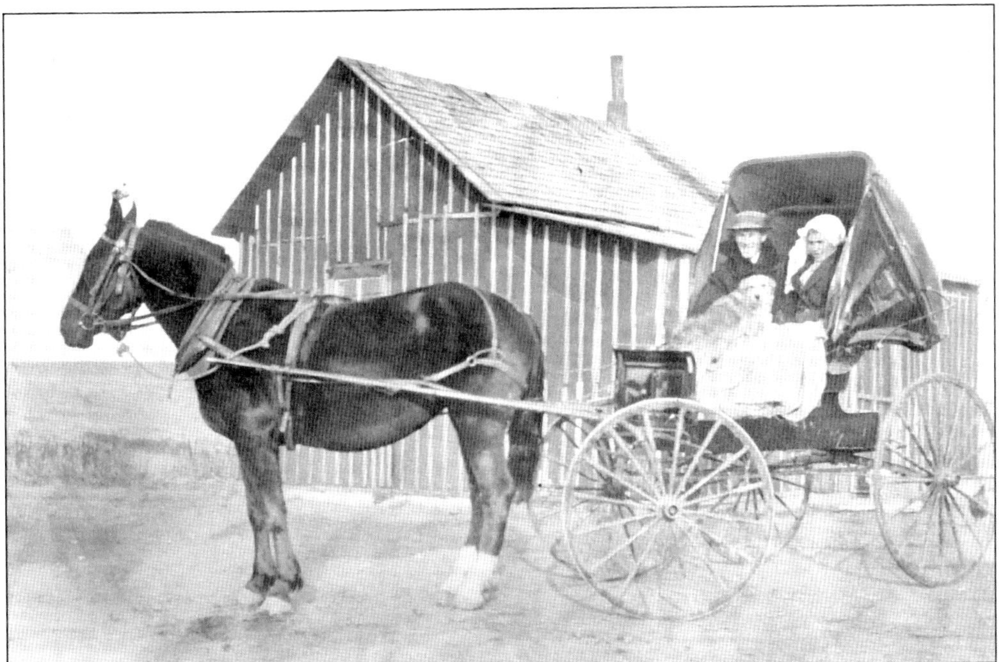

Dramatic changes have taken place over the last 100 years in the means by which Sheridan County residents get from one place to another. Some of the earliest homesteaders walked from the train station at Culbertson. Others, like this unidentified couple, were lucky enough to own horses and a carriage. In 1912, Sears sold a mail-order buggy similar to this one for $34.95 plus shipping. (Courtesy of Marlys Vogt.)

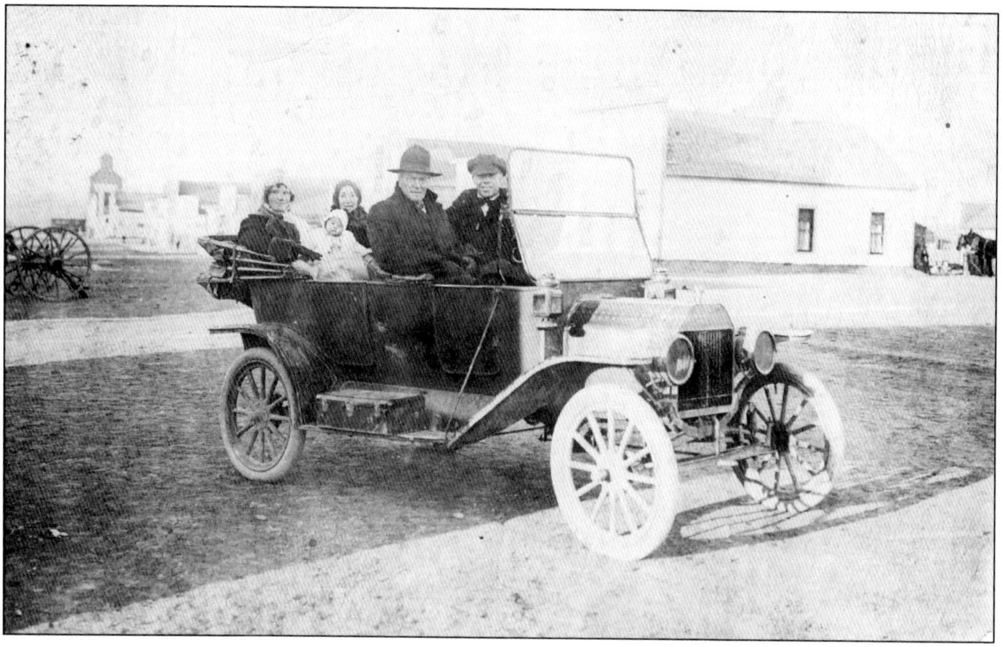

For most American families during the 1910s and 1920s, the purchase of their first car was a life-changing event and a source of great pride. As automobiles arrived in Sheridan County in the early teens, these prized possessions began to be featured prominently in family photographs. Shown above are Victor (driving) and Elsie Wilberg (holding baby Vernon in the backseat) giving a ride, possibly to Elsie's parents, Mr. and Mrs. E.E. Phelps, in Redstone around 1917. Before there were dirt bikes and four-wheelers, some local residents put their cars to the test in hill-climbing contests. The date and location of the below photograph are unknown, but the car on the right displays a campaign sign for R.C. Stanfield, a Culbertson resident. (Above, courtesy of Eugene Hagan; below, courtesy of Sheridan County Museum.)

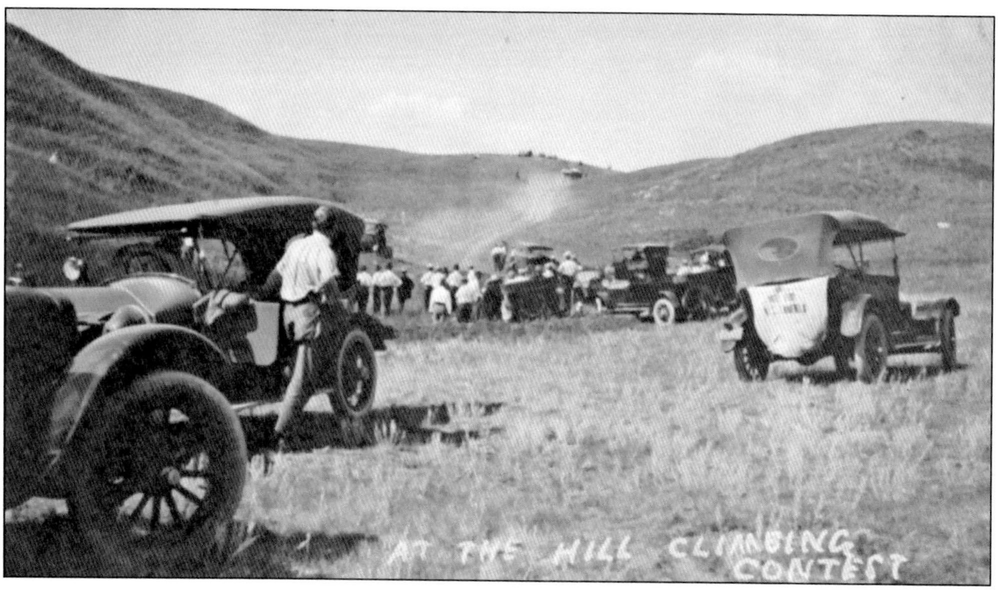

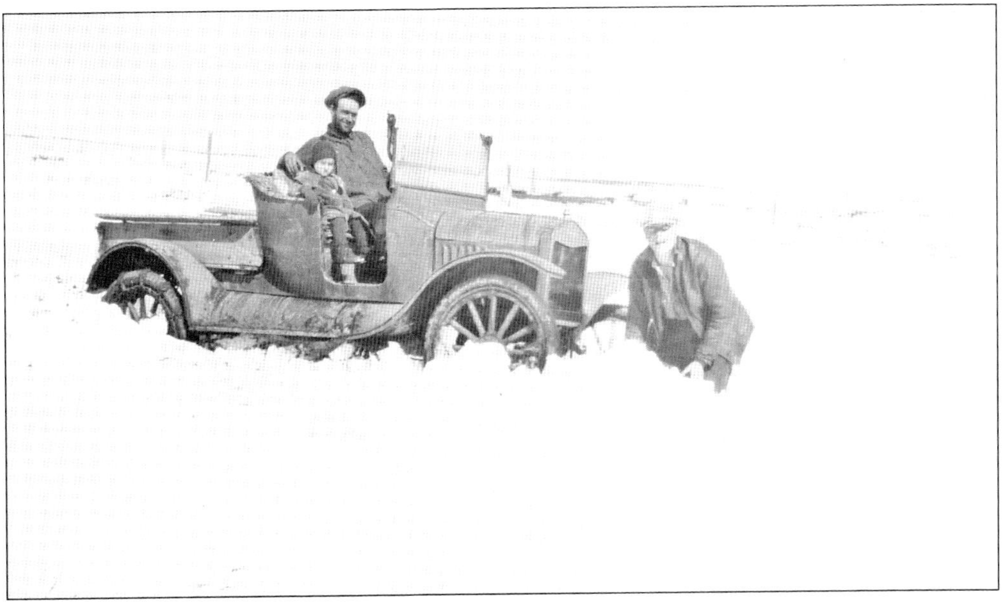

Transportation in Sheridan County was and still can be complicated during the winter. Above, Bob Hill is shown behind the wheel with young Walter Mattson. Hill and his brother were early settlers of the Raymond community, having come from Minnesota. Mattson's parents, Henry and Dagny, homesteaded northwest of the Hills. George LaGrange, who appears to be clearing snow in front of the vehicle, was just five when his parents came to Raymond in 1909. Pictured below is nine-year-old LeRoy Lodahl delivering mail in 1945. His father, Niels, was the rural Dagmar mail carrier for over 28 years. The winter of 1945 was especially snowy, and the Lodahls used what was then called a "snowmobile" to make their rounds. (Above, courtesy of Lois Dalthorp; below, courtesy of Elice Nelson.)

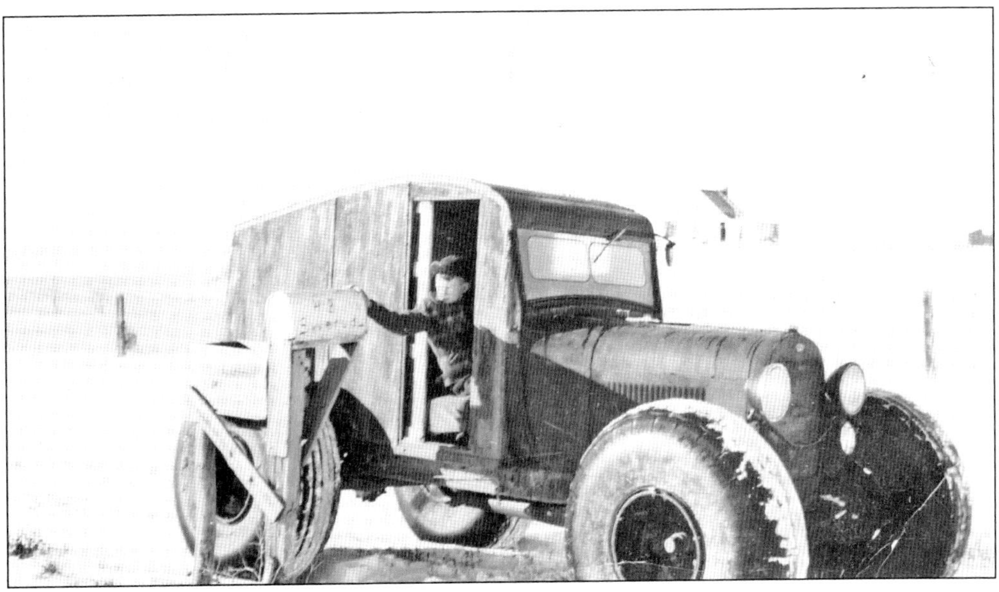

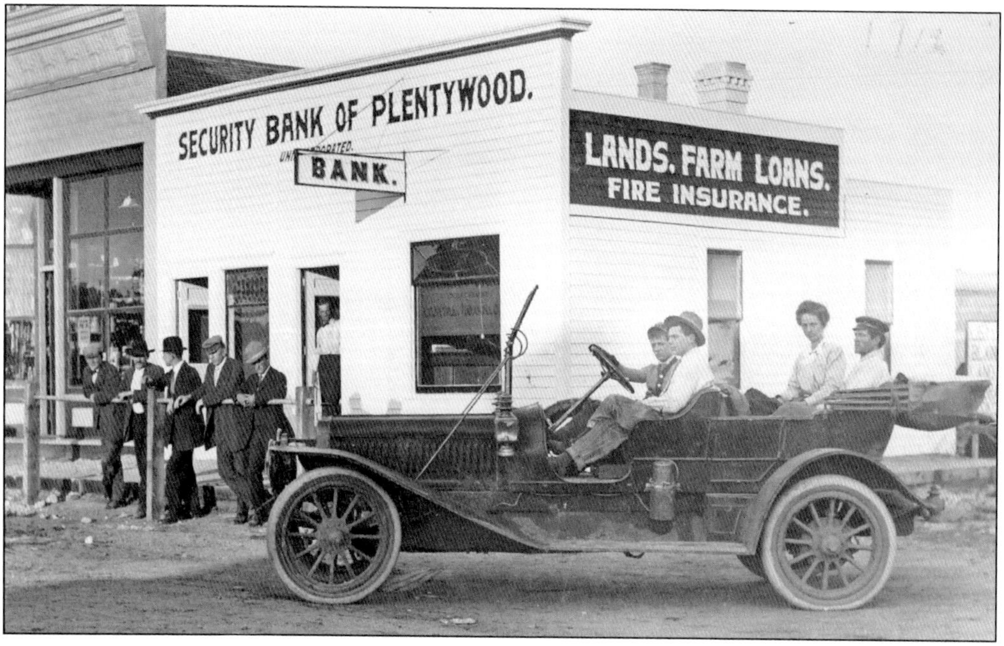

In the above photograph, the Bruvold family is shown in front of Security Bank of Plentywood in 1912. Alvin and Peder Bruvold homesteaded on land near Comertown in 1910. The Security Bank was in the area where the current Town Square is located. It later became a gas station run by Martin Nelson, and eventually the Peterson Garage. Pictured below is one of the first school buses in Sheridan County, pulled up outside of Medicine Lake's school. It was driven by Frank "Swede" Holmquist and his team of mules, Tom and Jenny. Observers can be seen in the second-story windows. (Both, courtesy of Sheridan County Museum.)

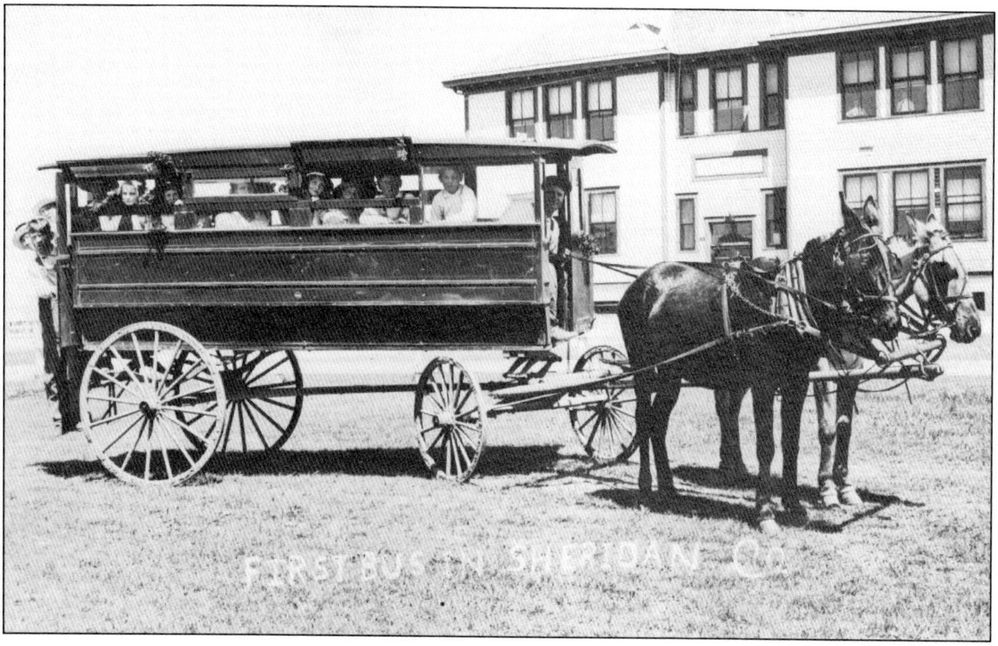

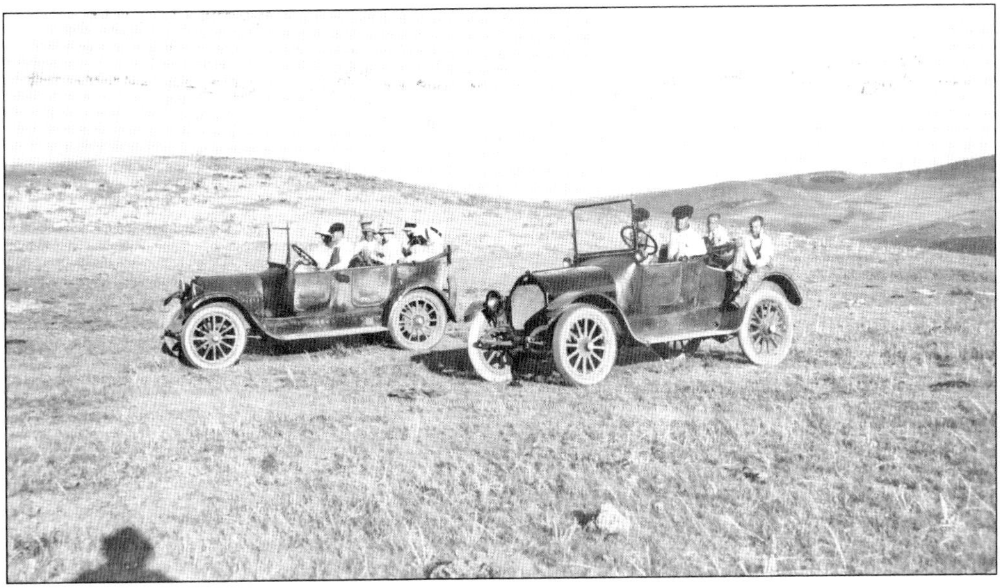

The James Michels family is shown above in 1920 seeking a location for their farmstead 18 miles west of Reserve in the area called Wolf Creek. In the Overland car on the right, Lloyd Michels drives, accompanied by brothers Vernon in front and Roy and Andy in back. The other vehicle, a 1914 Studebaker, is probably driven by James Michels, accompanied by his wife, Anna, Grandma Fugle, Aunt Mable, sons Fred and Jack, as well as the Freeman family. The photograph was taken by Fred Fugle, the only person in the area who owned a camera at that time. Below, the Michels men are shown on their Wolf Creek homestead. Posing here are, from the front, Clair, Jack, Fred, Andy, Roy, Lloyd, Vernon, and James Sr. Not shown are the other children: Francis (who died in infancy), Leah, Mark, Elsie, and Jim. (Both, courtesy of Clair Michels.)

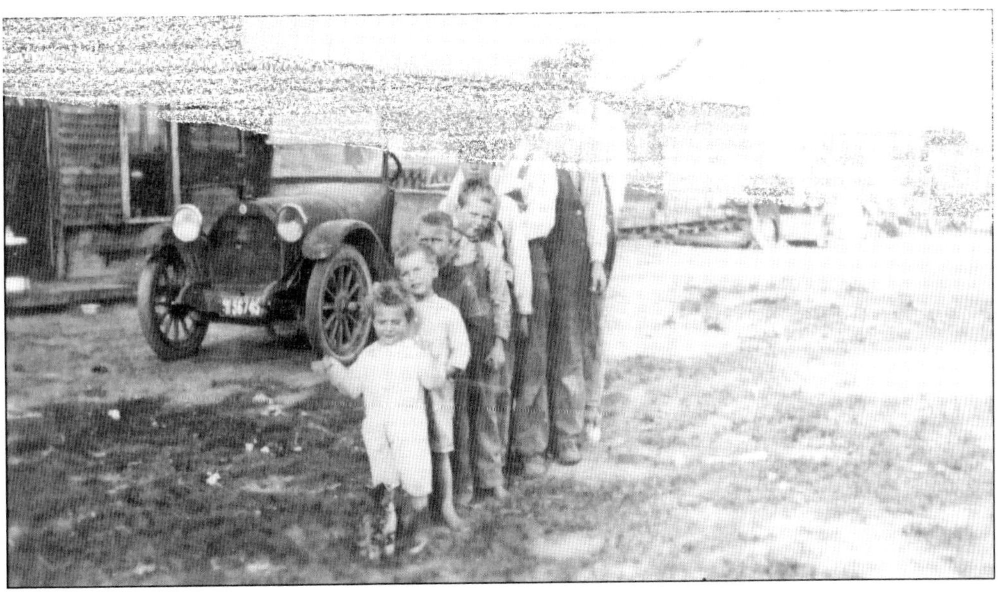

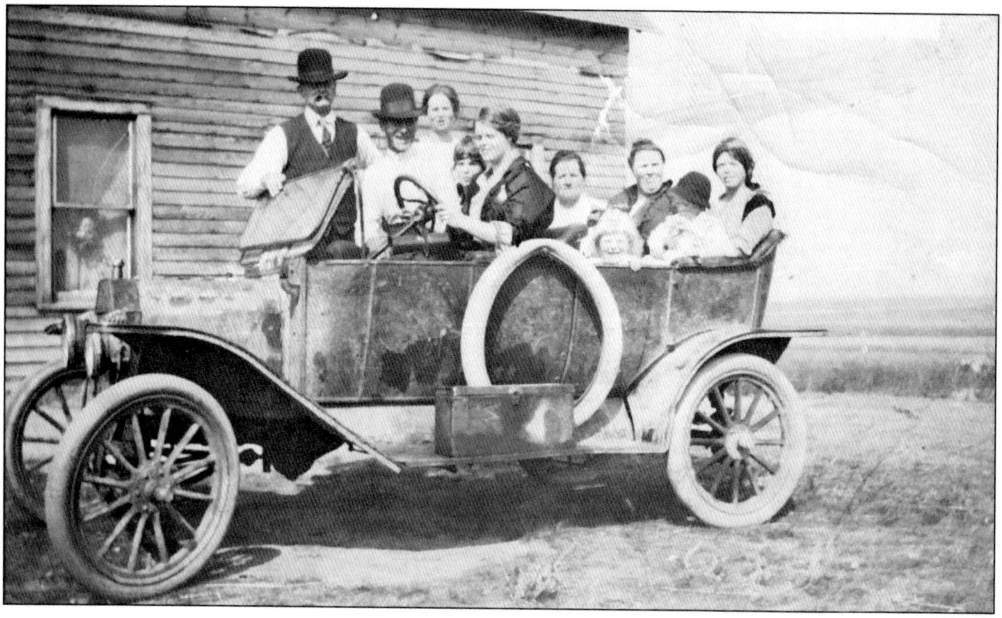

Annata Madill, born in Peterboro, Ontario, was the fourth of seven girls born to William and Caroline Madill. In 1910, the family homesteaded north of Raymond, near the Canadian border. Annata married August Westphal in 1917 and was one of the first women in the Raymond community who learned to drive a car. She is shown above preparing to chauffeur a group of Raymond friends and their children. Pictured in the postcard below are some of Medicine Lake's early cars, including Fords and Studebakers. The Vendome, probably named after the five-star Hotel de Vendome in Paris, had been in the town of Flandrem, but was moved to Medicine Lake's main street. The hotel was destroyed by fire around 1917. (Above, courtesy of Ila Syme; below, courtesy of Virginia Carpenter.)

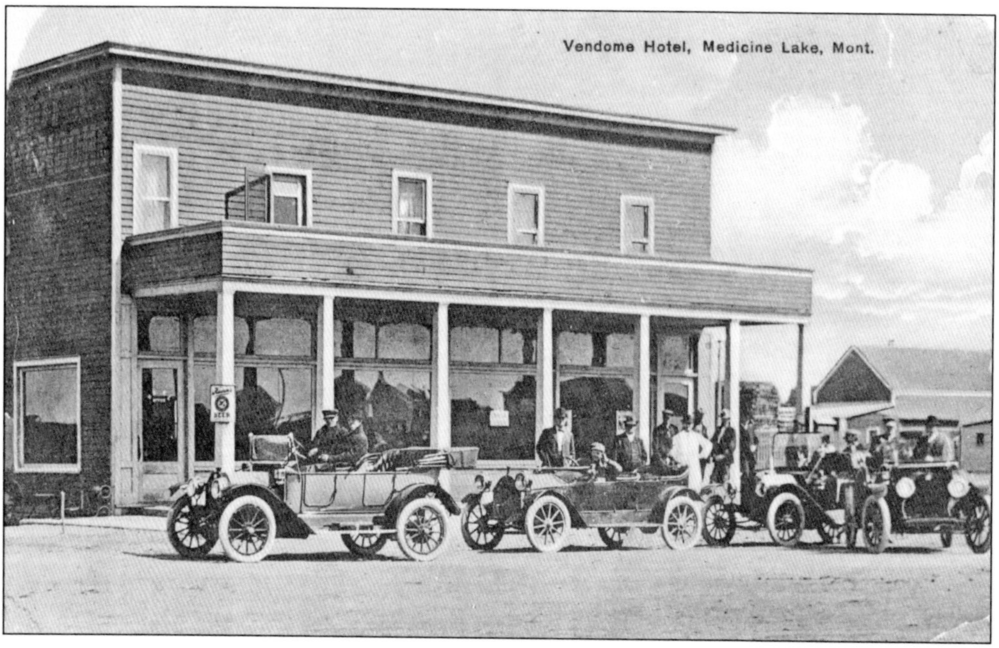

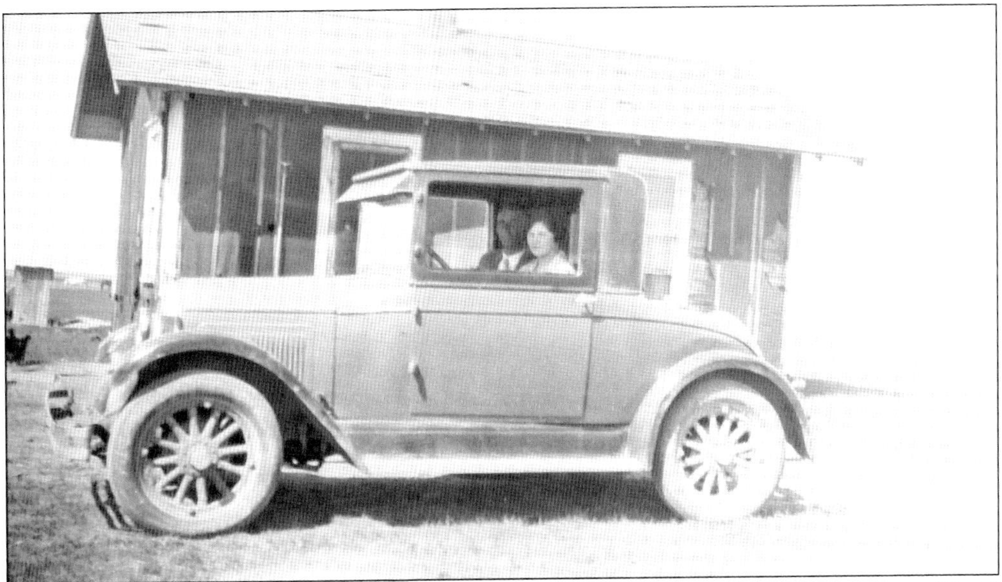

Albert Erdahl moved from Minnesota to the Malta area to homestead prior to his service in World War I. After his discharge in 1919, he worked on the Great Northern Railroad and farmed in the Homestead and, later, Medicine Lake communities. He is shown above giving his wife, Elmyra, driving lessons. The Erdahls later moved to Plentywood, where he served as sheriff from 1942 to 1963. Below, Maurice and Cora Plaisance pose by their car. The daughter of Norwegian immigrants Ole and Martha Risa of the Redstone area, Cora graduated from Plentywood High School and worked for several years at J.L. Sorem's grocery, in the location of present-day Cassidy's. Maurice Plaisance later owned the Kaiser-Frazer automobile dealership, selling Buicks and GMCs, as well as Oliver implements. (Above, courtesy of Evelyn Rice; below, courtesy of Karen Forster.)

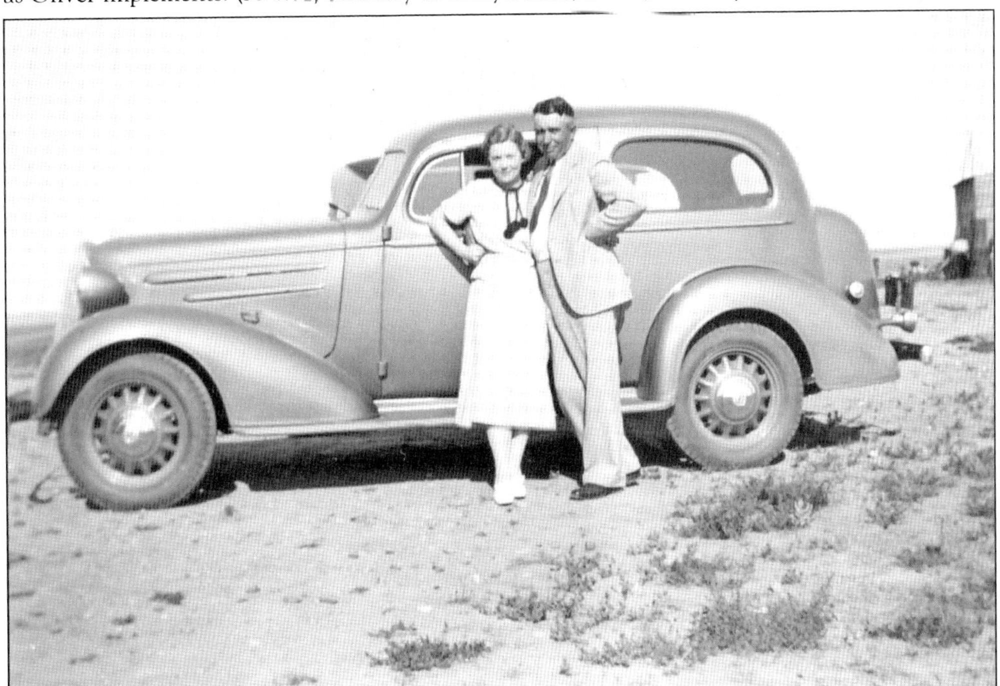

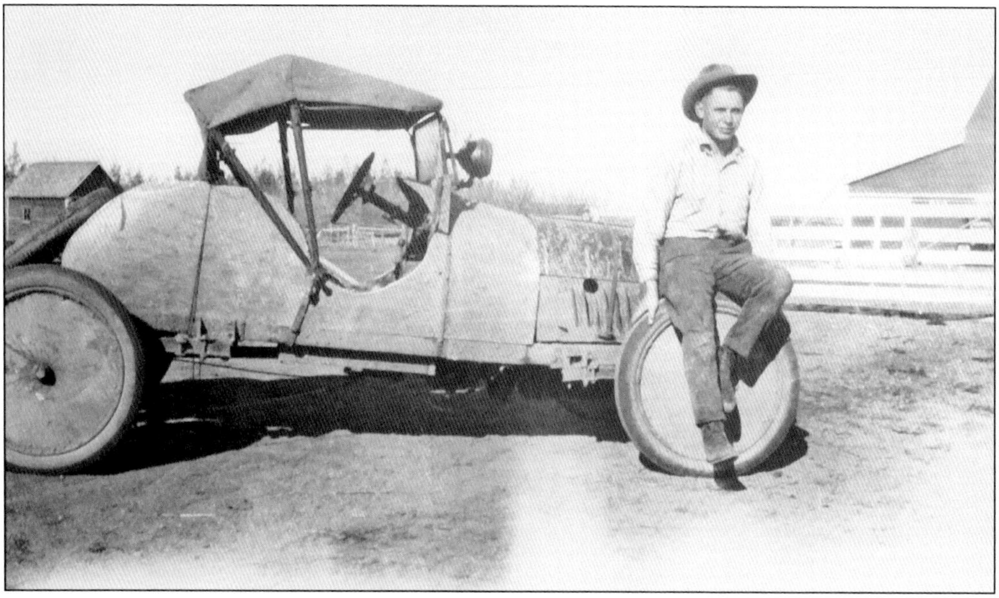

The families of John, Clair, and Grant Stoner, as well as their sister Minnie and her husband, Nibs Cox, settled in the Outlook community in 1909. Ray Stoner, son of John and Beula, is shown above with what he called his "racer." Stoner's father had offered to give him the family's old Overland if he could get it running. He did, and traded it to a Canadian for 40 bushels of flax and a cow, which he in turn resold. He used the proceeds of the sale to buy his Chevrolet 490, the name of which indicated its price when it was introduced in 1915. Stoner presumably paid less than that when he bought the used vehicle in 1924. The photograph below shows that, in the mid-1910s, horseless carriages shared the streets of Plentywood with the old-fashioned equine variety. (Above, courtesy of Eileen McCarty; below, courtesy of Marilyn Fishbeck.)

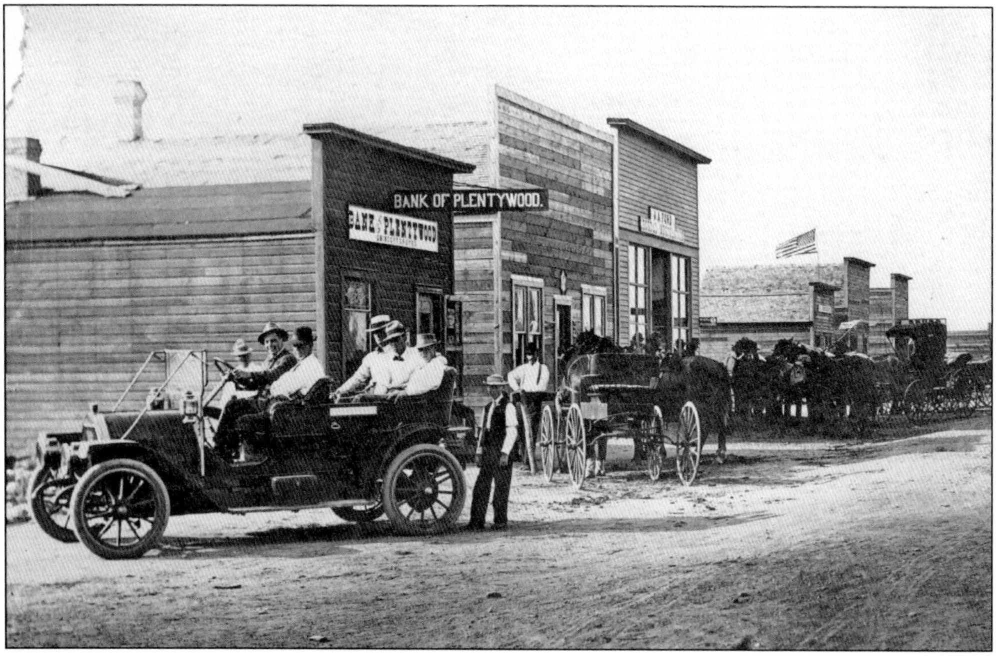

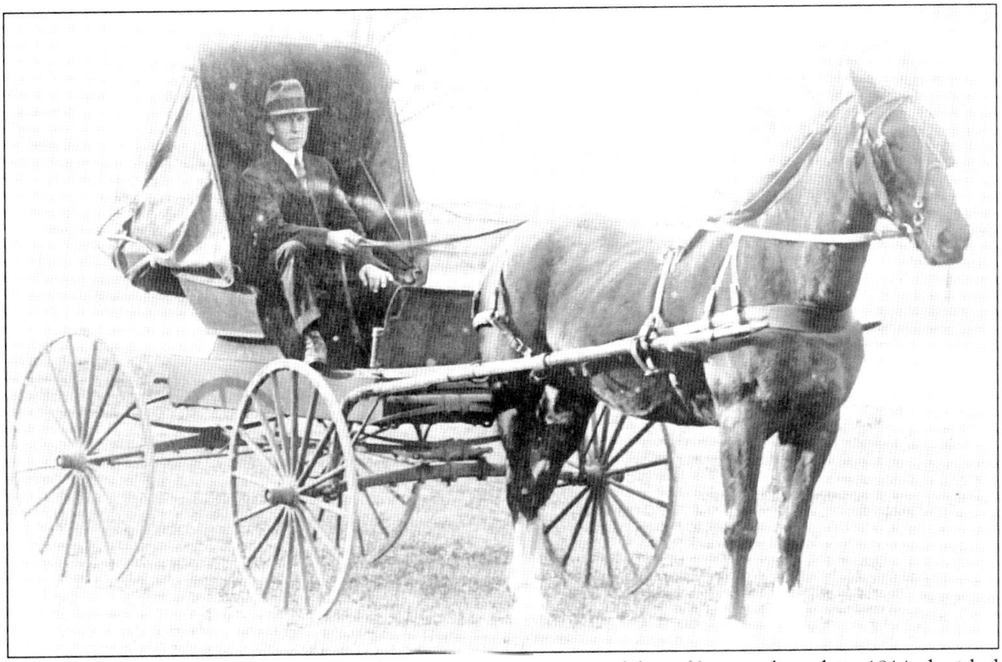

Otto Andersen, shown above in his first carriage, immigrated from Denmark and, in 1914, decided to go west. On the train, he met and accepted a dinner invitation from Chris Madsen of Dagmar. Anderson felt warmly welcomed and decided to remain in Sheridan County, homesteading west of Reserve. Among those who helped establish the Dagmar colony in 1906 was Skov Nielsen, pictured below with his family in the mid-1920s. They are, from left to right, Arne, Ove, Alf, Nielsene, Skov, and Vera. The transition from horse and plow to tractors took some adjustment for Nielsen. One day, while driving his new John Deere Model D tractor, he suddenly realized that he was approaching the fenced end of his field and shouted, "Whoa!" The tractor failed to respond and kept going, taking the fence along with it. (Above, courtesy of Rose Marie Lossing; below, courtesy of Joy Keil.)

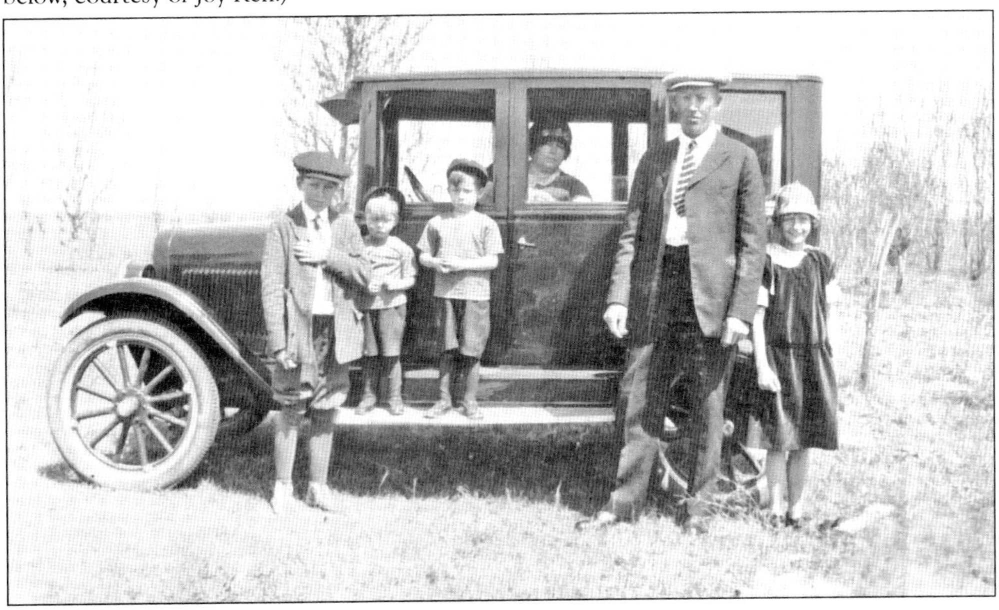

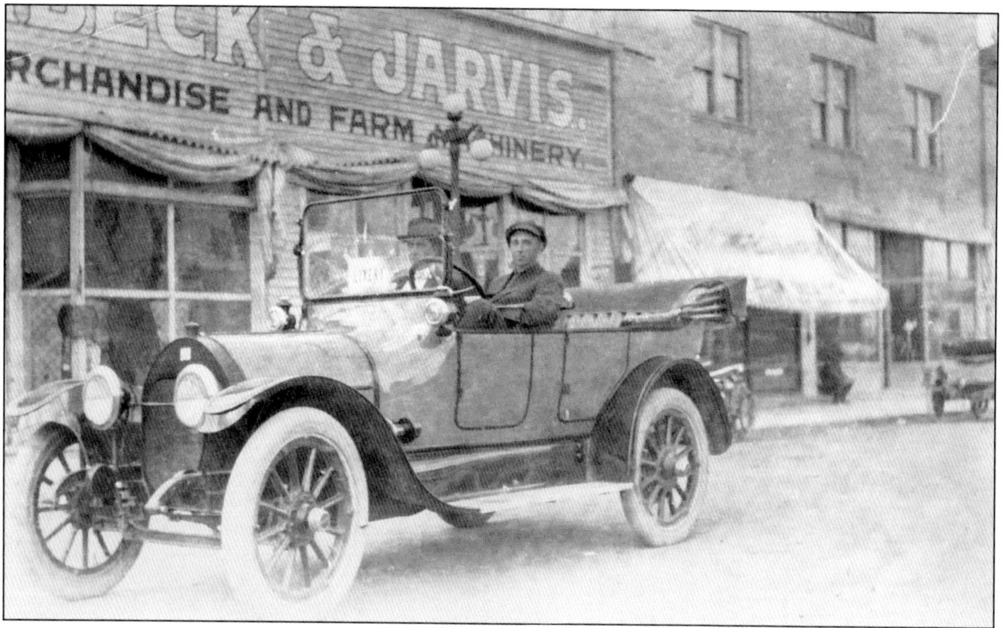

Charles "Rennie" Fishbeck is shown above in 1912 driving his Stanley Steamer, for which he paid $1,600. The car, one of the first in Plentywood, is shown outside his father and uncle's business, Fishbeck & Jarvis Realty Company. Frank Fishbeck Sr. was a prominent businessman and the first citizen from Sheridan County to serve in the Montana state senate, having been elected in 1914. Rennie Fishbeck died during the 1918 flu epidemic. Below, Sig Klofstad (left) and Clarence Wagnild pose at a mine near Raymond. The men are using Klofstad's ragtop coupe to haul coal. The Klofstads and Wagnilds were neighbors in the area southeast of Outlook. (Above, courtesy of Marilyn Fishbeck; below, courtesy of Dorothy Wagnild.)

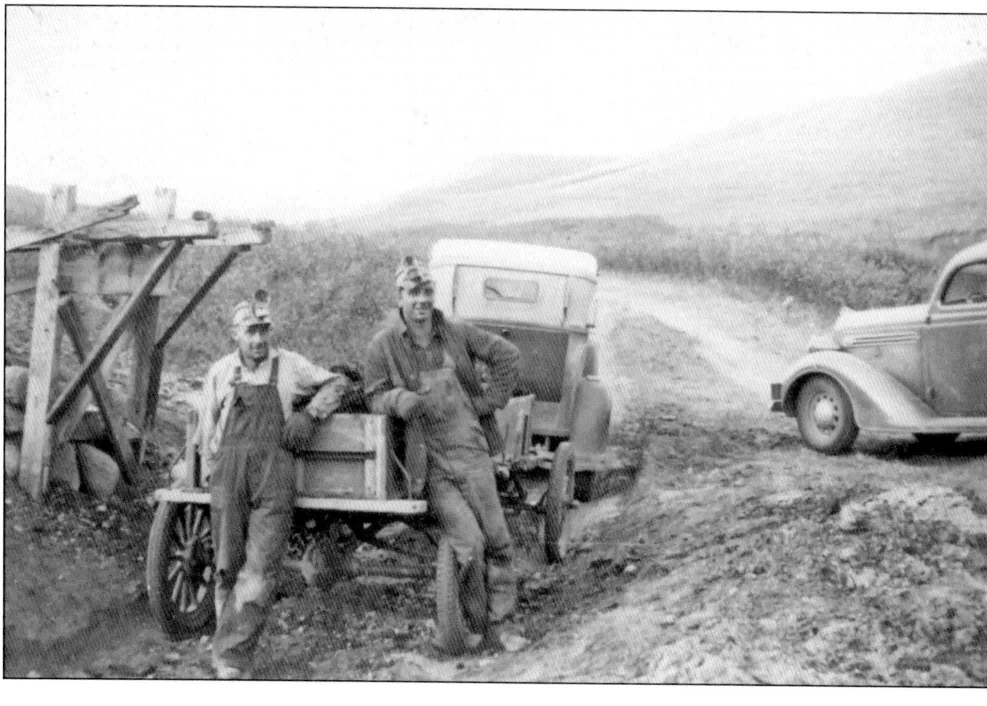

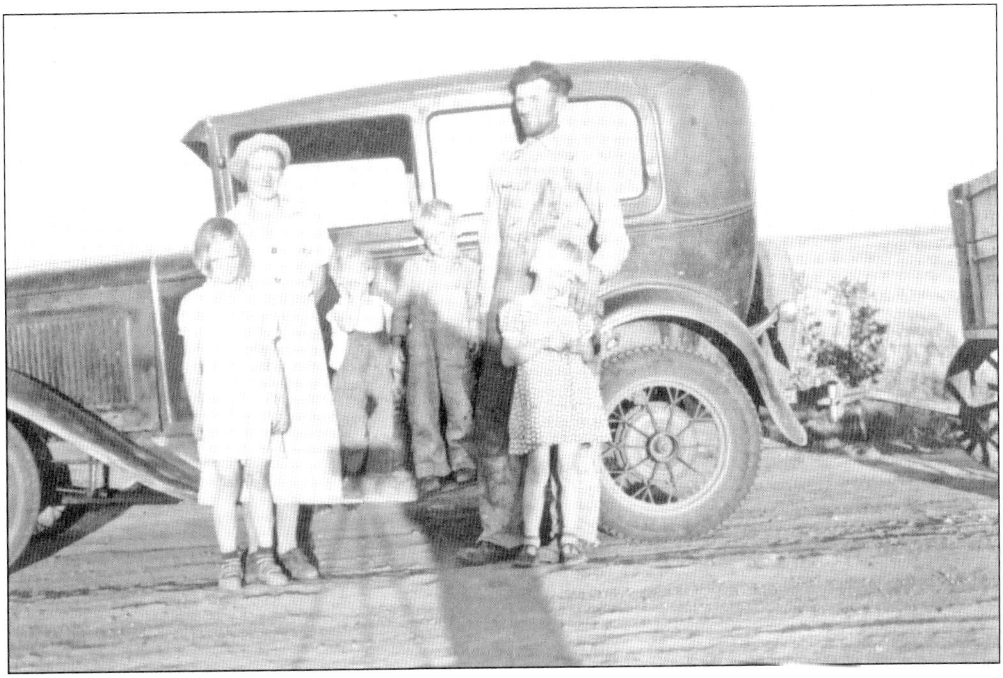

Niels and Signe Moller Lodahl were Danish immigrants who married in 1929 and raised their family on the former Nels Willumsen farm in the Dagmar-Volmer community. The family is shown above using their car to tow a wagonload of water from the Dahlstrom well one mile north of their farm. They are, from left to right, Elice, Signe, LeRoy, Ove, Niels, and Vera. Even in the 1940s, many families still used icehouses or iceboxes to refrigerate their food. Shown below in 1948 is Frank Frasier, whose City Dray Line hauled ice to businesses and residences in Plentywood. The ice was cut from the Raymond Dam into 43-inch-square blocks. (Above, courtesy of Elice Nelson; below, courtesy of Lillian and Lyla Frasier.)

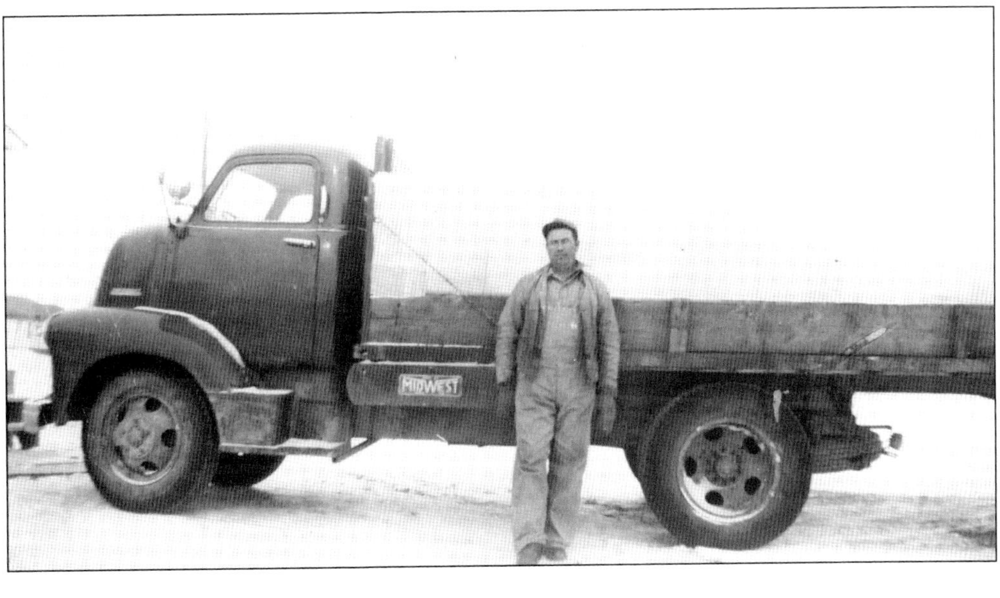

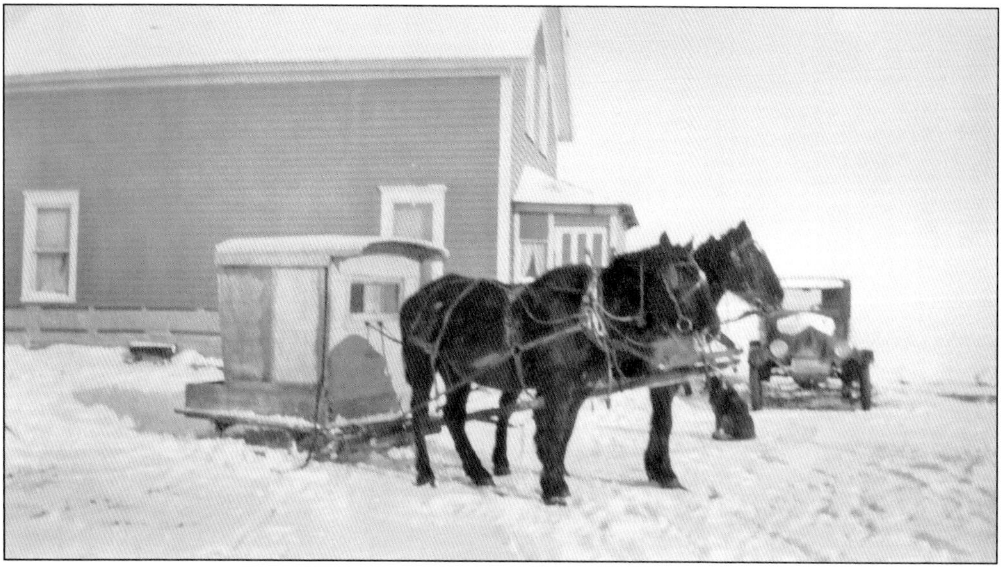

The enclosed sled pictured above was called a pung, derived from an Algonquian word. Earl Nickerson built it to take his children, June and Jack, to the Nickerson country school in the winter during the 1920s and 1930s. Years later, farm children were sometimes treated to an unexpected airplane ride when Taral "Thor" Thorstenson surprised their families by landing in a field and taxiing up to the house unannounced. Thorstenson's parents homesteaded north of Raymond in 1906, and he trained as a pilot during his service in World War I. Back home in Sheridan County, Thorstenson was a flight instructor and mechanic. The photograph below was taken at the Richard Whitney home, south of Outlook, when Thorstenson made an unexpected visit in 1959. (Above, courtesy of Jack Nickerson; below, courtesy of Arlene Whitney.)

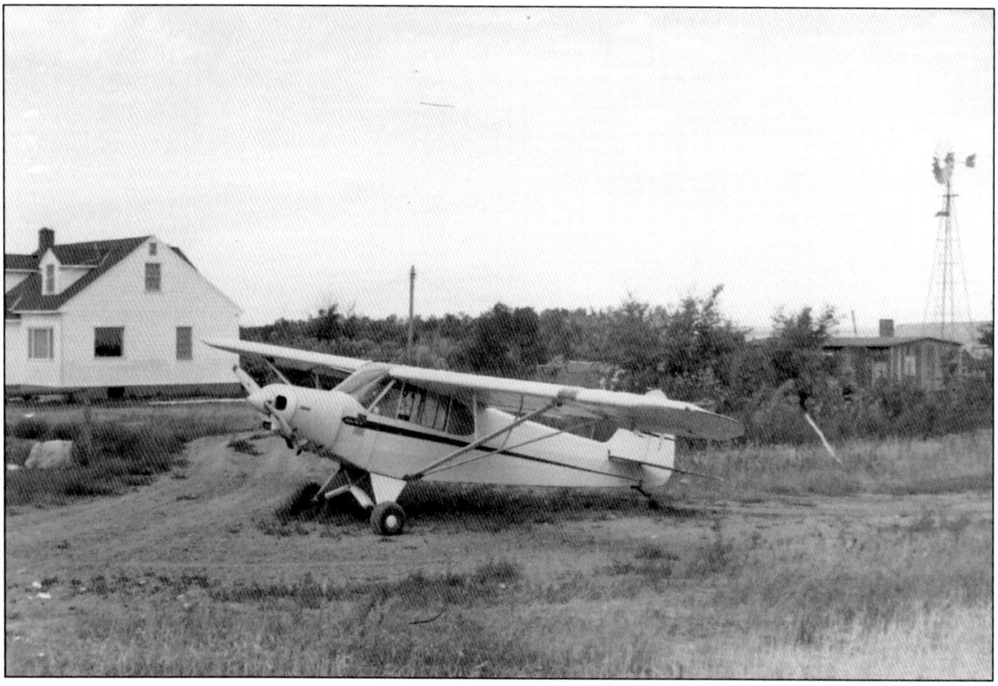

Six

Home Sweet Home

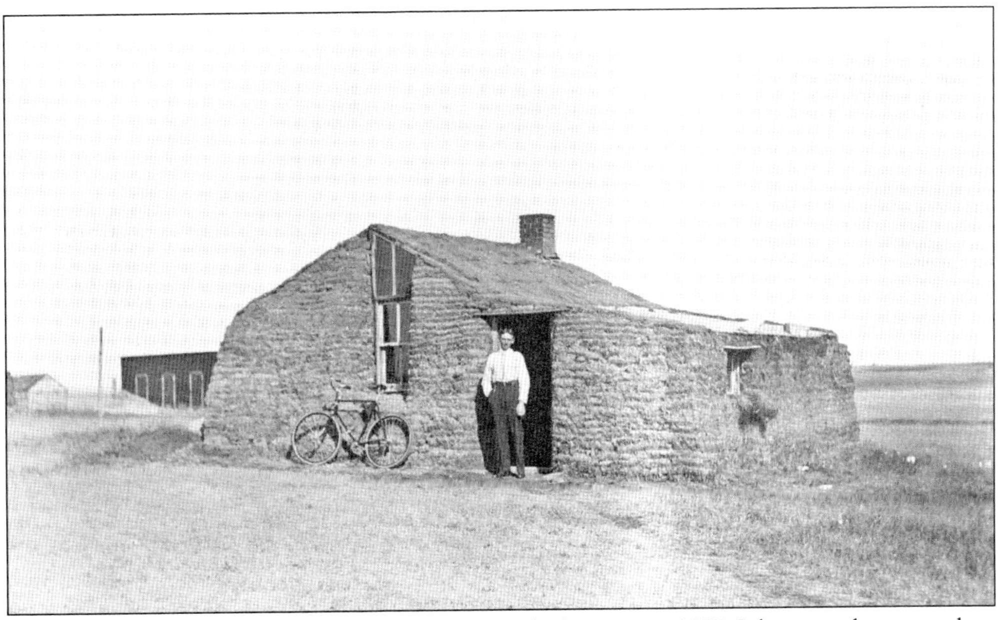

Danish immigrant Walter Olsen came to the Coalridge area in 1907. Like many homesteaders, he built a sod house, although he was said to have added an unusual feature: air-conditioning, in the form of a hand-cranked ceiling fan. An entrepreneur, Olsen owned a garage in Westby, operated a light plant that provided electricity for the town, and also became a Ford dealer. (Courtesy of Heather Shoal.)

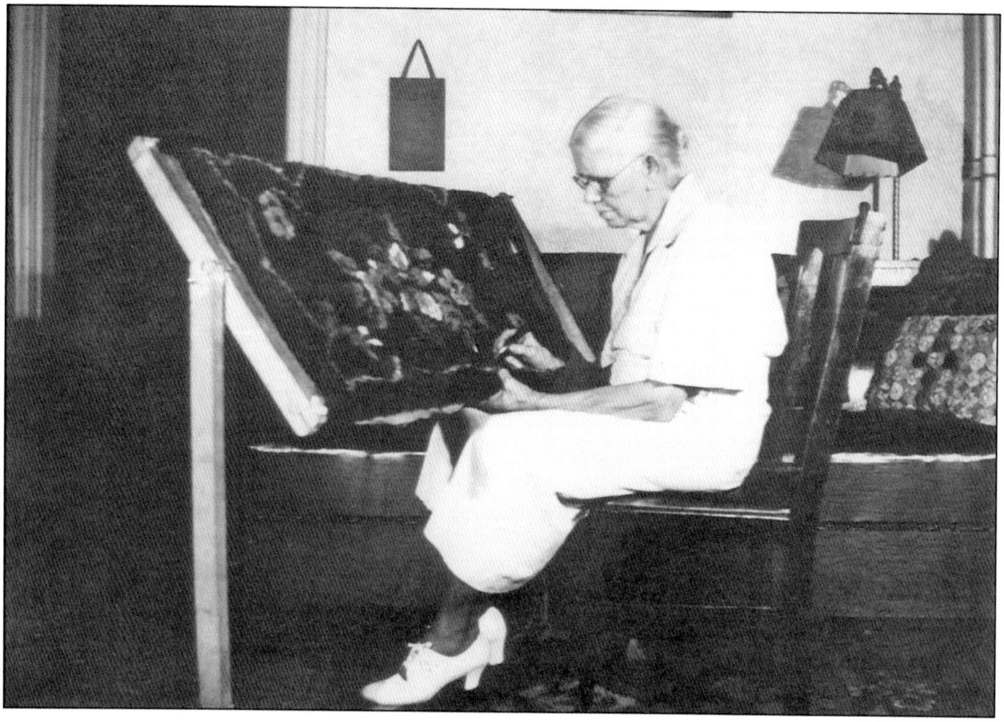

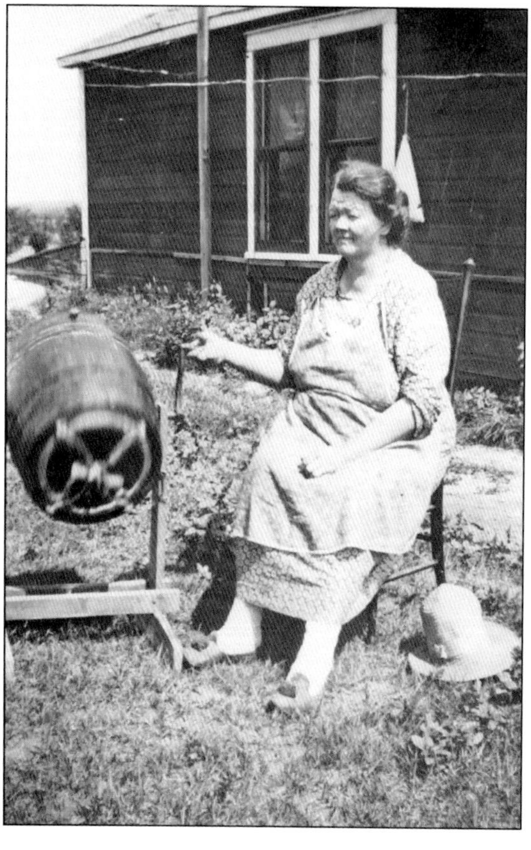

Amelia Phelps is shown above doing needlepoint work. She was born in New York, the fifth of Frederick and Emelia Ball's 12 children. When she was 18 months old, the family moved to Minnesota, leaving her with an uncle and aunt in Wisconsin after promising that they would return for her. They never came back, and she did not learn her parents' true identity until she was 12 years old. She married E.E. Phelps, a carpenter, and they eventually settled in the Wolf Creek area. Phelps worked on many buildings in his community and in Redstone. In the left photograph, Olga Nelson churns butter outside her home. She and her husband, Herman, homesteaded east of Reserve, living in a sod house before building a wood-frame home. (Above, courtesy of Gordon French; left, courtesy of Shirley Nelson).

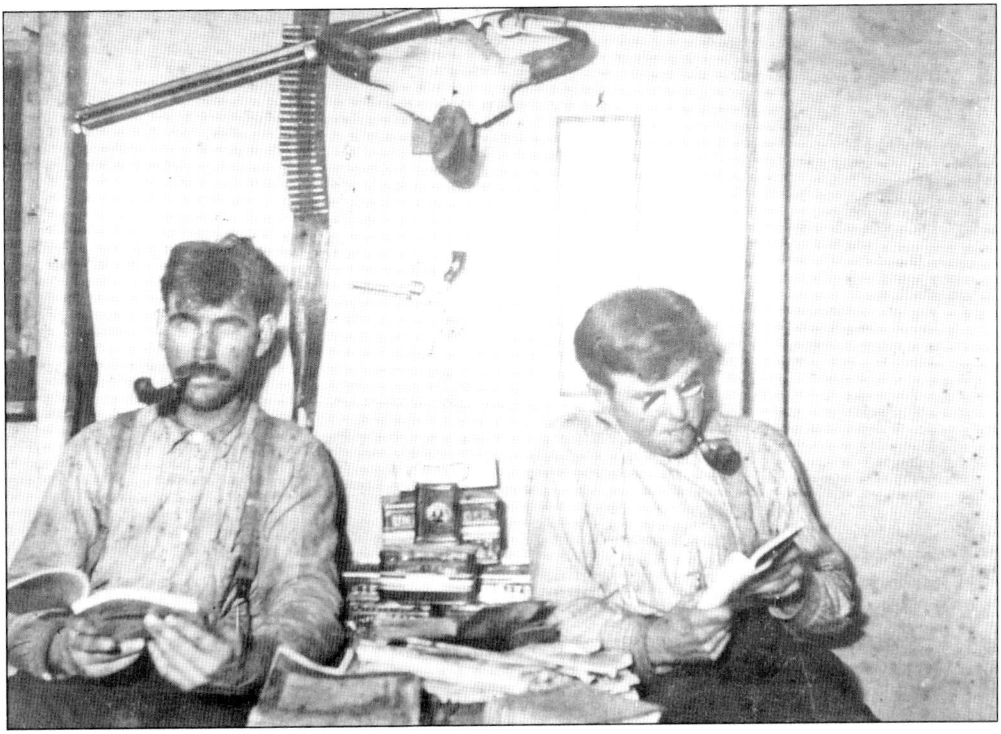

Bob Hill (left) and Henry Mattson are pictured above enjoying a quiet evening at the Hill homestead. When Mattson came to the Outlook community, it had not yet officially opened for homesteading, so he squatted on the land until 1908, a common practice at the time. His property was four miles east of present-day Outlook. At that time, the area was called Greenville and had its own post office on land owned by the Hass family. Mattson met Dagny Hanson, who had come from Canada to visit her brother, one of Mattson's neighbors, and they were married in 1920. Right, Bob Hill's brother Ed is shown protecting his home sweet home, a tar paper shack. (Both, courtesy of Lois Dalthorp.)

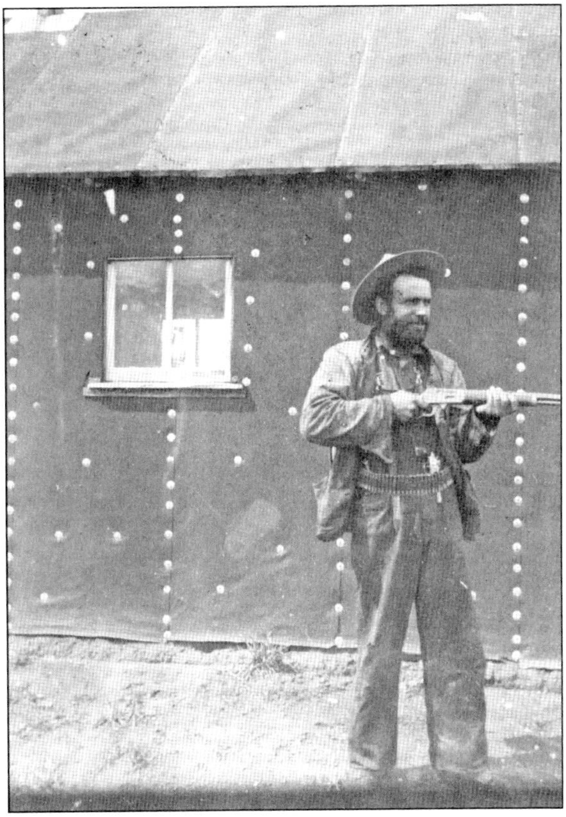

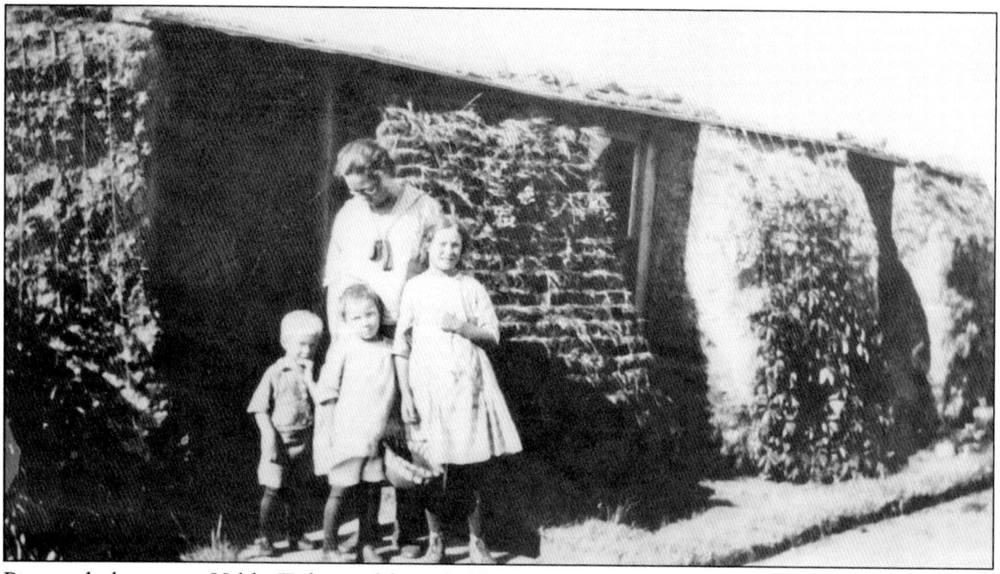

Pictured above are Hilda Tefre and her children, Howard (left), Sylvie (center), and Norma. Andrew and Hilda Tefre were Norwegian immigrants who came to Sheridan County in 1919, homesteading west of Reserve. Their two-room, 12-by-24-foot sod house was built by two uncles. The house was framed by two-by-fours spaced four feet apart, and this frame was then covered with lumber. Finally, the outer sod layer was added. Because of a miscalculation in the building process, the house leaned roughly 10 inches out of square, but served the family well until 1938. A fifth generation of the Tefre family is growing up today on the original property. Below, John Lindblom (right) is shown with an unidentified visitor outside his partially sodded homestead northwest of Raymond. (Above, courtesy of Howard Tefre; below, courtesy of Chester Lindblom.)

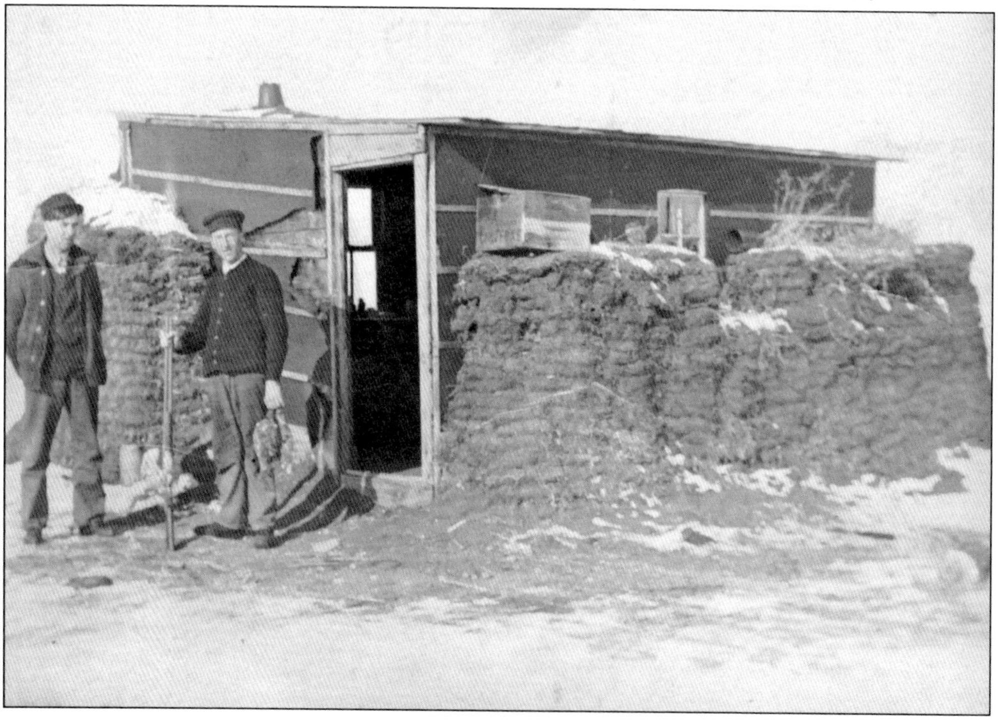

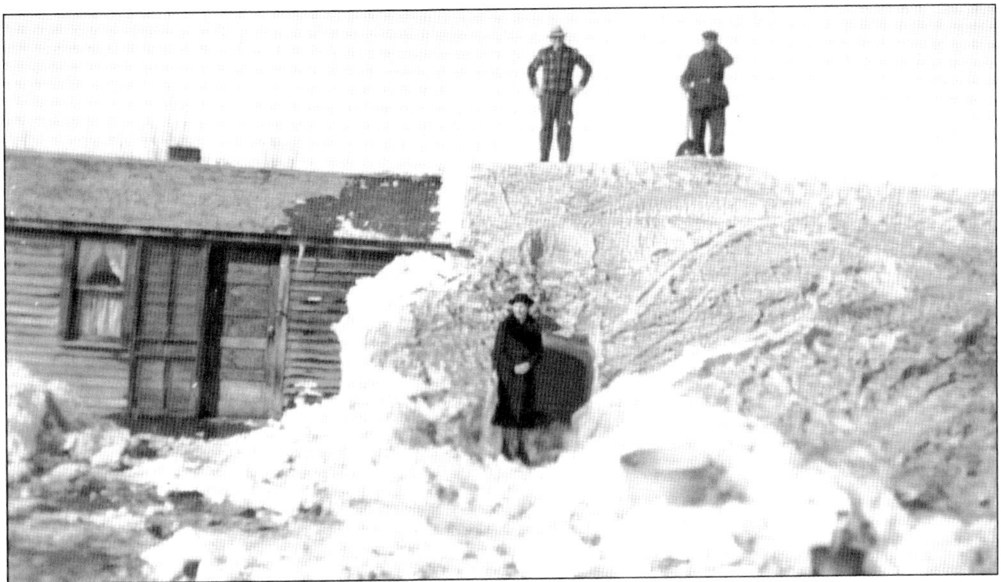

A March 1943 blizzard covered the east side of Frank Dietrich's house, as shown above. Neighbors came to check on the family and found that the Dietrich boys had climbed out of a window, shoveled a pathway to the door, and begun excavating a cave. Dietrich had come from Minnesota in 1907 with his future brother-in-law, Henry Karsten. They filed on adjoining homestead claims northwest of Plentywood, near the McCoy and Goodman families. Below, Martin Rostad of Comertown is shown hauling a load of what appears to be stable muck on a stoneboat harnessed to a reluctant steer. (Above, courtesy of Helen Stoner; below, courtesy of Merlin Rostad.)

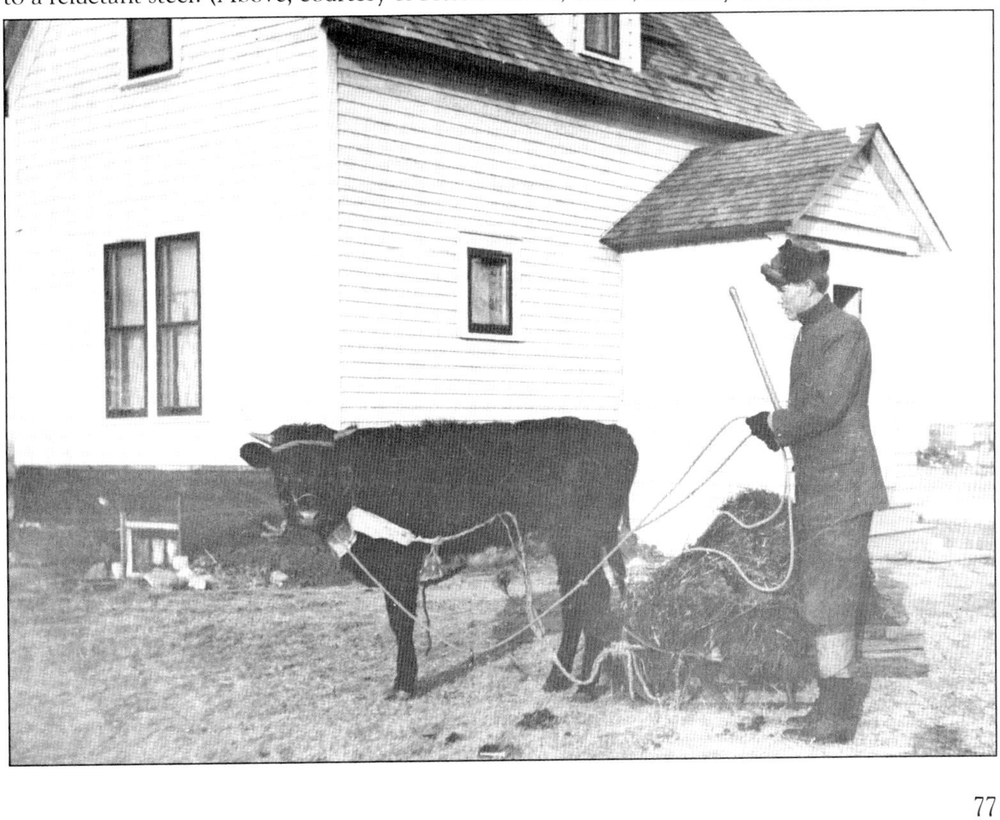

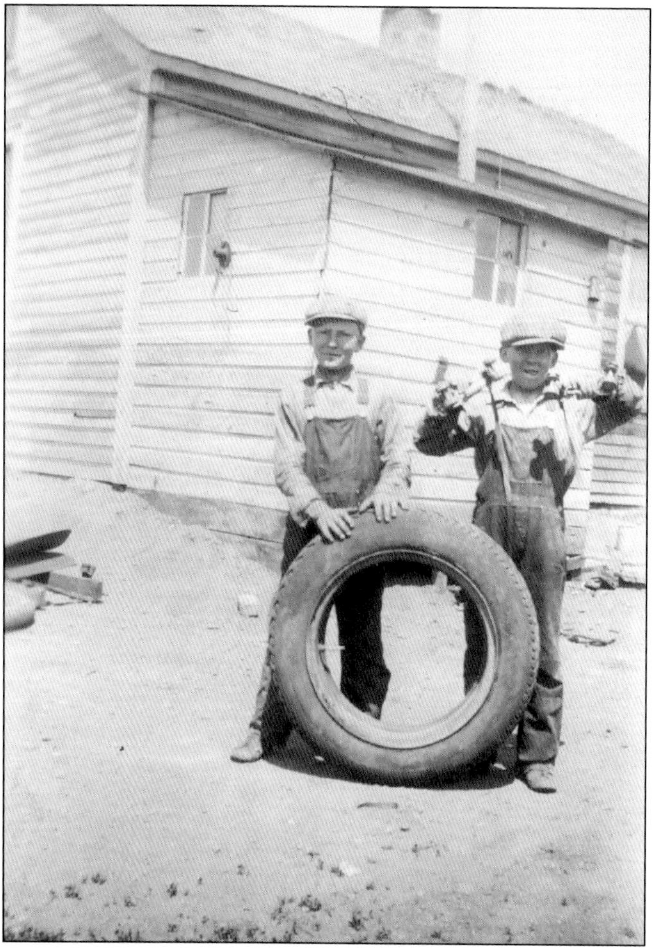

In the left photograph, taken in the mid-1920s, brothers Carl (left) and Melvin Kampen play outside their home on the farm west of Reserve. Their father, Ole, had immigrated from Valdres, Norway, in 1905 at the age of 19. He married Anna Froystad in 1915 and they homesteaded in Sheridan County a few years later. When the Kampen family disembarked the train at Reserve, according to Carl Kampen, their first act was to unload the stove, set it up on the street, and make a meal for the group of "hungry Norwegians." Below, some early-day residents of Dagmar are gathered at the home of Alfred and Valborg Strandskov Jensen. (Left, courtesy of Mary Anne Fowells; below, courtesy of Norman Jensen.)

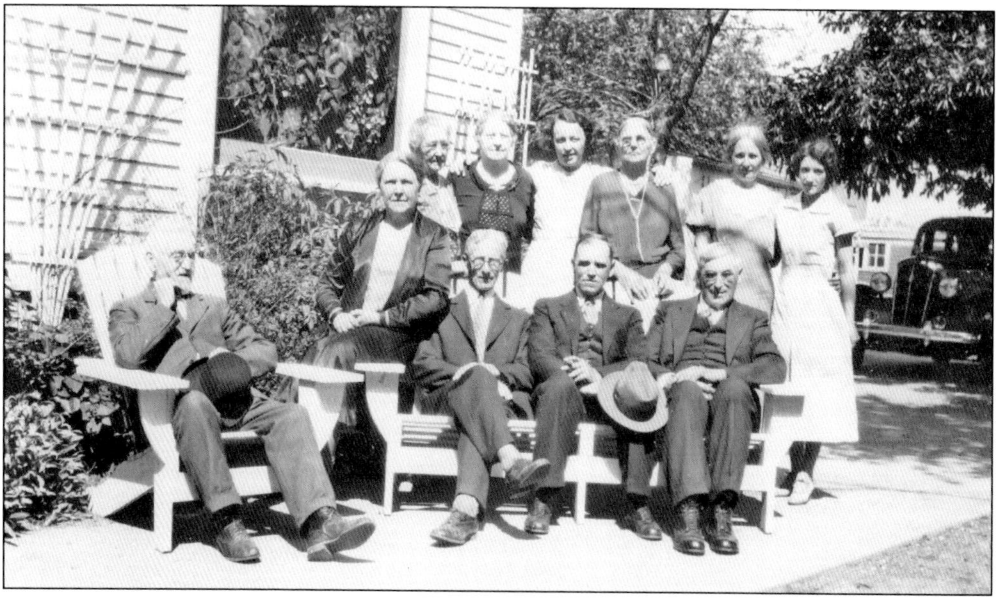

Oscar and Sarah "Sadie" Wagnild were married in Caryville, Wisconsin, in 1913 and came to what they called Rosedale Farm, southeast of Outlook, where he had homesteaded in 1910. The photograph at right is inscribed, "Sadie at 24, Oscar at 26, enjoying honeymoon days on their farm, October 10, 1913." The Wagnilds and their five children lived in this house until it burned to the ground in 1932. Norwegian immigrant Lars Johnson homesteaded north of Plentywood in 1906, bringing his new bride, Guri, to the homestead in 1911. Below, posing outside of the house he built for her are the Johnson family and three of Lars and Guri's brothers. Shown here are, from left to right, Lars, Elmer, Guri, Garnet Johnson, Knut Johnson, Lars Aarhus, and Gulliek Aarhus. The Johnsons later had five more children. (Right, courtesy of Helen Stoner; below, courtesy of Gary Klofstad.)

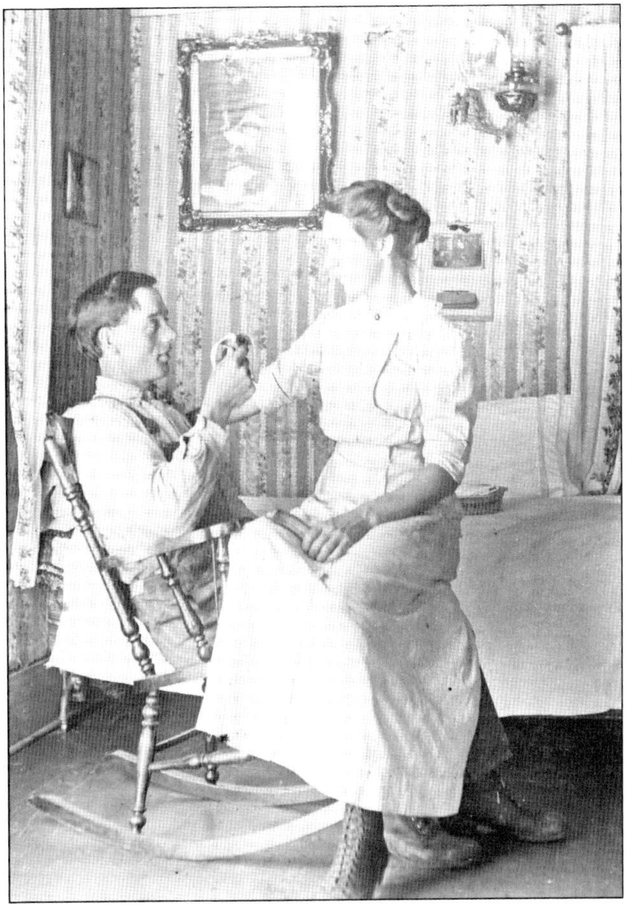

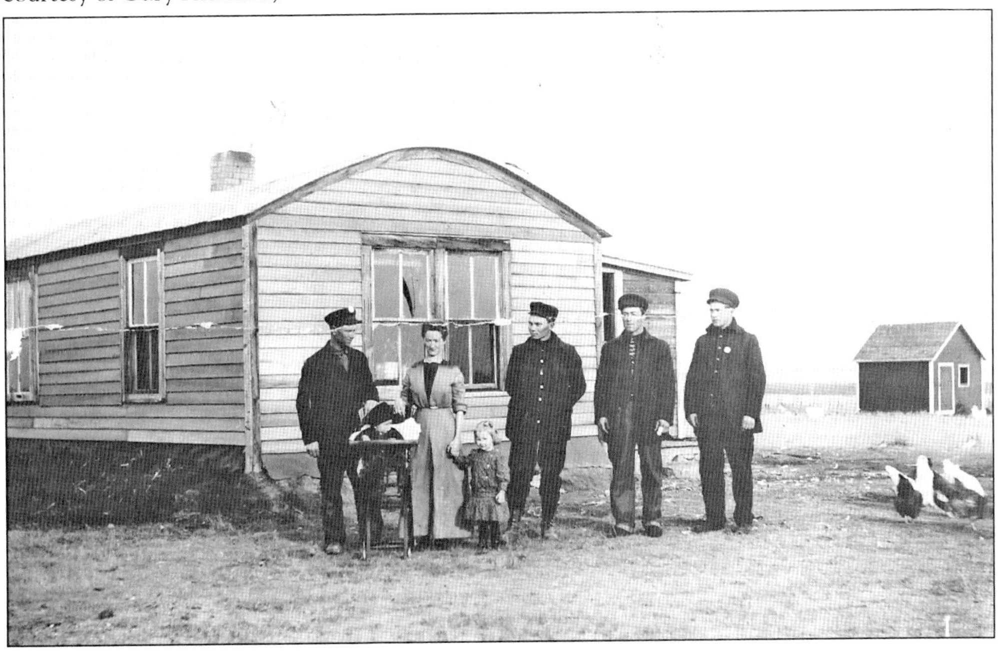

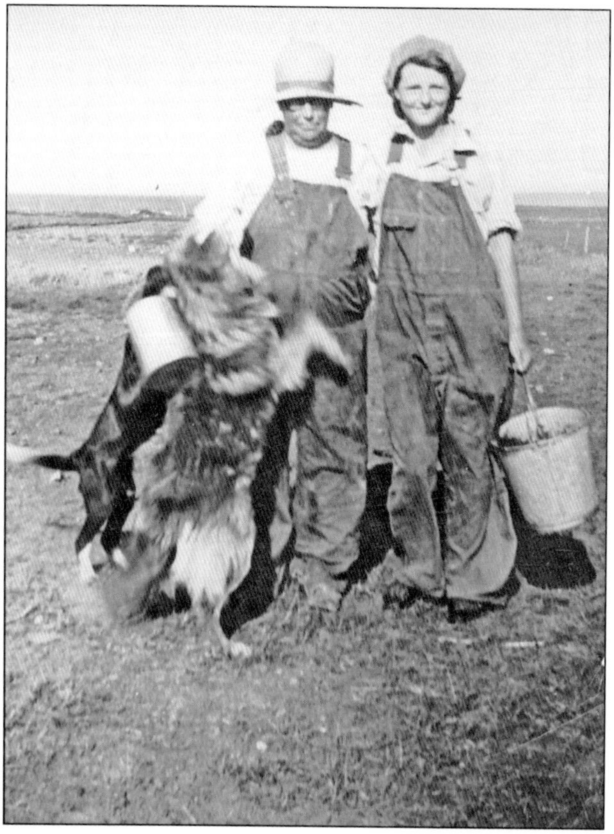

Pictured at left are Christine Benson (left) and neighbor Lillian Boyd in their farm clothes. Christine and Oscar Benson and their five sons came to Montana by train in 1907. Two of the boys, Walter and Herbert, rode in what was called an "immigrant car," a boxcar loaded with a family's possessions including, in the case of the Bensons, cows and chickens. Christine was a practical nurse and midwife who traveled from her homestead northwest of Plentywood to deliver many of the area's babies during the 1910s and 1920s. The Benson farm was near the future Carroll Dam, shown below in 1942 after an unusually heavy, two-inch rainfall. The storms caused water to cross the cement spillway, a preview of coming disaster. (Left, courtesy of Harold Benson; below, courtesy of Helen Stoner.)

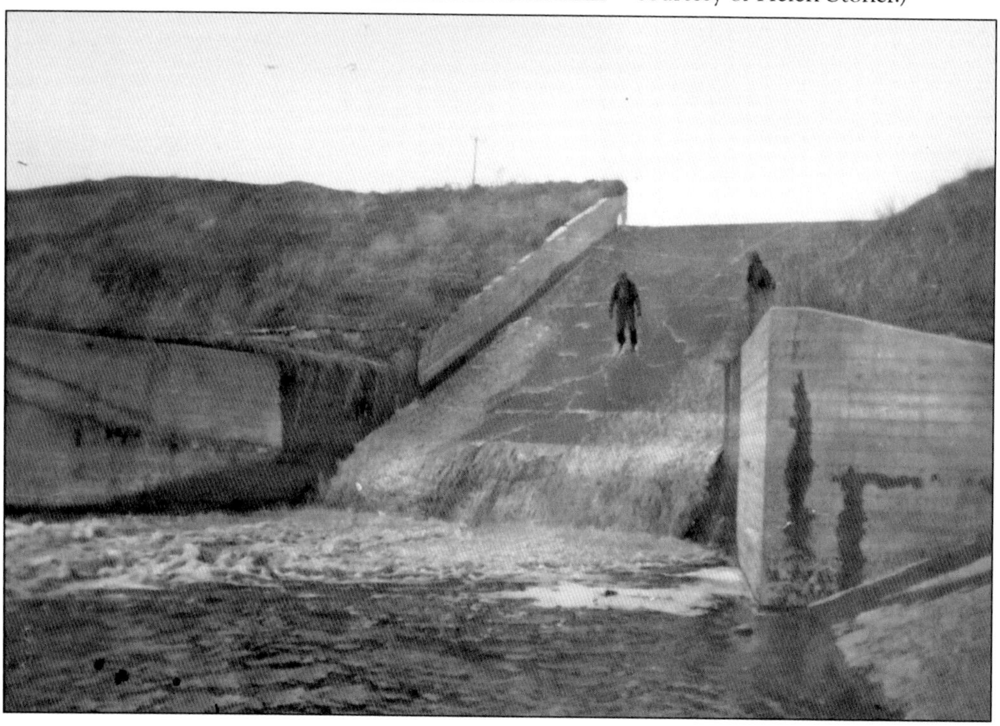

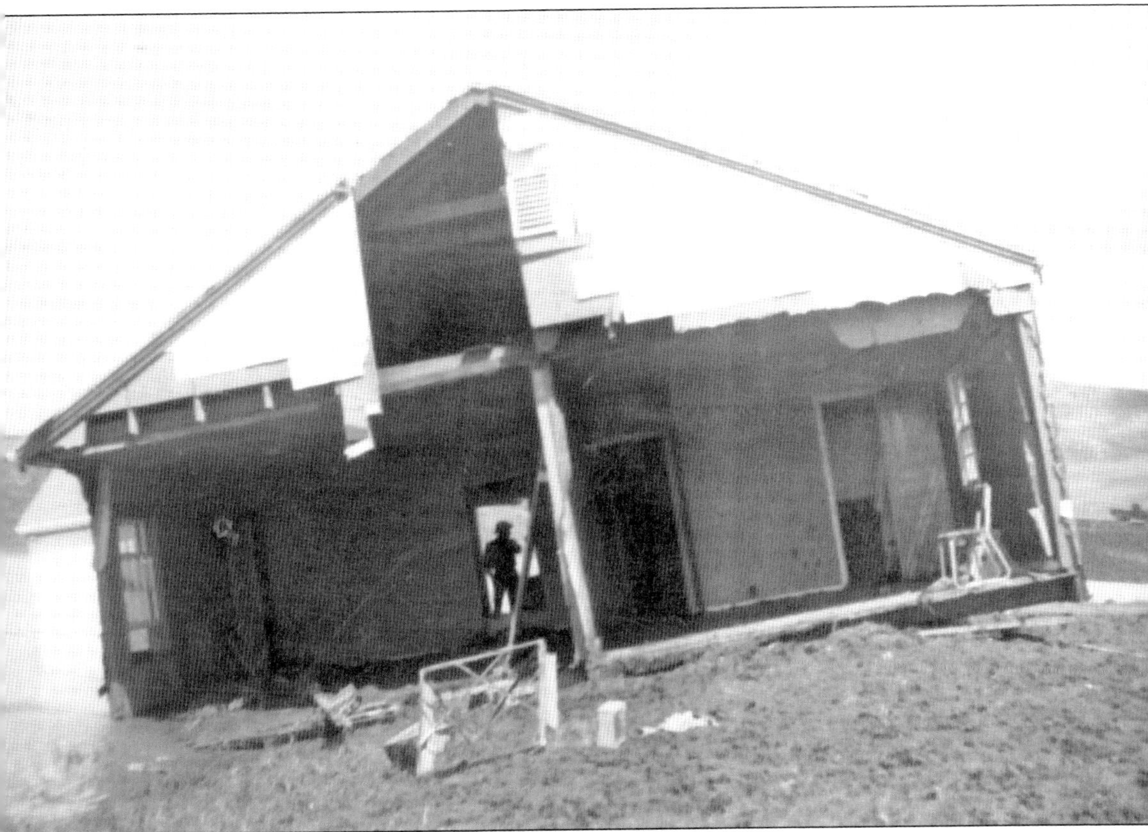

A torrential downpour of more than five inches fell throughout the day of July 6, 1946. On the farm homesteaded by his parents, Herb Benson heard the roar of water and walked toward Carroll Dam, where he saw water flowing over not only the spillway, but the dam's walls. Benson drove his truck through treacherous mud to the Hub Bar in Outlook, where he called his brother, Dr. Oscar Benson Jr., urging him to warn the family. Should the dam break, the family's house would be in the path of the flood. Benson and local pharmacist E.I. Miller sped to the Goodman ranch west of Plentywood, where the children had already gone to bed in the basement. The Goodman family took refuge on a hill and, when lightning illuminated the landscape, they watched the flood roaring through the valley, sweeping their home from its foundation. The Goodman home, shown here in the aftermath, was salvaged and moved back to the ranch, but Carroll Dam was never rebuilt. (Courtesy of Ardelle Hart.)

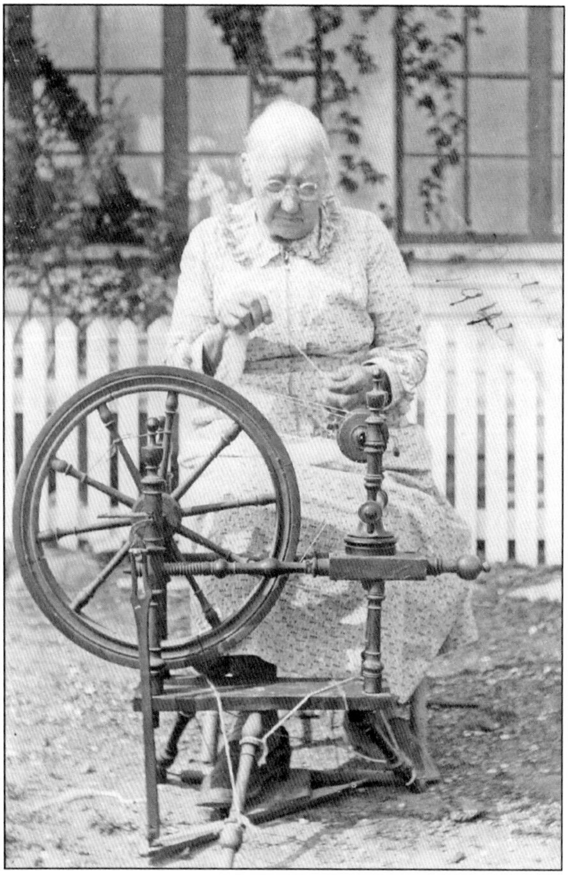

Maren Strandskov Jacobsen of the Dagmar community is shown at left in 1940 at the home of her daughter and son-in-law, Marie and Jens Lind, west of Reserve. She is demonstrating for her grandchildren how to use a spinning wheel. Below, a group of friends and teachers gathers at the Martin Rostad home in Comertown in the late 1920s. In the first row, at center, is Henry Raaen, a graduate of St. Olaf College in Minnesota. Raaen homesteaded in 1910 and taught school in Daleview and in the Olson country schools before accepting a position as the first Plentywood school principal. He continued to farm, served for a time as Sheridan County deputy assessor, and eventually became Sheridan County school superintendent. (Left, courtesy of Bernice Jacobsen; below, courtesy of Mina Mittelstaedt.)

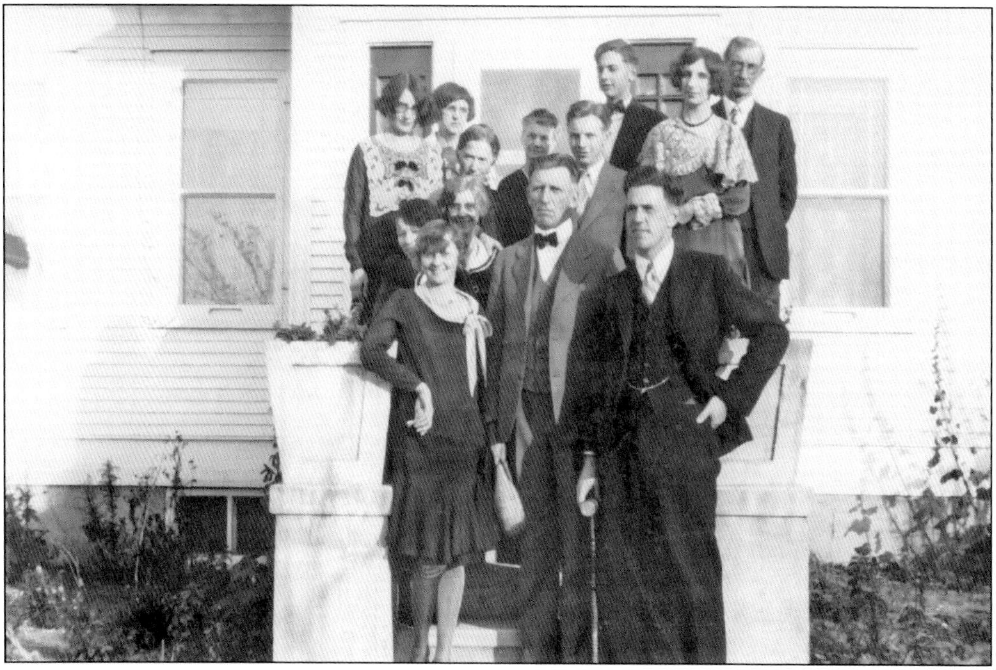

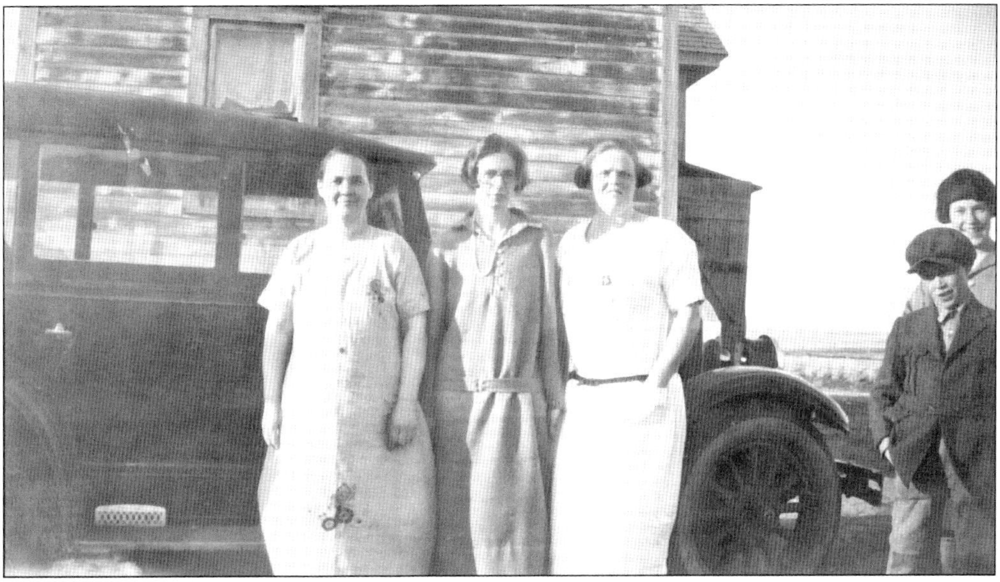

In the above photograph, members of the Raymond community gather for an afternoon visit. Shown are, from left to right, Clara Melle, Agnes Lindblom, Anatta Westphal, Albert Lindblom, and Anna Melle. Below, friends from the Plentywood, Outlook, and Raymond communities gather at the Grain Terminal Association convention in St. Paul, Minnesota. They are, from left to right, (first row) Elsie Medders, Wanda Wankel, Kate Benson, and Herb Benson; (second row) Lyle Medders, Jack Westphal, Bob Wankel, and Louis Melle. Medders was the only child of Roy and Lila Medders, who had homesteaded in the Dooley area in 1916. During the 1918 Spanish flu epidemic, Lila helped Dr. Joseph Charles Storken care for sick patients, even bringing some of them into her own home. (Above, courtesy of Ila Syme; below, courtesy of Harold Benson.)

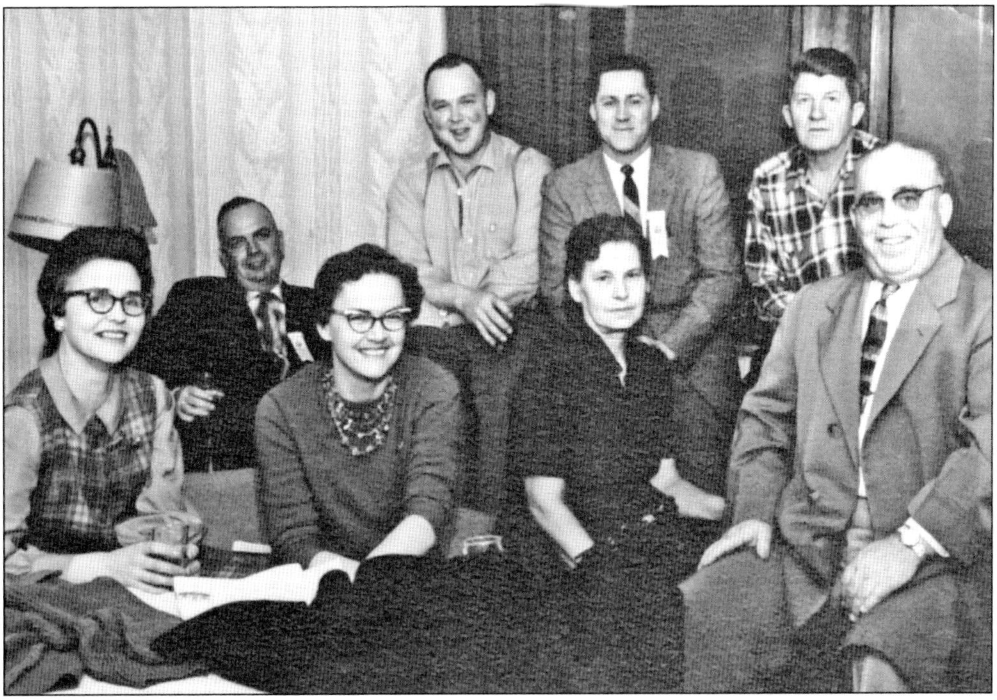

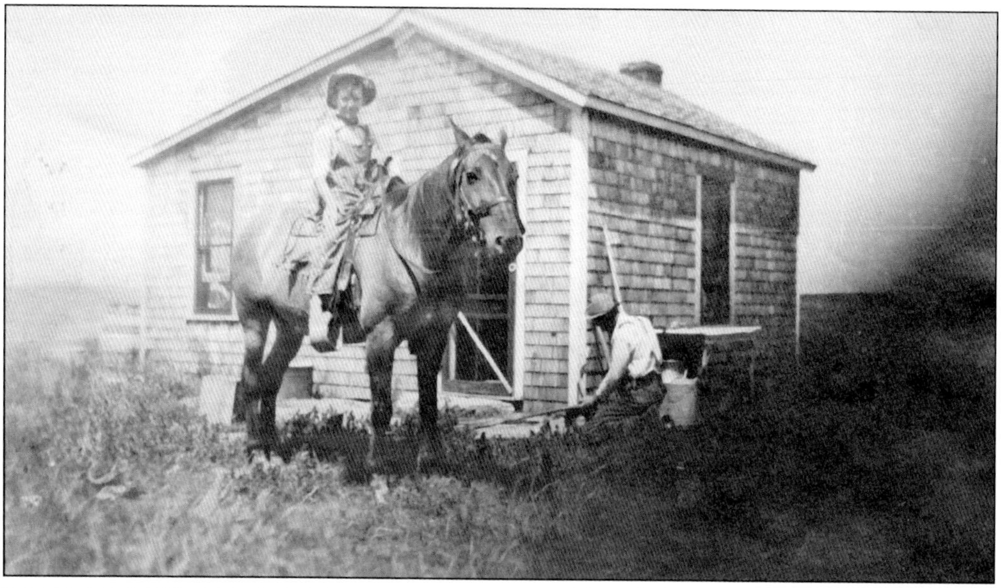

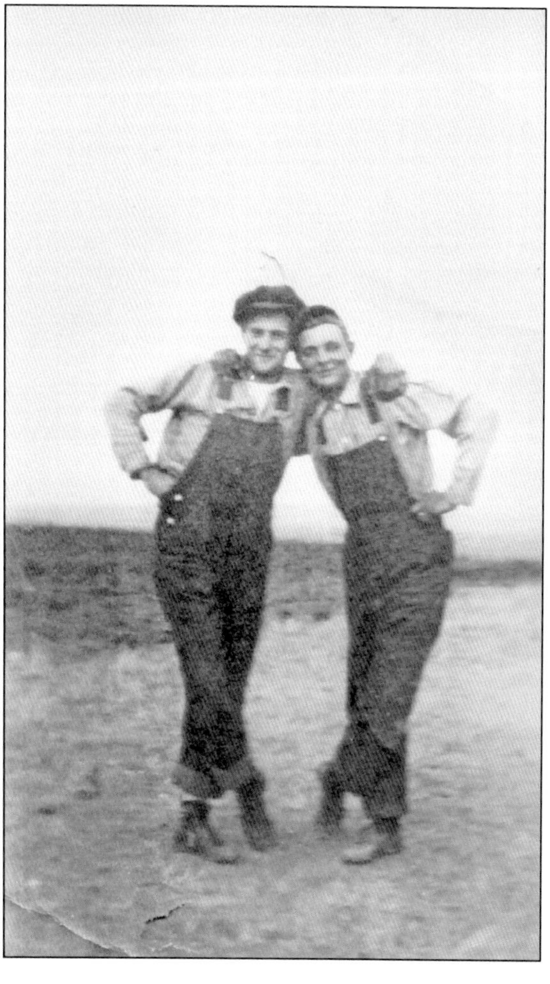

Peter Keldsen emigrated from Denmark in 1907, staked his homestead claim in the Westby area in 1910, and became a naturalized citizen four years later. Above, Keldsen works to repair a mower sickle outside his home as a neighbor, Bill Stageberg, poses on his horse. One of 10 children, Stageberg was from North Dakota, but came to attend the McElroy School, where his older sister Pearl was a teacher. Left, Joe Wirtz Jr. and John Ladd Jr. pose on the Ladd farm. By the time John and Aurelia Ladd came to Sheridan County in 1914, Outlook had already moved to its present site when the Soo Line came through. The Ladd family purchased land that included the old townsite and built a two-story home over an abandoned basement. (Above, courtesy of Ken Keldsen; left, courtesy of Chester Wirtz.)

Seven

Growing Up in Sheridan County

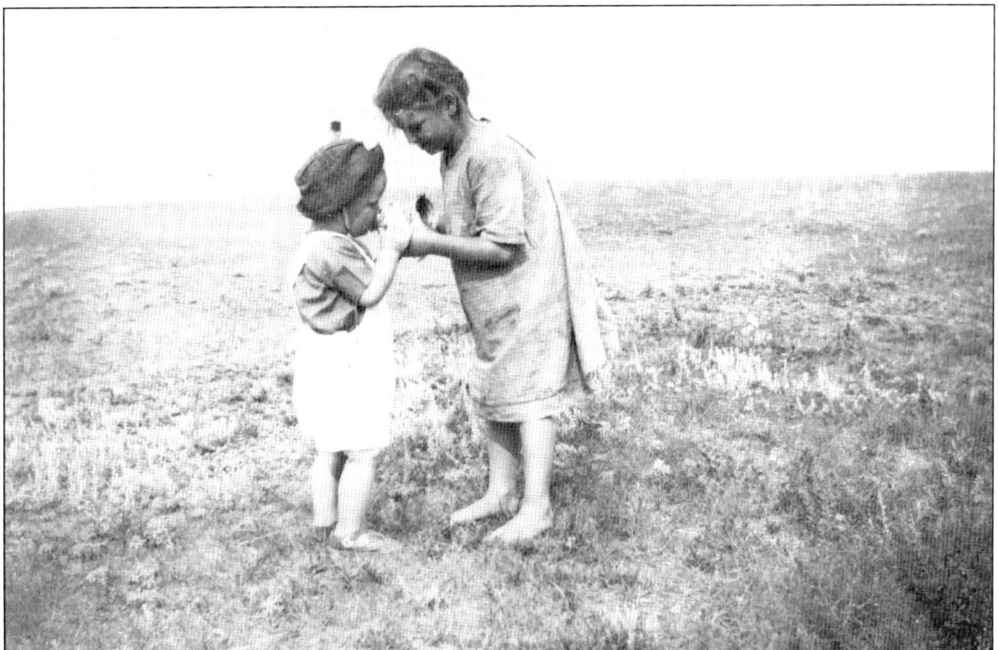

Gladys Nelson helps her little brother, Harold, get a drink on their farm southeast of Antelope around 1915. Their parents, Herman and Olga Nelson, were Swedish immigrants who eventually had five children. The eldest, Nels, helped his mother maintain the farm so Herman could supplement the family's income by working in the trade for which he had been trained as a young man: tailoring. (Courtesy of Shirley Nelson.)

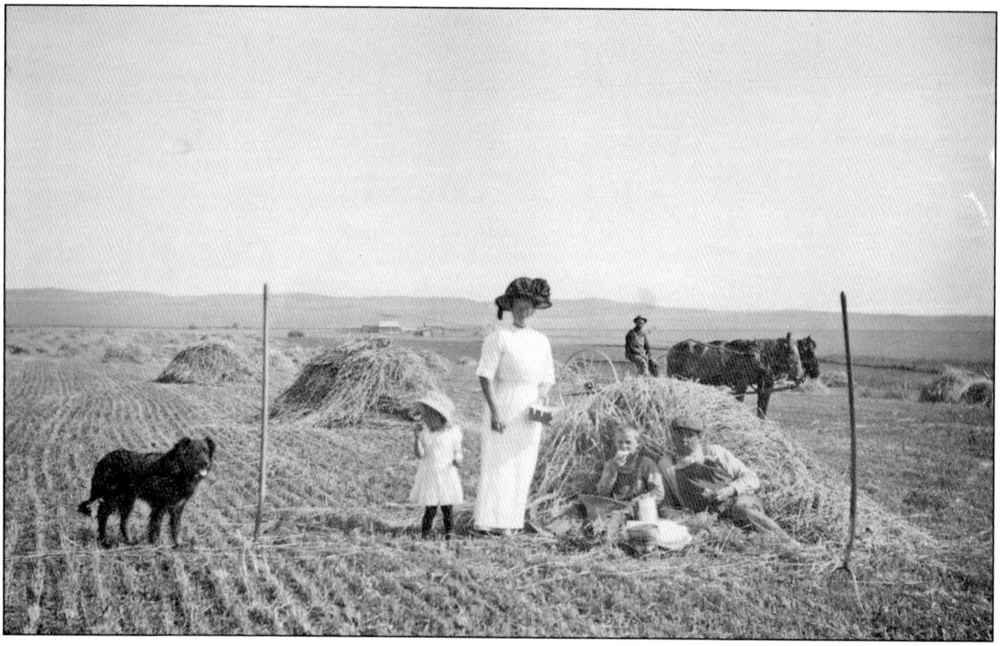

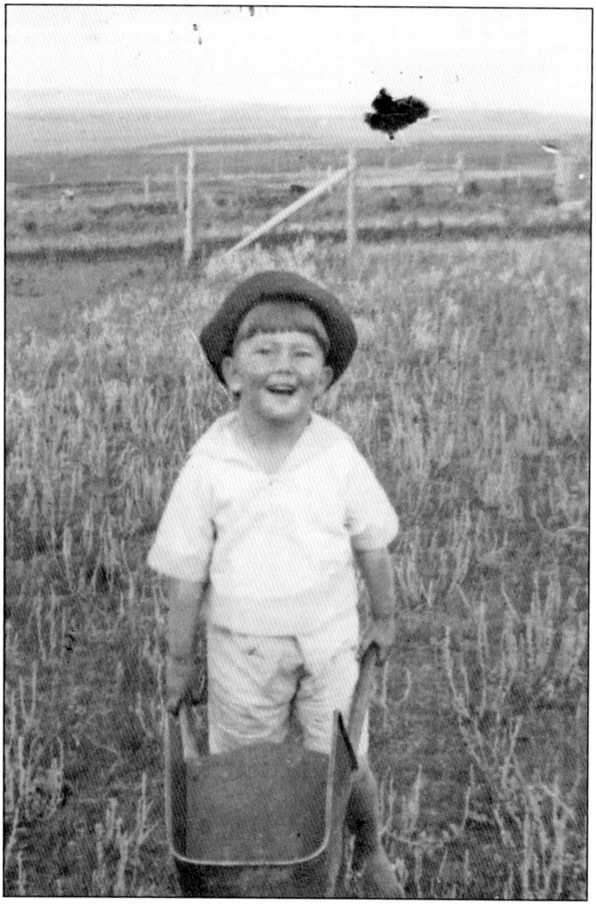

For many children, growing up in Sheridan County meant participating in farmwork. In the 1915 photograph above, Helen Lundeen and her daughter Agnes bring lunch to the field, where straw is being stacked. Martin Lundeen and his son, Erick, rest against the straw stack, and an unidentified man, possibly one of Lundeen's brothers, drives the team of horses. A Danish immigrant, Martin Lundeen had originally planned to make a fortune in Montana and then return to his family in Denmark. Instead, it took four years for him to make enough money to bring them to America. Left, young Harvey French is shown with his wheelbarrow on the farm of his parents, Hugh and Mildred Phelps French, south of Redstone. (Above, courtesy of Don McCrory; left, courtesy of Ardelle French.)

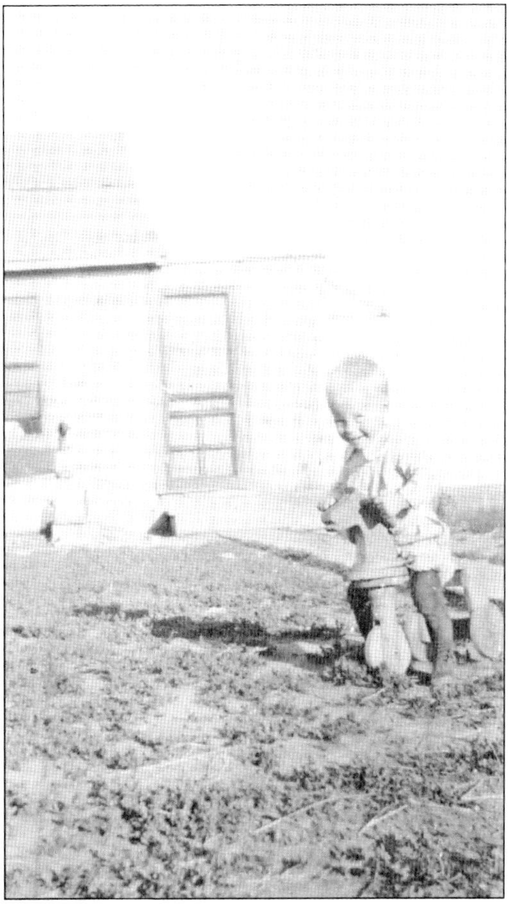

Wilbur Damstrom, born in 1918, is shown in the right photograph riding a wooden tricycle in the yard of his family's homestead east of Antelope. His parents, Henry and Minnie, made monthly wagon trips to Culbertson for supplies. On the way home from one such trip, the family was caught in a whiteout blizzard. Henry released the reins, trusting that his team of horses would lead them home, and the family arrived safely. One of four children, Wilbur, along with his wife, Eloyce Anderson Damstrom, eventually took over the farm. Shown below are the Bishop children, whose father was the manager of one of Medicine Lake's four lumberyards. (Right, courtesy of Craig Damstrom; below, courtesy of Virginia Carpenter.)

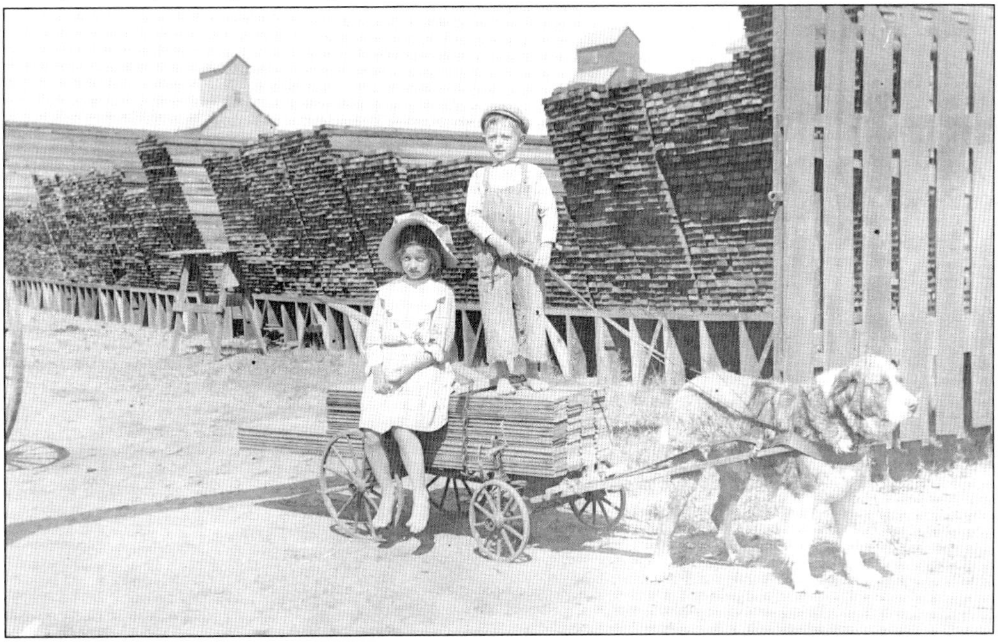

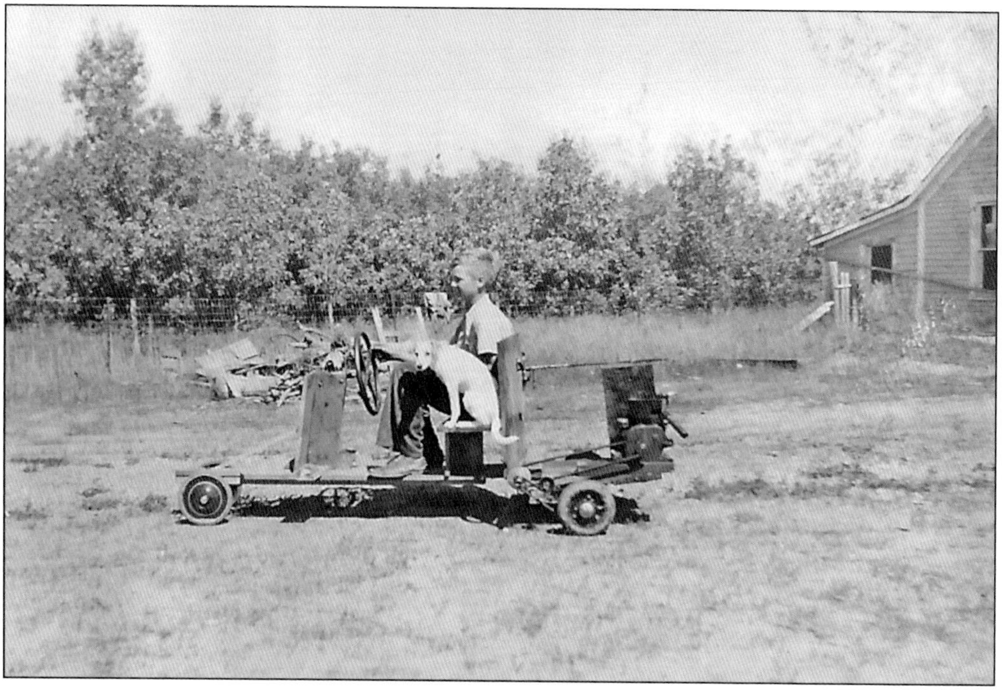

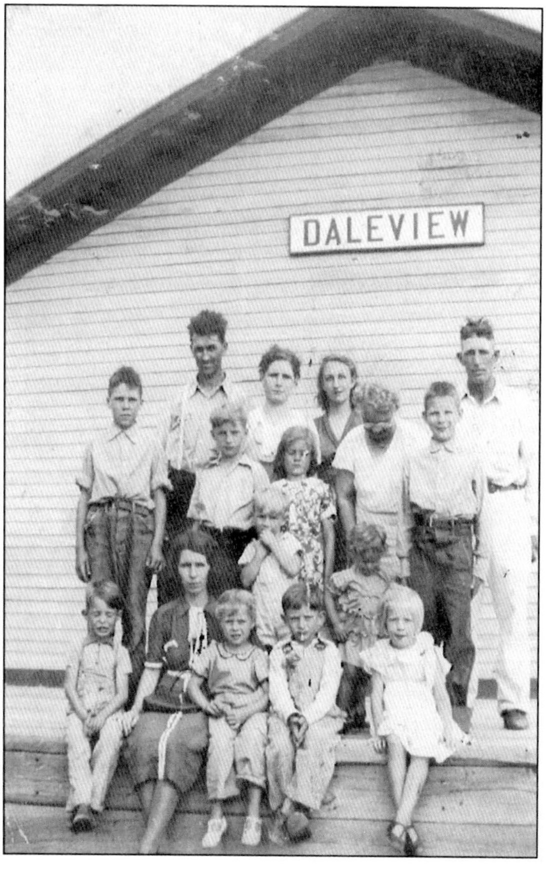

Eddie Angvick of Reserve is pictured above with his dog, Nancy, in a go-cart he made when he was 12 years old. He used an old washing machine motor and wheels that he found in the Plentywood junkyard and attached them to a six-foot wagon. He could reach speeds of roughly 16 miles per hour (and lived to tell about it!). At left, the Lester family of Daleview gathers for a photograph at the train depot during a family reunion in 1936. They are, from left to right, (first row) Forrest Lester, Thelma Berglund, Elsie Berglund, Jim Bodahl, and Charlotte Lester; (second row) Larry Bodahl and Geraldine Lester; (third row) Don Berglund, Robert Bodahl, Phyllis Lester, Sarah Lester, and Bob Berglund; (fourth row) Walter Berglund, Veldon Bodahl, Elaine Berglund, and Art Lester. (Above, courtesy of Marbea Lane; left, courtesy of Phyllis Johnson.)

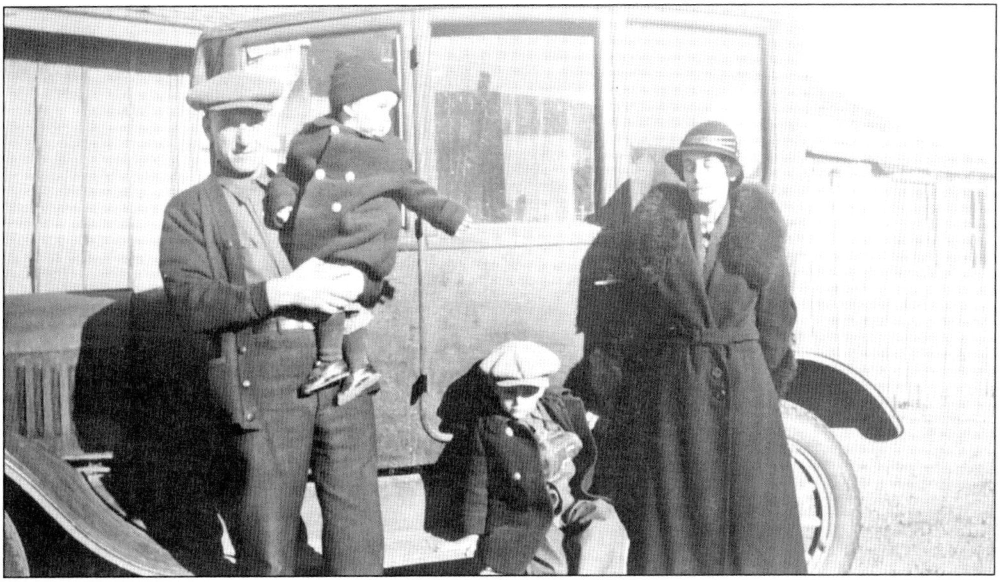

Pictured above in 1933 are Calvin (second from left) and Arnold Nelson with their grandparents Sam and Sarah Walkeden. Originally from England, the couple met after immigrating to Canada and eventually homesteaded northeast of Raymond. One of their daughters, Nancy, married Nels Nelson and gave birth to Arnold, and then Calvin, dying shortly thereafter of scarlet fever. The Walkedens helped raise the two boys, who enjoyed growing up near their cousins, the children of Floyd and Edna Walkeden Willard. The kids in the 1937 photograph below are, from left to right, one of the Lindly brothers, whose father was a local pastor; Arnold Nelson; baby Nancy Willard, who was named in honor of her aunt; another Lindly boy; and Calvin Nelson. (Both, courtesy of Ginny Larson.)

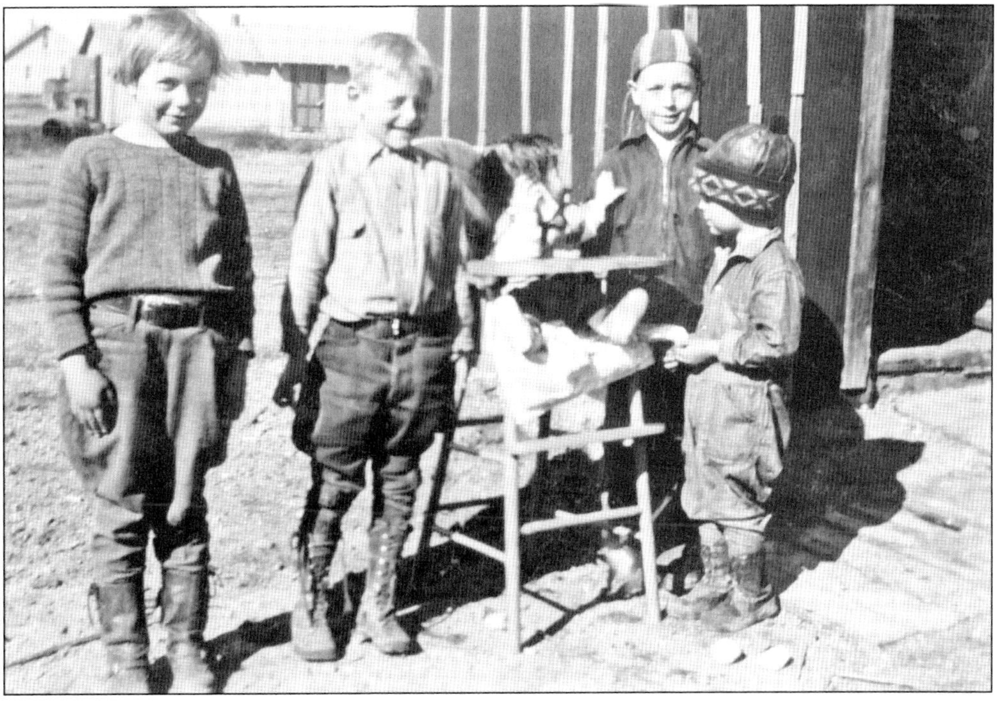

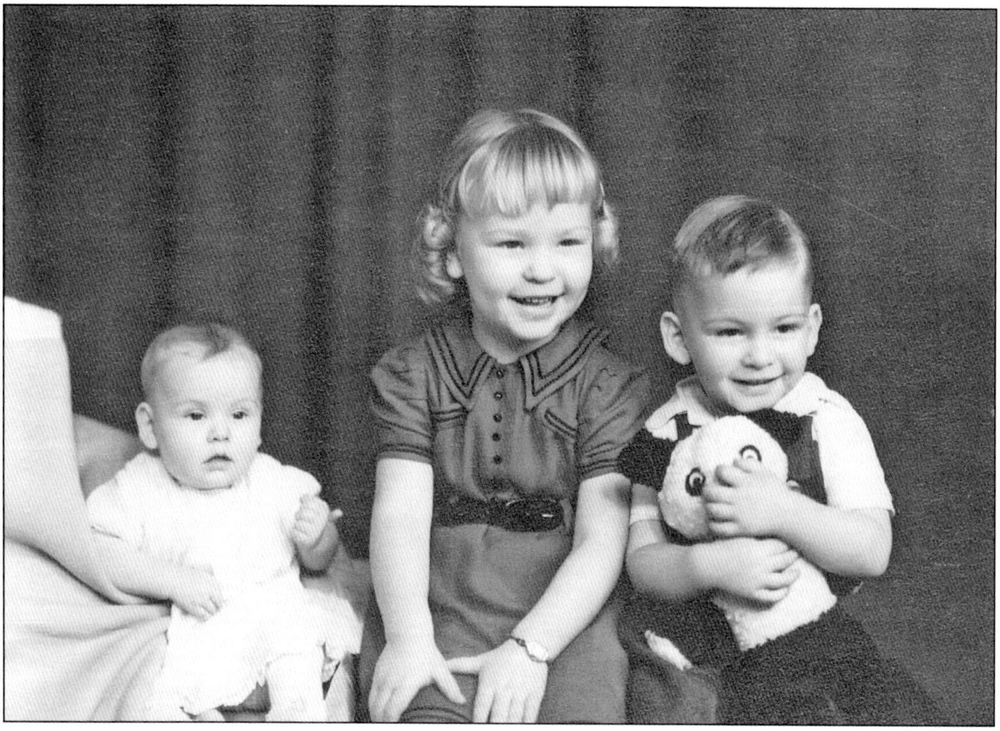

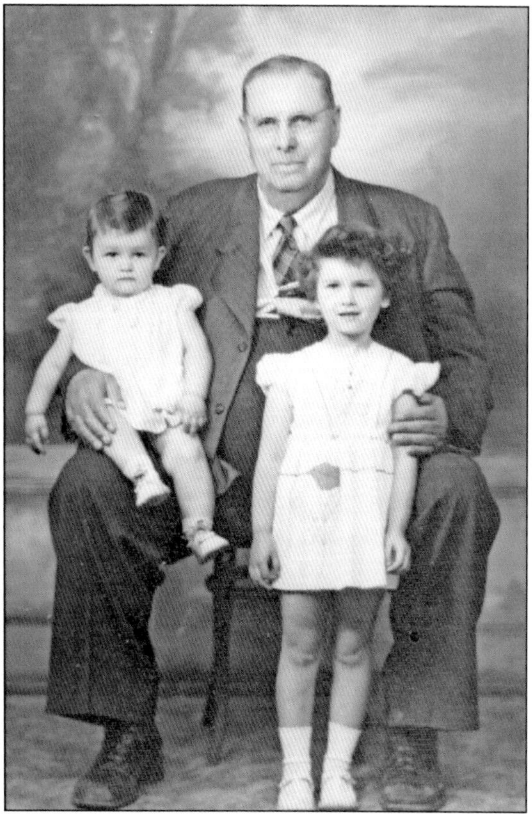

Pictured above in 1942 are Karen (left), Sharon (center), and Roger Nelson, the children of Harold and Edith Robinson Nelson of Medicine Lake. Both parents were born on their families' homesteads: Harold, east of Reserve, and Edith, east of Medicine Lake. They lived in Los Angeles and Seattle before returning to Sheridan County in 1943, where four more children were born. Left, "Big John" Wolter poses with his granddaughters Linda (age one) and Johnette (five). The girls, daughters of George and Hazel Wolter Whittaker, were later joined by little sister Julie. Johnette married John Grefe, lives in the Wanso community, and serves as a Lutheran pastor. Linda married Roger Nelson and went on to serve as a state representative and later a senator in the Montana Legislature. (Both, courtesy of Linda Nelson.)

Lucille (left), John (center), and Cora, children of Lars and Beatrice Angvick, are shown in the right photograph playing on the swings at their farm in the Reserve community in 1926. Lars Angvick grew up in Wisconsin and became the head of his household at age 15 when his father passed away. Following his marriage to Beatrice Vincentsen in 1919, the couple moved to the farm he had bought after it was relinquished by a homesteader. Angvick became known as the father of soil conservation in Montana as a result of pioneering contour strip cultivation on his farm. Pictured below on their farm near Westby are Ellen Keldsen, baby Ken, and daughter Elsie in 1928. (Right, courtesy of Marbea Lane; below, courtesy of Ken Keldsen.)

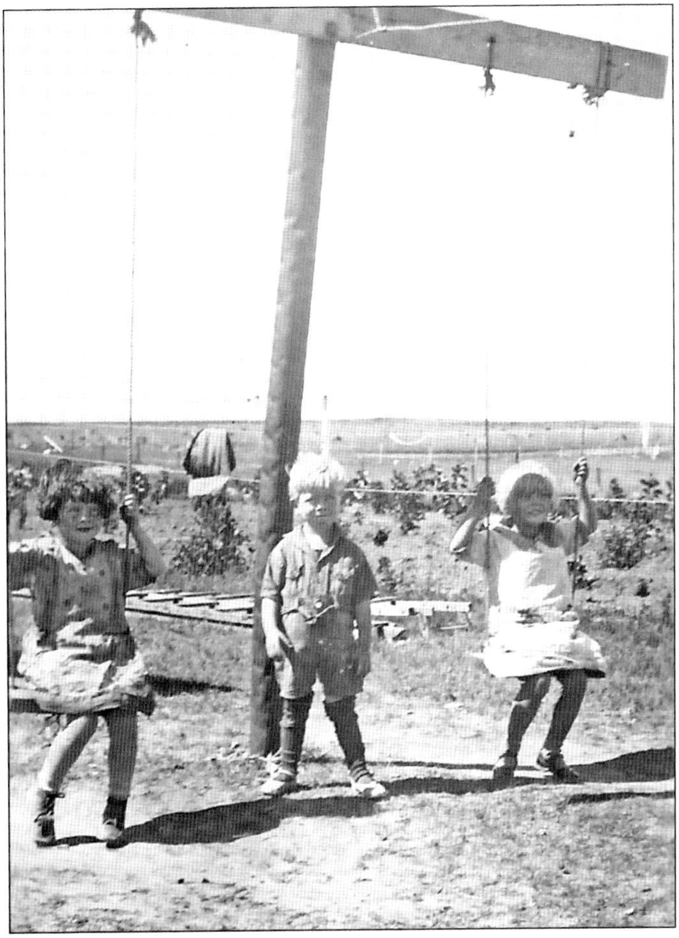

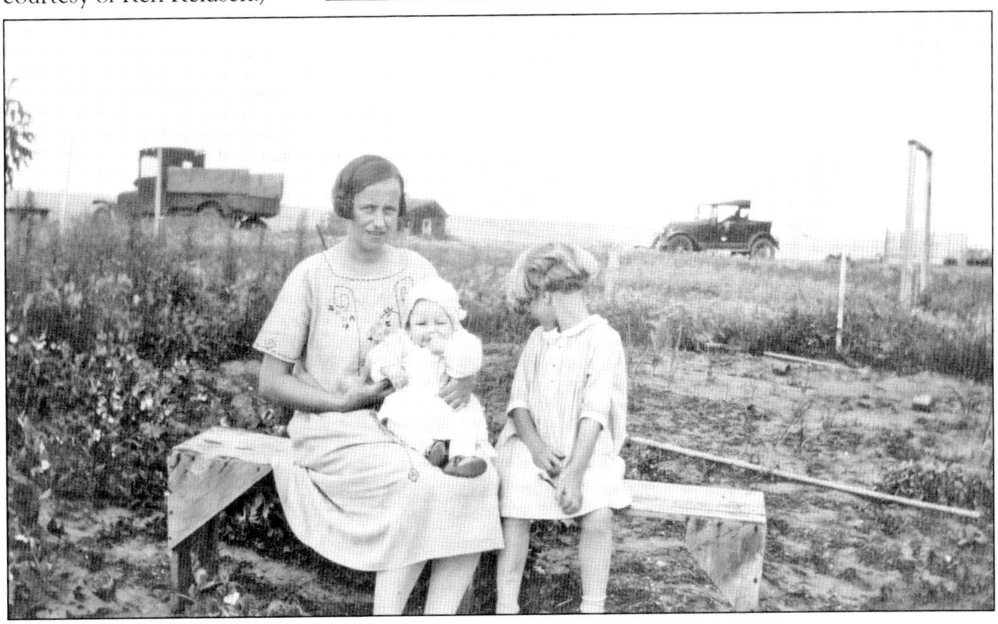

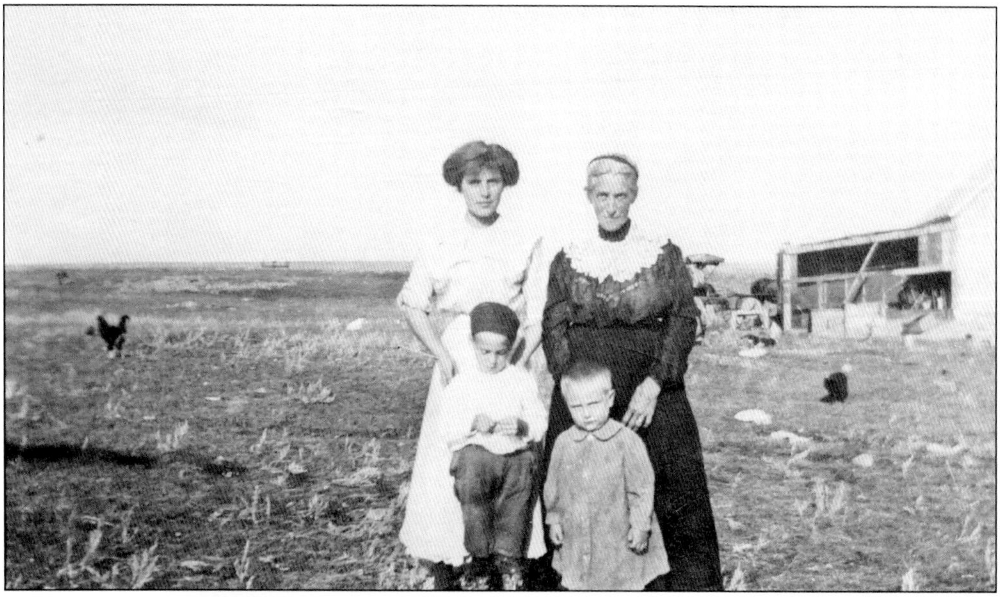

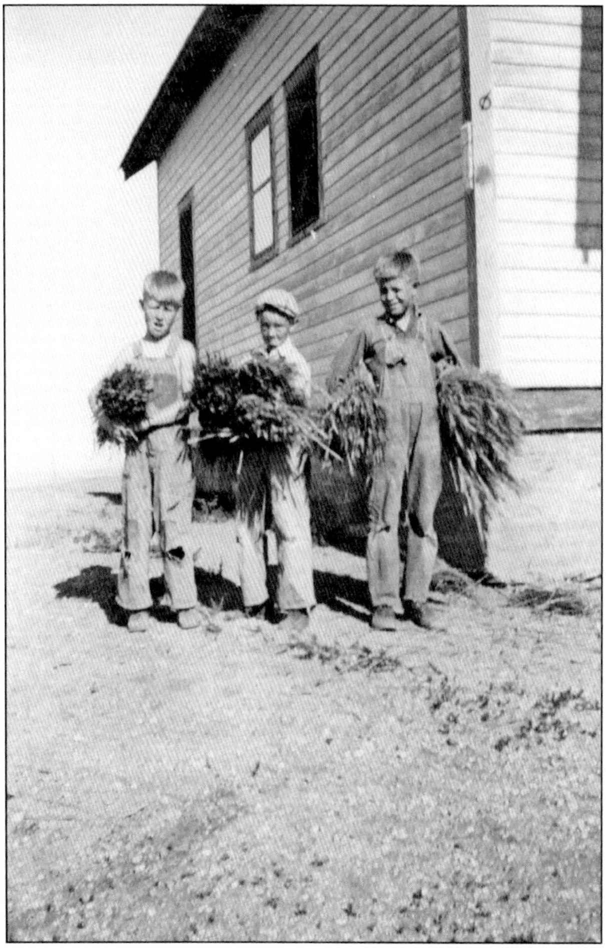

Children's lives were not always without turbulence during the early years in Sheridan County. Shown above are Floyd (left) and William "Bill" Willard with their grandmother Ellen Willard and cousin Stella Willard in 1912. Their father, uncle, and grandmother homesteaded in Sheridan County, but their mother, Bertha, who was not well, remained in her hometown in North Dakota, keeping the boys with her. When their mother passed away, the Willard boys came to live with their father, only to lose him to blood poisoning in 1914. Their grandmother raised them to adulthood. In the left photograph, Ray Clemetson (left), Chester Olson (center), and Lloyd Clemetson hold the Clemetsons' entire crop of 1937, cut with a scissor. The awful harvest led Ray and Lloyd's father to comment, "Our children, they're the only crop we have left." (Above, courtesy of Ginny Larson; left, courtesy of Marlys Vogt.)

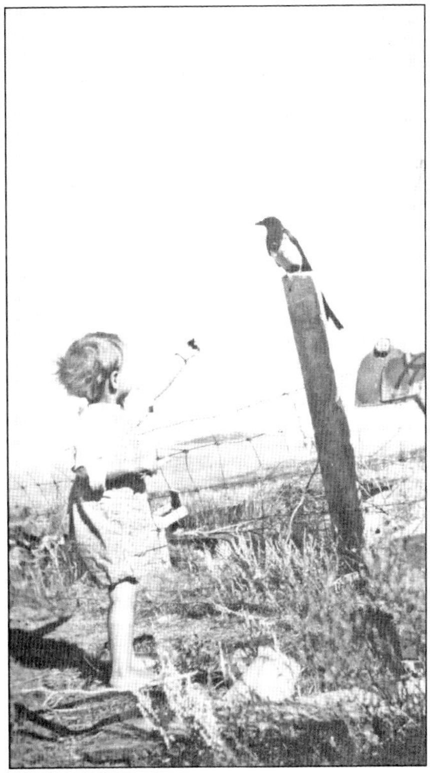

In the right photograph, Catherine Sebastian, about three years old, offers a cracker to a tame magpie. Below, her sister Anna Louise completes her milking chores. They were two of ten children born to Frank and Rena Sebastian, both originally from Indiana. Frank homesteaded 17 miles southwest of Plentywood in 1911. Later, Rena Builtman came to Sheridan County, where she worked as a waitress in a Plentywood restaurant before filing a homestead claim just to the west of Frank Sebastian's property. They were married in 1914. Later, Rena's sister Agnes joined her in Sheridan County and married Archie Mann. The Sebastian children's help was needed on the farm, where the family grew grain, raised poultry and pigs, and milked cows. They sold their butter to the Ingwalson grocery store in Plentywood. (Both, courtesy of Millie Marsh.)

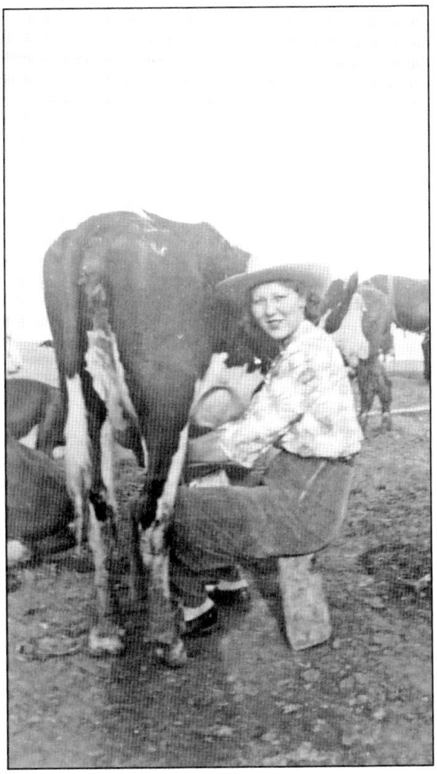

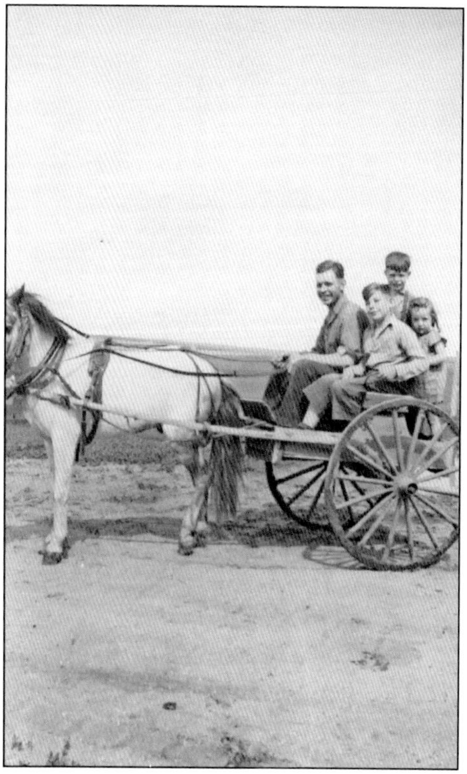

Ray Stoner of rural Outlook is shown at left with his children in a cart being pulled by Tony the pony. Seated in front is Vernon, with siblings Gaylen and Eileen in back. Stoner had come to Sheridan County with his parents in 1909 and later married Harriet Carroll, whose parents farmed land that would eventually become the site of Carroll Dam. Pictured below is Frank Frasier with daughters Roseann, age one, and Janet, three, on Easter morning in 1949. Frasier owned and operated City Dray Line, which hauled ice, coal, sand, gravel, and oil-well supplies. Frasier was at one point the largest individual coal dealer in Montana. He and Lillian Eggen Frasier later had a third daughter, Lyla. (Left, courtesy of Eileen McCarty; below, courtesy of Lillian and Lyla Frasier.)

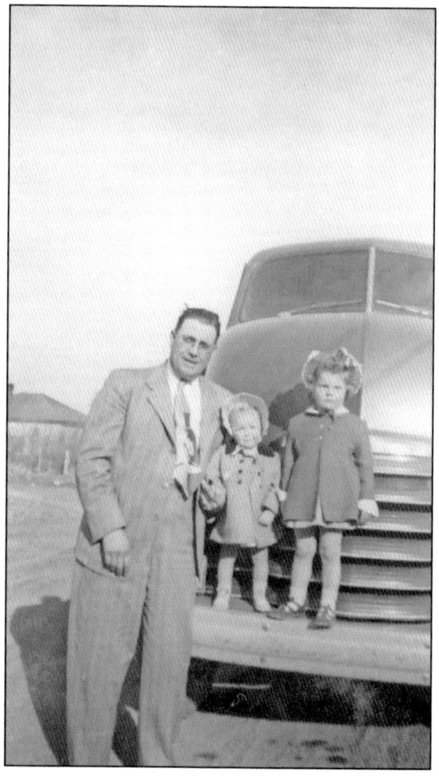

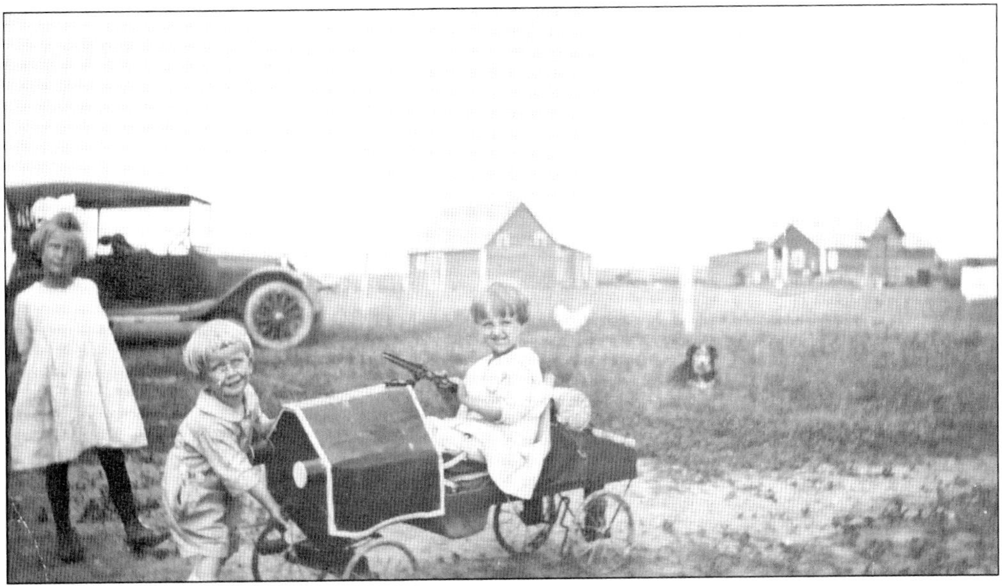

Dorothy (left), John (center), and Helen Poe, the children of C.J. and Marie Bielen Poe, are shown in the above photograph driving their car in the 1920s. The family later added another daughter, Virginia. C.J. came to Montana in 1906 and lived in Flandrem before it was moved and renamed Medicine Lake. He and a business partner owned a combination jewelry and drugstore, and Poe served as Medicine Lake's first elected mayor. A skilled druggist, he was also a "deputy doctor," assisting with bone-settings and surgeries. The children of Medicine Lake tended a Victory garden during World War II, shown below. Gardens like this one and others in Sheridan County supplied vegetables for canning and later use in school hot-lunch programs. (Both, courtesy of Virginia Carpenter.)

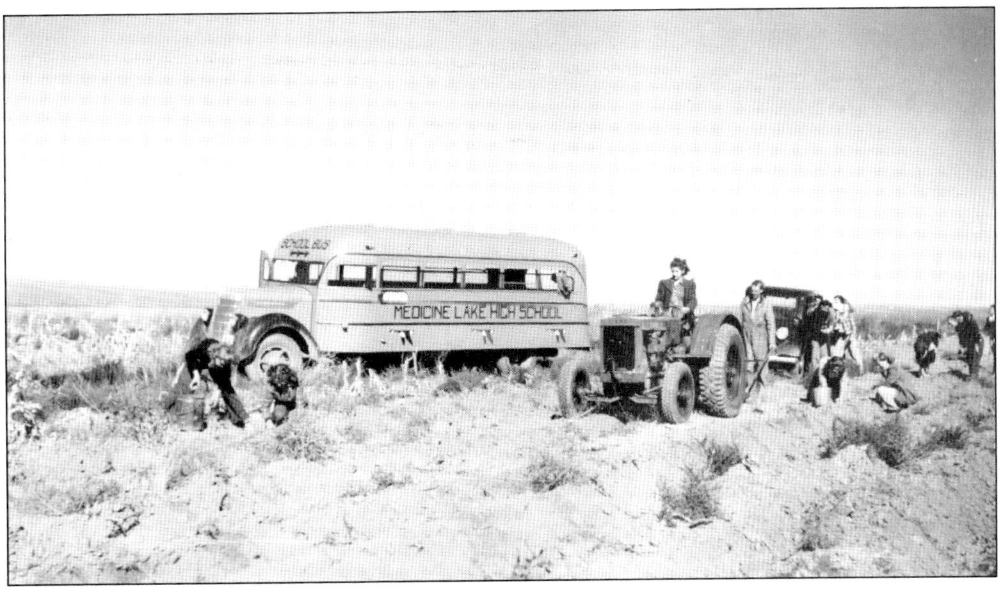

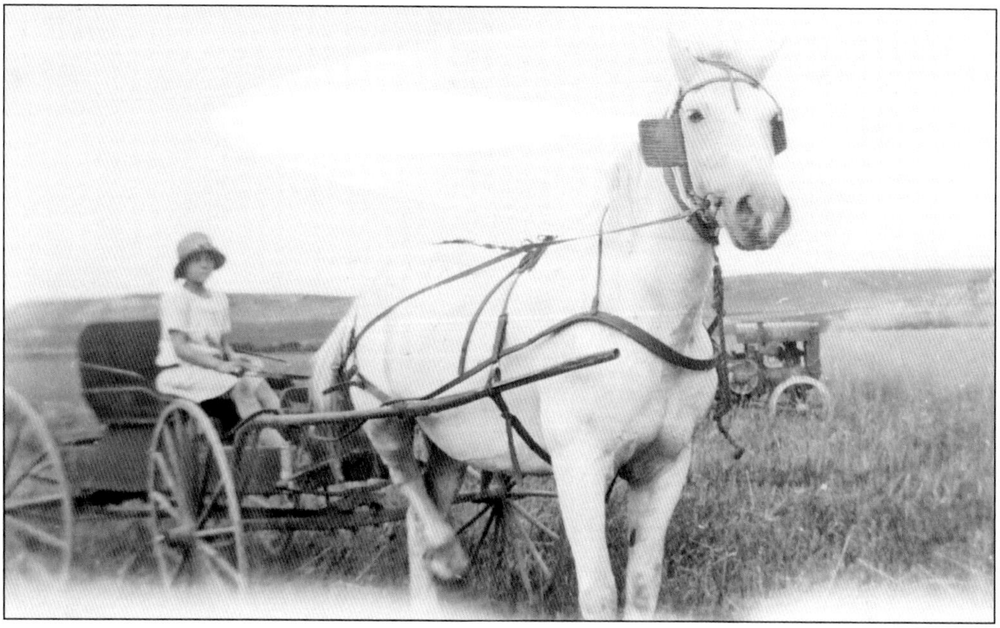

Pictured above is nine-year-old Lillian Eggen driving her favorite horse, King, to deliver lunch to her father in a field on what is now the J Bar E Ranch near Archer. As John Eggen enjoyed his meal, Lillian climbed on the binder, which cut oats for use on their farm. Lillian's mother, Tillie Lee Eggen, and her sister, Clara, had come to Montana when they were in their twenties and homesteaded on adjoining quarter sections 10 miles west of Plentywood. Among their neighbors were Andrew and Molly Eggen Fadness, who had come to the area in 1899 by covered wagon and lived for two years in a space dug out of a hillside, with straw as its floor covering, until they built a house. Molly was John Eggen's sister, and after Eggen homesteaded in the neighborhood, he and Tillie began courting. They were married in 1913. (Both, courtesy of Lillian and Lyla Frasier.)

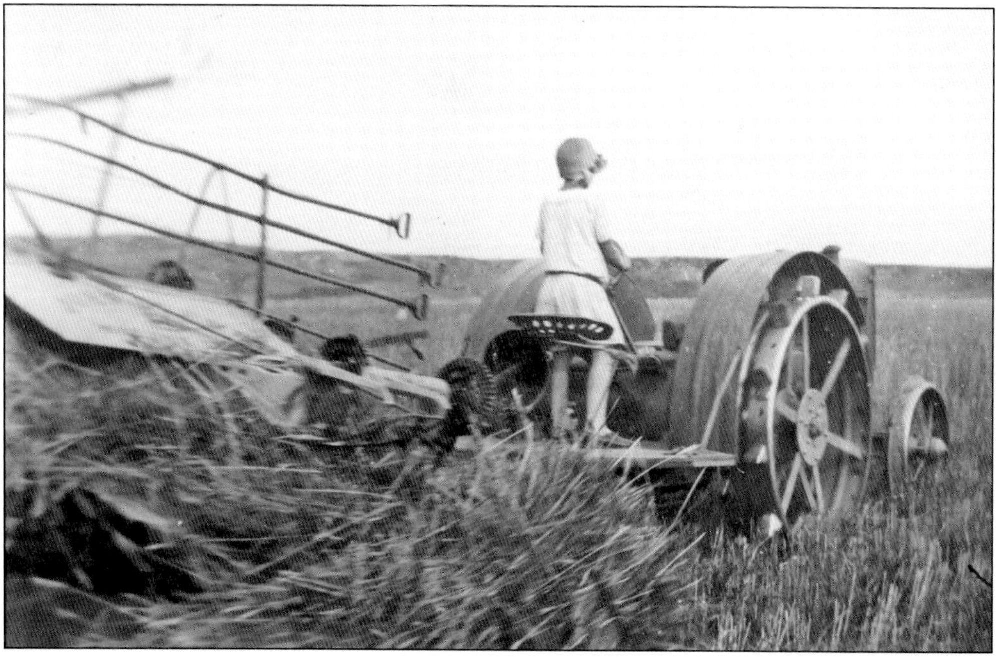

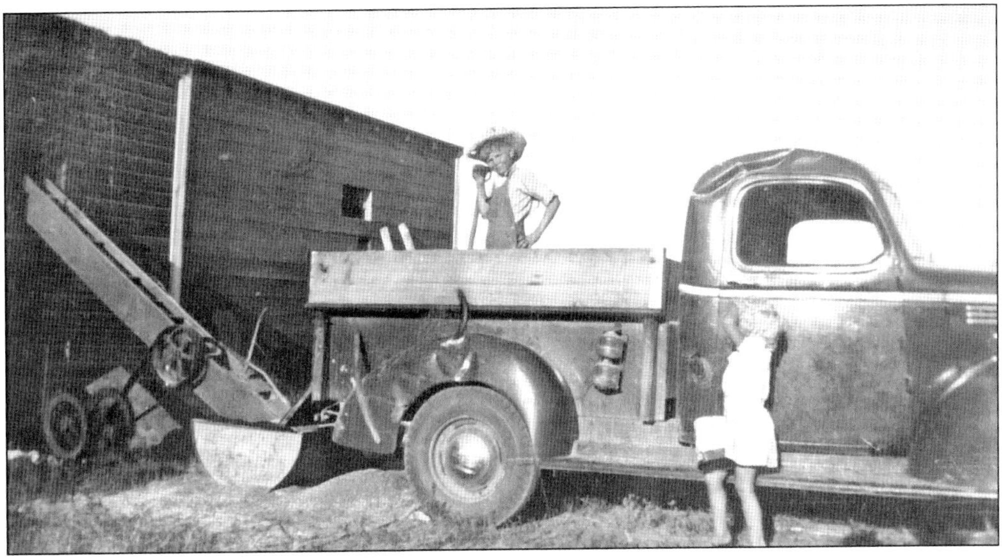

In the above photograph, Orvis Nelson, age 10, shovels grain from a truck bed into an auger. His grandparents, Ole and Inga Nelson, had homesteaded east of Homestead in 1906, constructing a sod house and, a few years later, building an addition to accommodate their growing family. The Nelson farm was struck by not one, but two tornadoes in subsequent years, destroying their barn and other buildings, but sparing the house. A fifth generation of Nelson descendants is growing up on the farm today. Below, 10-year-old friends Ken Keldsen (left) and Clifford Hammer of Westby shock barley in 1938. (Above, courtesy of Orvis Nelson; below, courtesy of Ken Keldsen.)

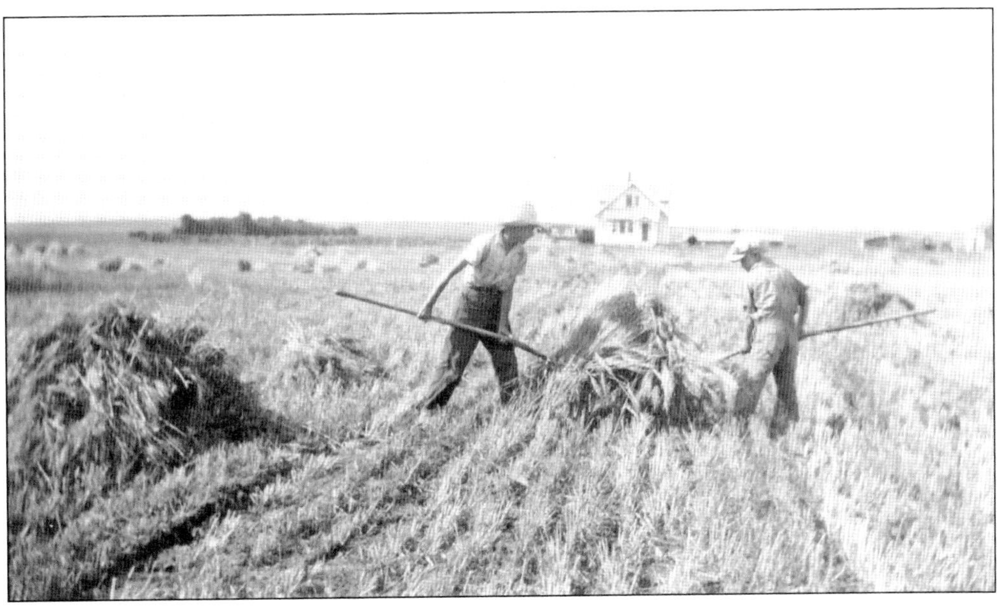

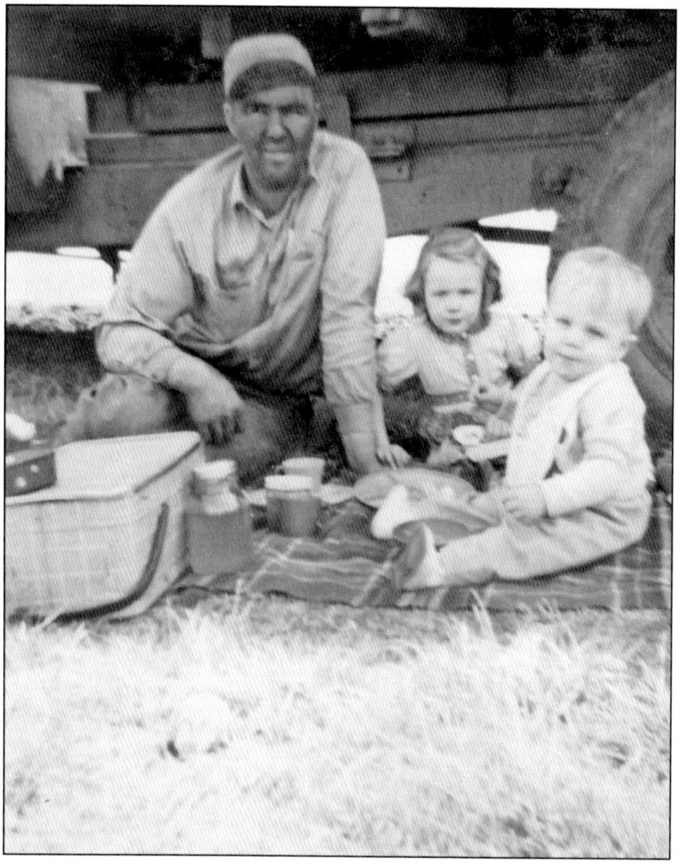

During busy seeding and harvest seasons when the sun rose early and set late, sometimes the only way young children had a chance to see their fathers was to go to the field. In the photograph at left, Howard Nielsen shares lunch with his children, Susan, age four, and Allen, one, in 1958. They would be joined later by siblings Eric and Cheryl. Their father was the eldest of eight children born to N.P. and Vita Hansen Nielsen, and he carried on the family farm in the Coalridge community when his parents moved to Plentywood in 1961. Below, a picnic lunch is under way during harvest at the Nels V. Nelson farm east of Reserve. (Left, courtesy of Irene Nielsen; below, courtesy of Shirley Nelson.)

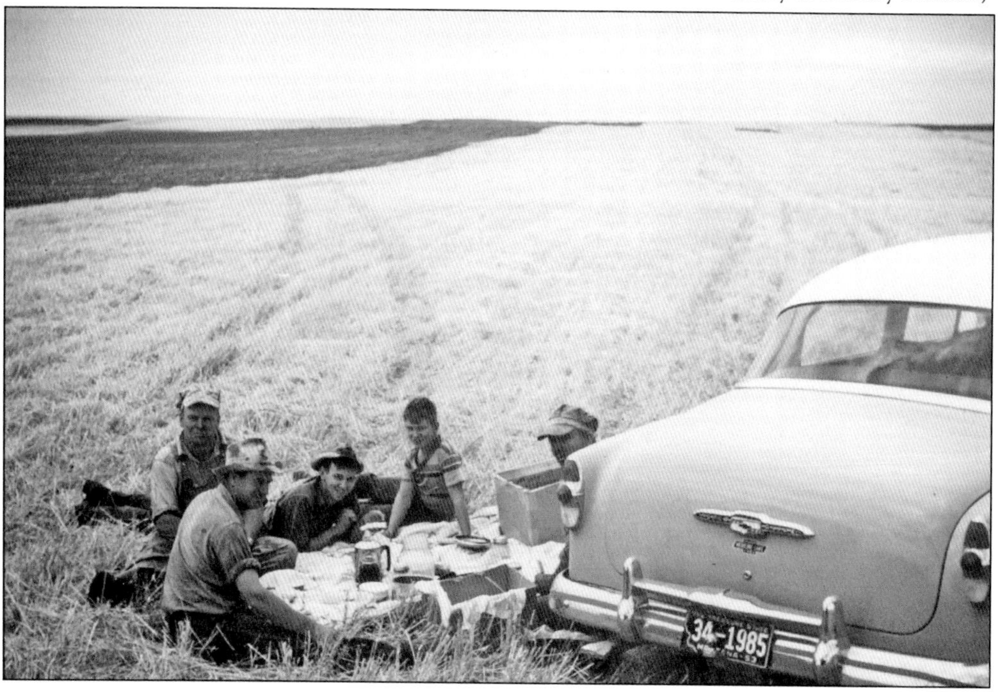

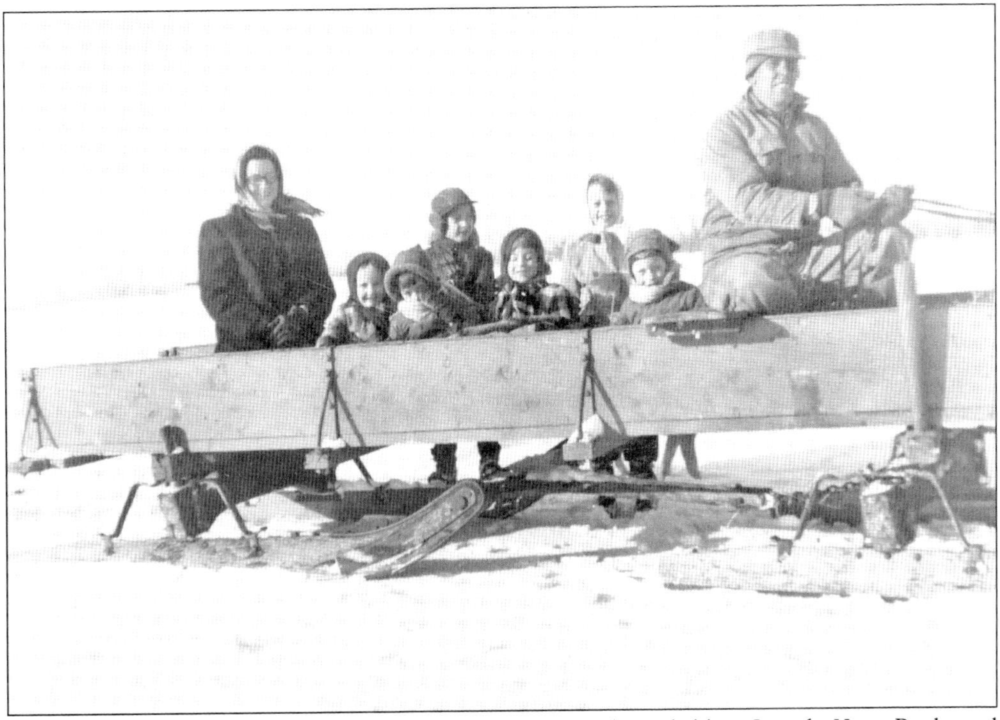

Pictured above are Max and Florence Schlag Rasmussen, their children Janyth, Kent, Ruth, and Jon, and cousins Vicki and Wanda, in 1955. Florence grew up in the Redstone community and graduated from Redstone High School before attending college in Havre. She then returned to work in Plentywood for five years. Max was the eldest of four children born to Albert and Sarah Hovet Rasmussen. In the photograph below, taken in the 1940s, Selmer Espeland's sons shovel snow on Nereson Road near McElroy. The boys' grandparents Martin and Anna were Norwegian immigrants who settled in Iowa and later moved to North Dakota. After Martin's death, Anna and her four sons came to the Westby and McElroy areas. (Above, courtesy of Florence Rasmussen; below, courtesy of Richard Espeland.)

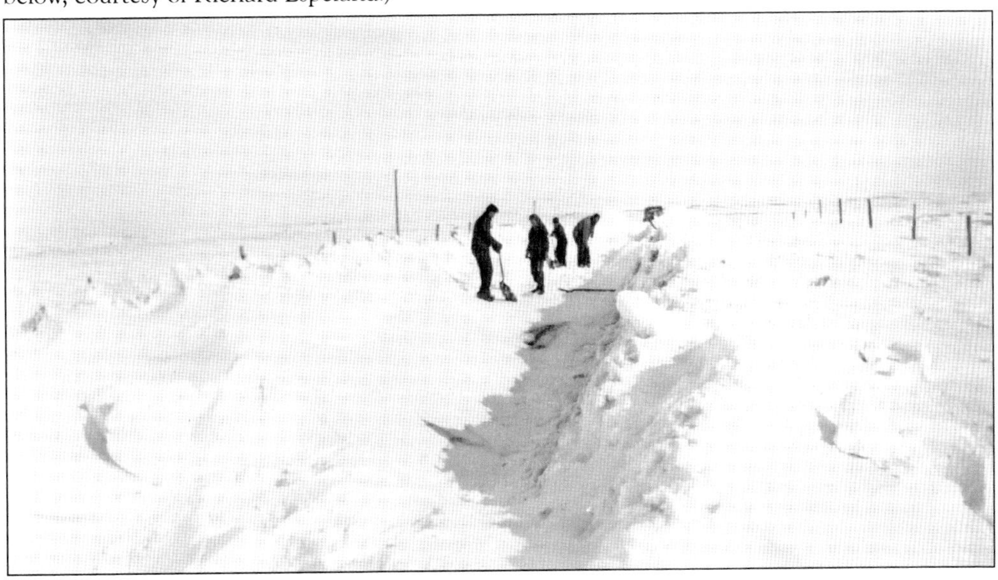

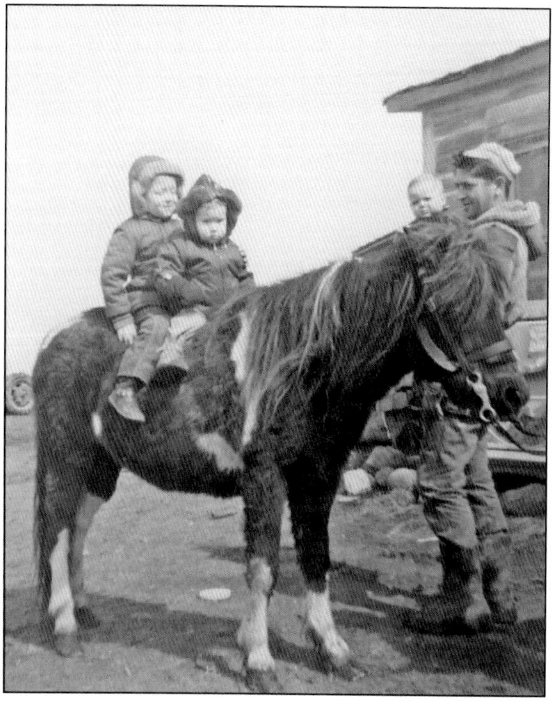

At left, Bob McCall holds his son Marty, as Monte (front) and Mickey take a pony ride in 1958. Sister Melody later joined the family. Both Bob and his wife, Betty Olson McCall, grew up on farms in the Comertown area and graduated from Comertown High School. Bob joined the Air Force, served in the Korean War, and was later stationed in Massachusetts and Morocco before returning to Sheridan County following his discharge. He served as Plentywood's postmaster, and Betty worked at the Anthony's store for many years. Below, Dooley kids Marcial LaVerdure (left) and Duane Falk enjoy a summer horseback ride in 1945. Jack Smith can be seen in the background. (Left, courtesy of Betty McCall; below, courtesy of Bertha Anderson.)

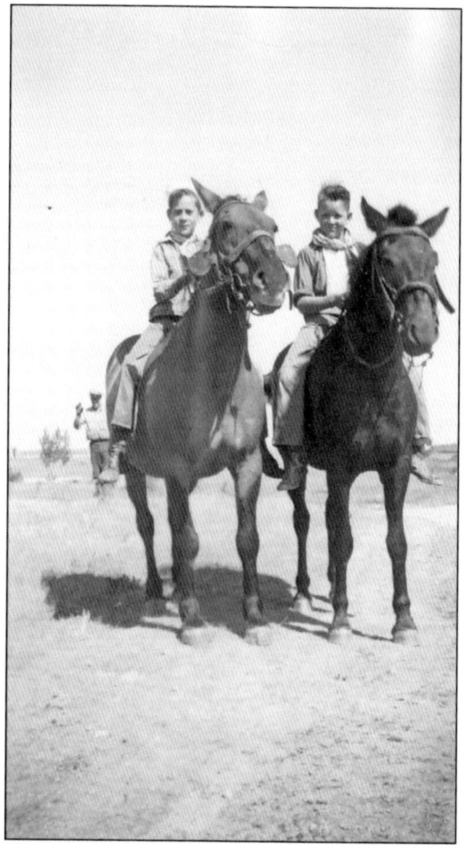

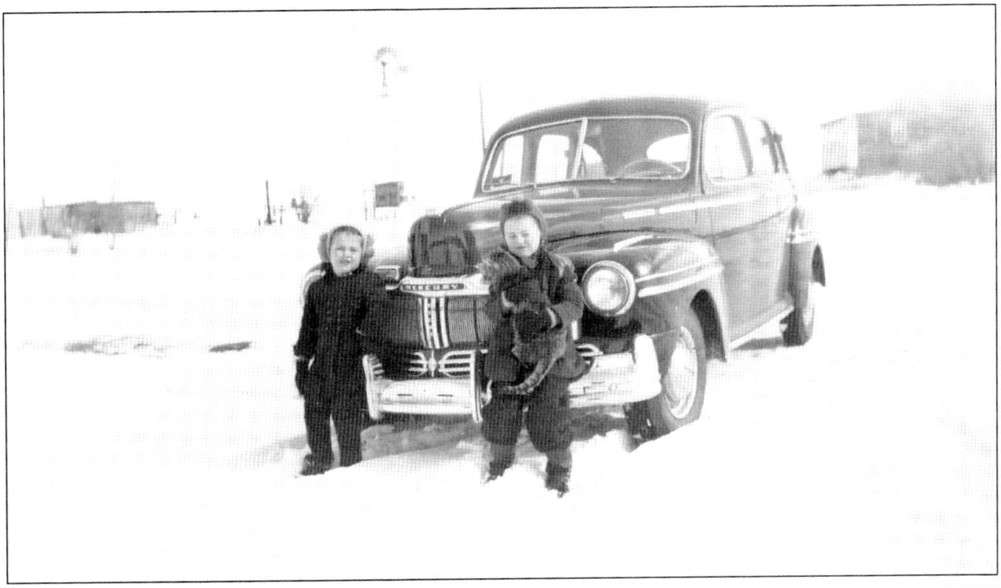

Standing in front of their parents' 1948 black Mercury are Bernice (left) and Arlene Whitney with Snooper the cat. Their father, Richard Whitney, was the son of Charles and Jonna Whitney, who had homesteaded south of Redstone in 1910. He worked on the farm with his father and brother doing fieldwork, caring for livestock, breaking horses, working on threshing crews, and, in the winter, mining coal. He met Elizabeth Juul, the daughter of homesteaders from the Outlook community, when she worked on the Vince Bergh ranch, and they were later married. Shown right at a July 4, 1950, parade are, from left to right, Doris "Peggy" Hilyard, Charlene Hilyard, May Hilyard, Marbea Lane, Carla Lane, Joyce Kresback, and Linda Peterson. (Above, courtesy of Bernice Van Curen; right, courtesy of May Budke.)

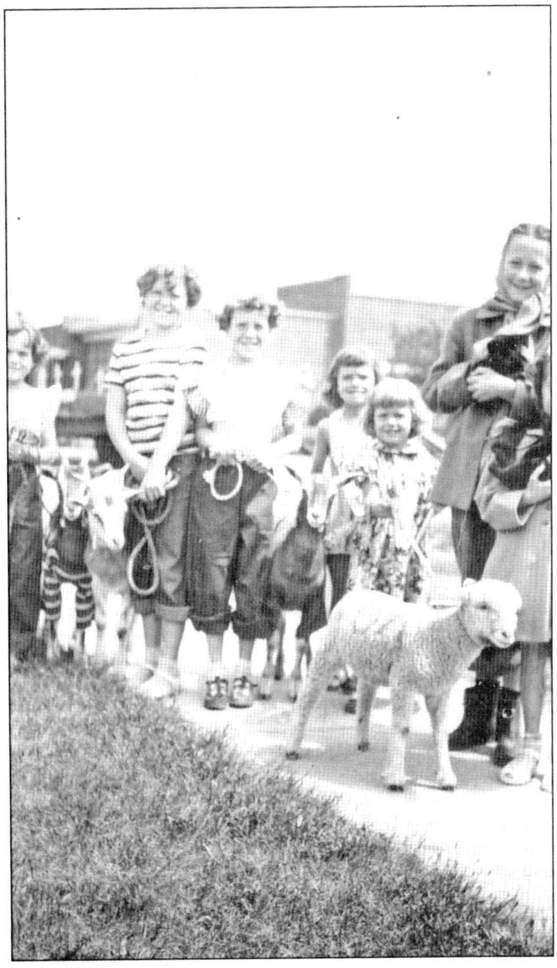

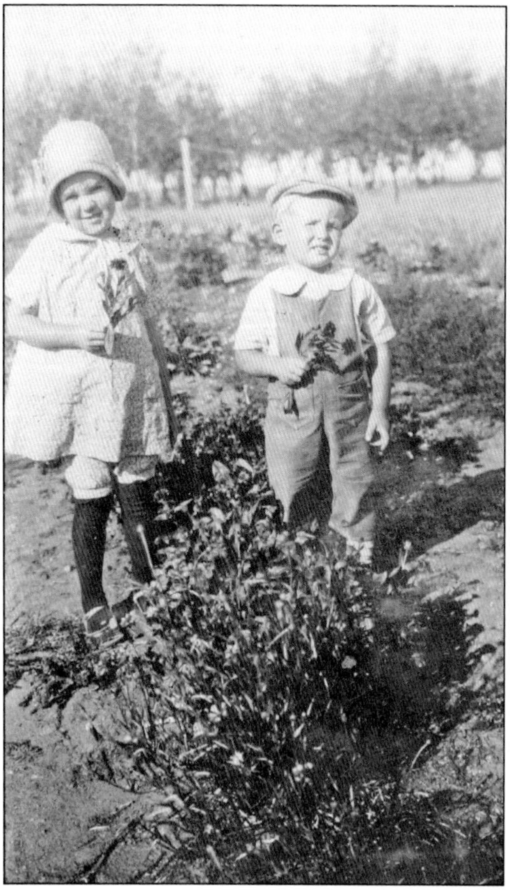

Left, siblings Edith (left) and Jens Sundsted are shown picking flowers at home in the Dagmar area. Their parents, Thomas and Ella Johnson Sundsted, raised their seven children on a homestead they had bought from another homesteader and proved up. Below are the children of August and Anatta Madill Westphal in 1923, braving snowy weather to be photographed standing next to their family's car. They are, from left to right, Ila, Eugene, Loretta, and Hazel. Their siblings Jack and Luella later joined the family. Westphal, his four brothers, and their mother, homesteaded northeast of Raymond in 1908. The Madill family lived north of the Westphals, having come to the United States from Canada in 1910. (Left, courtesy of Jens Sundsted; below, courtesy of Ila Syme.)

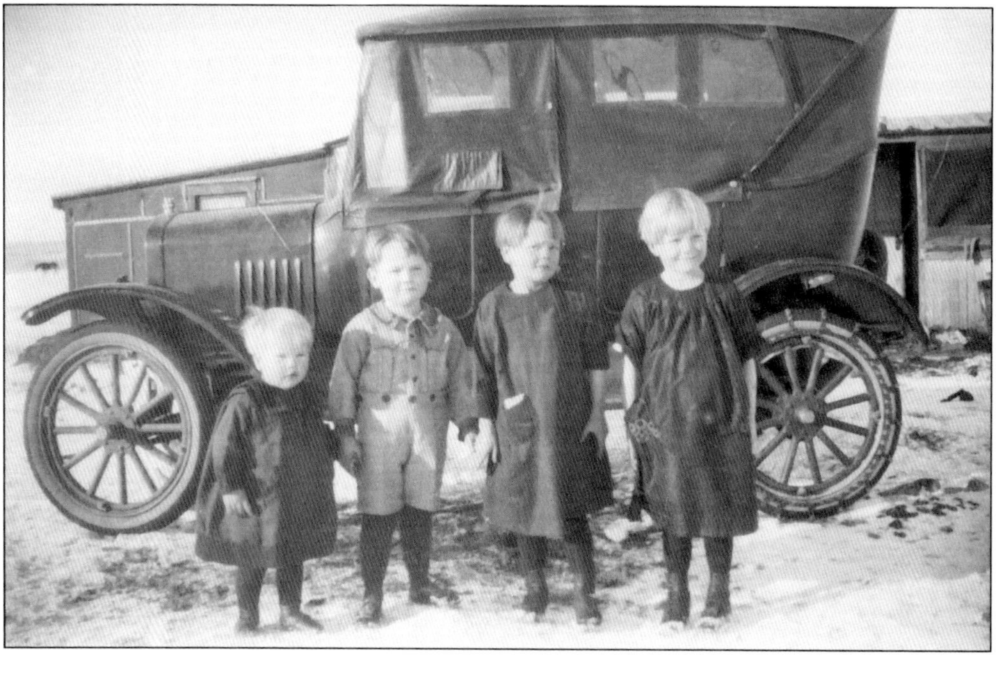

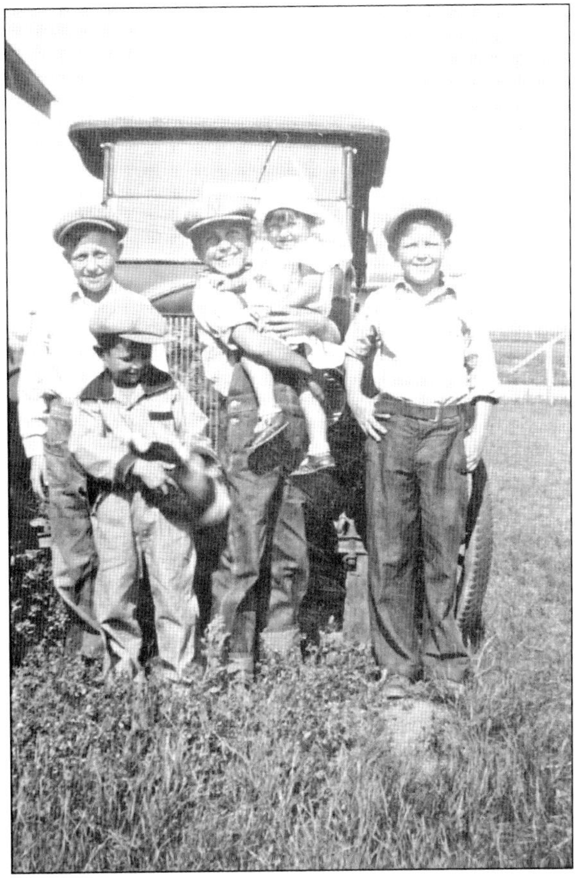

Shown at right are the children of Carl and Esther Lund of Plentywood around 1931. They are, from left to right, Norman, Sanford (holding dog), Morris (holding baby Betty Ann), and Conrad. A sister, Anna, had died a few years before as the result of an accident while she was playing with friends. Below, Norman Lund poses with his family during his military furlough in 1942 or 1943. Shown here are, from left to right, Betty Ann, Esther, Norman, and Sanford. Little sister Arna is in front. Lund, a glider pilot, gave his life at just 24 years of age in the Normandy invasion on D-Day in June 1944. (Both, courtesy of Arna Golterman.)

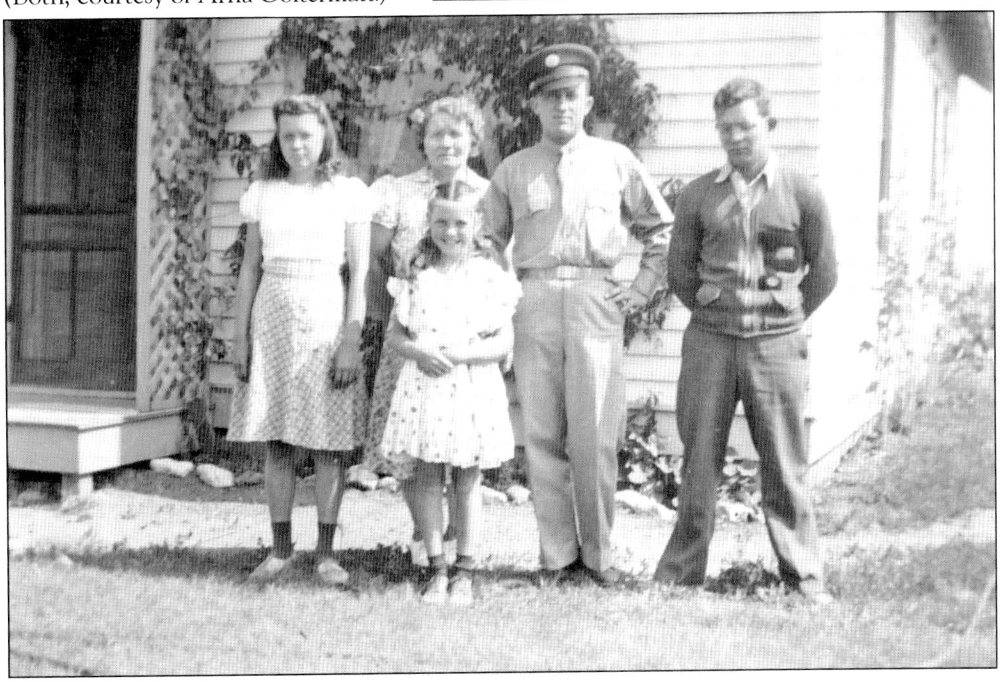

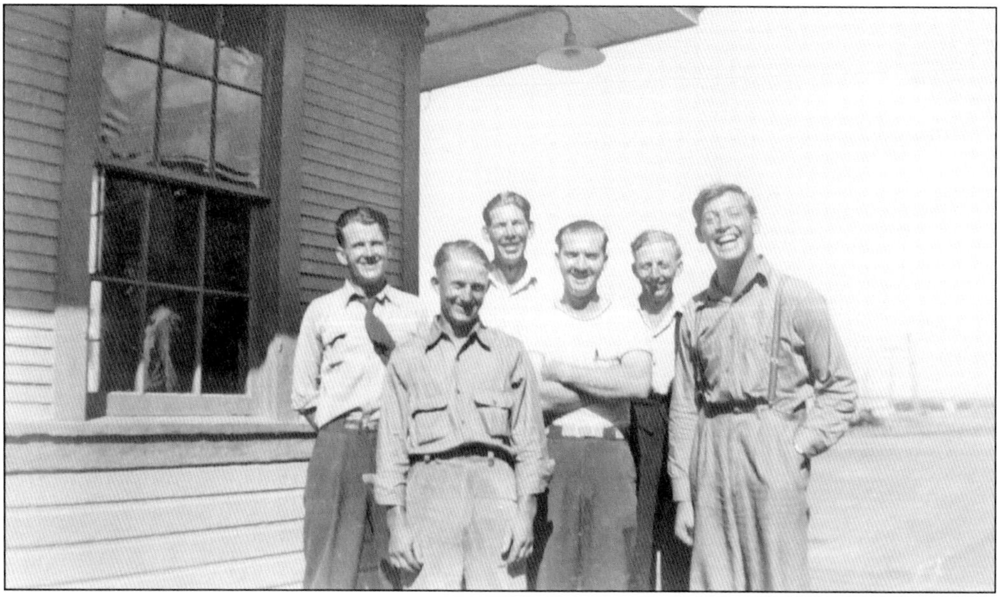

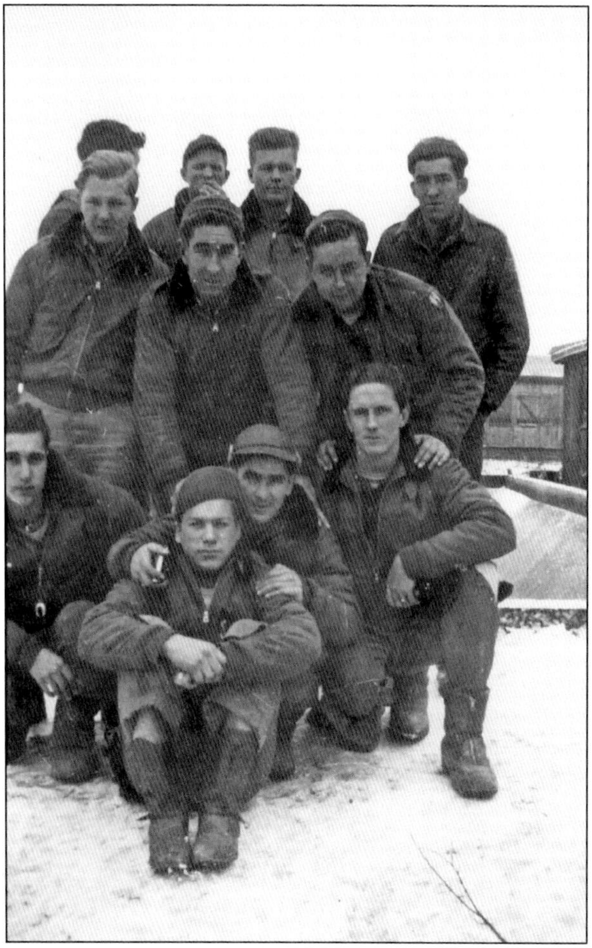

Many young men and women who grew up in Sheridan County spent their early adulthoods in service to their country. On July 8, 1941, the young men in the above photograph were inducted into the armed forces. Shown here are, from left to right, Willard Craig Saxton (Antelope), Lionel Edward Borley (Medicine Lake), Alvin S. Tommerup (Westby), Clifford LeRoy Ibsen (Reserve), Richard Roland Fenster (Medicine Lake), and Junior Allen Hess (Antelope; he had transferred from Missoula). In the photograph at left, Jorgen Egeland of Reserve (second from the right in the back row) poses with his Air Force crewmates during World War II. Egeland and one other man were the only survivors of this crew, as they were scratched at the last minute from a bombing raid that ended when the plane was shot down over Germany. (Above, courtesy of Sheridan County Museum; left, courtesy of Gertrude Sundsted.)

Eight

Fun, Games, and Entertainment

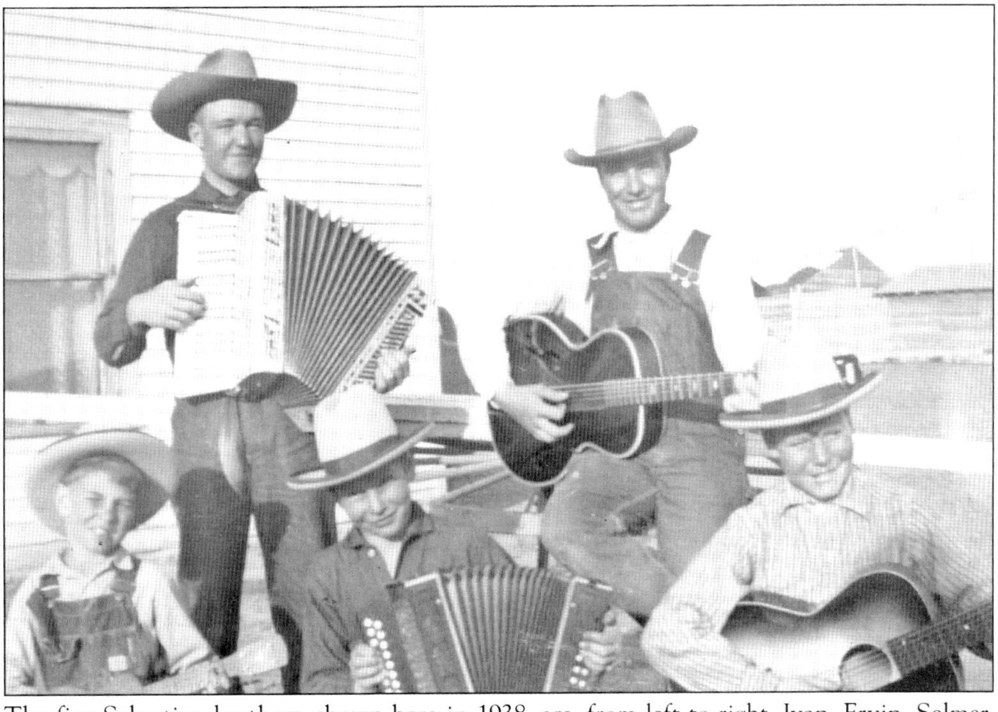

The five Sebastian brothers, shown here in 1938, are, from left to right, Ivan, Ervin, Selmer, Francis, and Clem. Tragically, two brothers would die in separate vehicle accidents and a third in a spray-plane crash. In happier times, the family enjoyed celebrations, such as a memorable early-1940s dance held in their newly rebuilt barn. (Courtesy of Millie Marsh.)

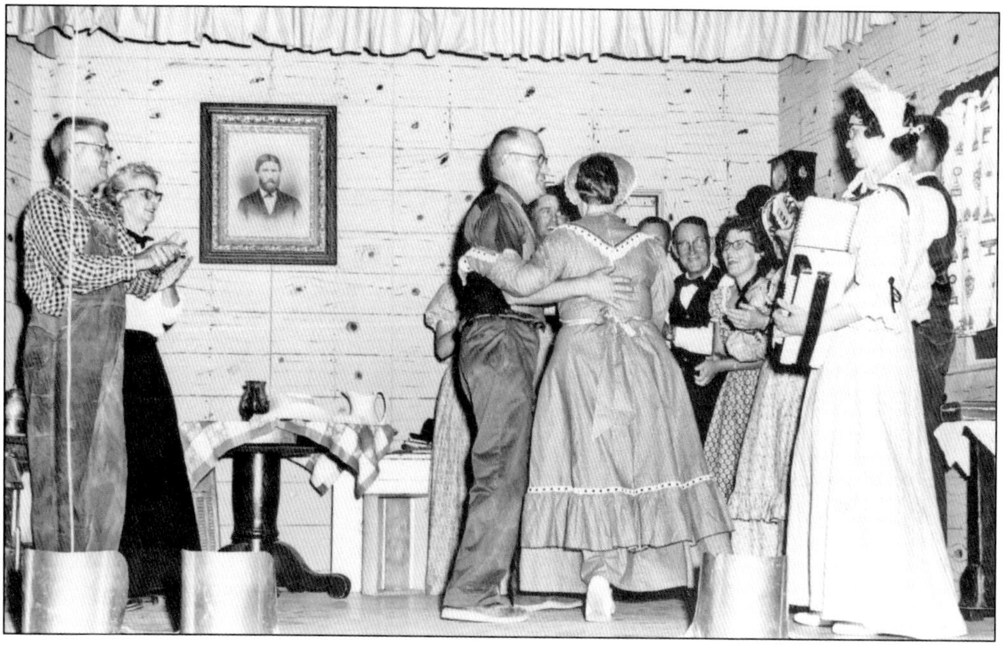

Community plays have been an enduring form of entertainment in Sheridan County. Pictured above is a play at the Reserve Hall in 1961. As Jack Anderson dances with an unidentified partner, Marlene Nielsen Bummer accompanies them on her accordion. More recently, plays at the Antelope Community Hall have become a popular autumn tradition. Below, Plentywood friends enjoy an evening cup of coffee. They are, from left to right, Nina Sachow, unidentified, Myrtle Anderson, Nancy Schott, Lillian Schott, Marie Hilyard, Norma Pederson, Gladyce Thomsen, unidentified, and Joann Thomsen. (Above, courtesy of Marlene Bummer; below, courtesy of Millie Marsh.)

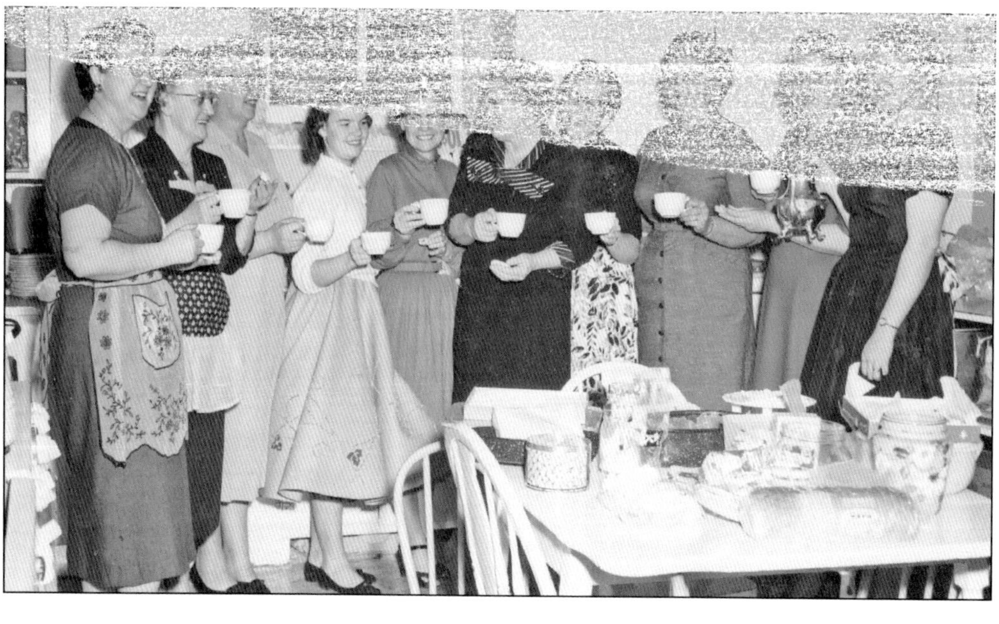

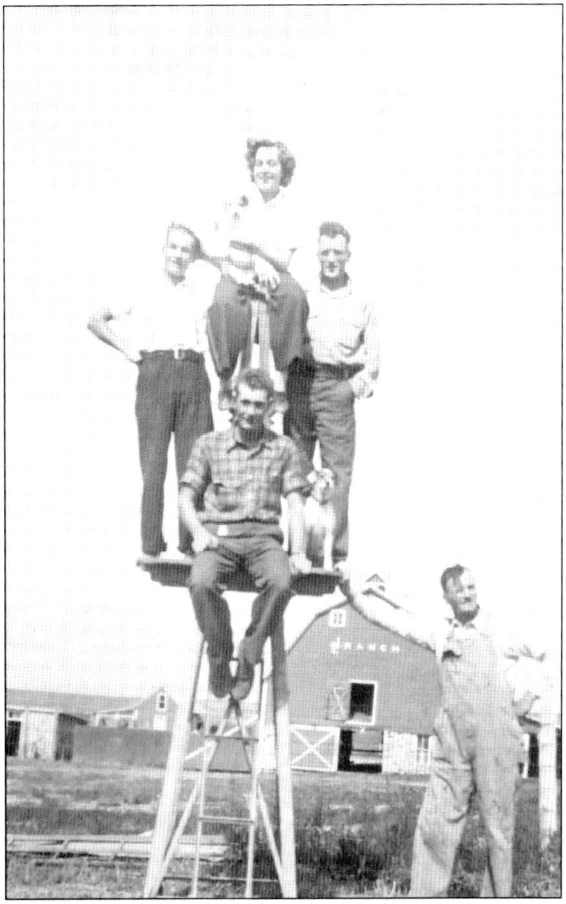

Right, members of the Eggen family of Archer pose on a Sunday morning in the fall of 1938. John is on the ground, and his son Joe is seated next to Toots the dog. Standing on the platform are, from left to right, Eugene, Lillian (holding her puppy), and Ed Bolino, who worked for the family. Painted on the barn's cupola (but not visible here) are the dates 1889 and 1909, the former signifying the arrival year of the property's original owners, Andrew and Molly Fadness, and the latter being the year the barn was built. Below, Cora Angvick boats on Medicine Lake in 1942. She was the eldest of five children born to Lars and Beatrice Vincentsen Angvick. (Right, courtesy of Lillian and Lyla Frasier; below, courtesy of Marbea Lane.)

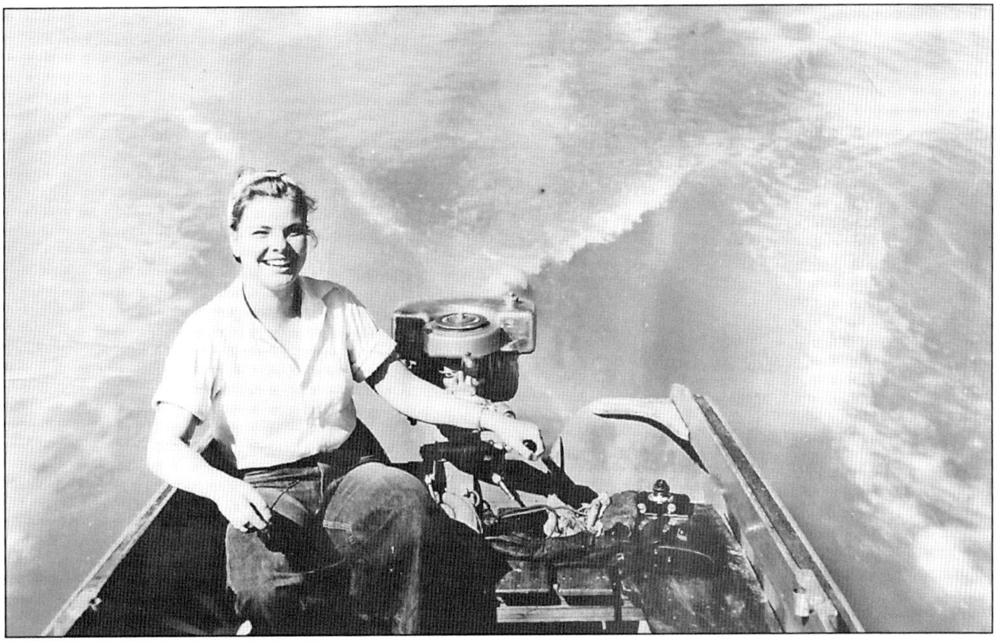

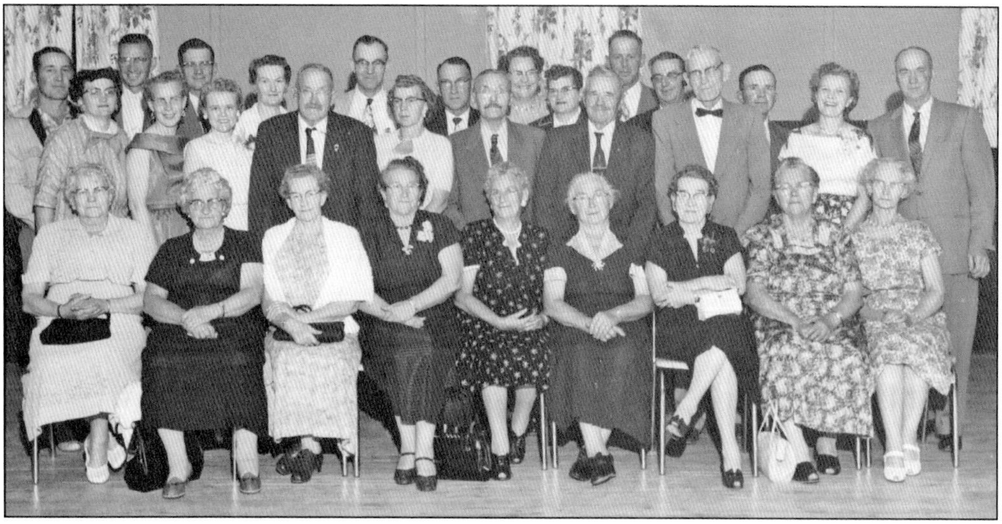

In the above photograph, members of the Danish Sisterhood Lodge No. 156, along with their husbands, gather at their banquet in Plentywood in 1958. According to Elsie Jensen, the organization was not a secret society, but a social group for friendship and fellowship. Members of the group are, from left to right, (first row) Johanne Petersen, Inger Petersen, Andrea Pedersen (husband, Niels, behind her), Alexandra Larsen, Christine Paulsen (husband, Rasmus, behind her), Clara Olsen (husband, Jens, behind her), Emma Andresen (husband, John, behind her); Anna Susag, Rosa Nielsen (husband, Niels J., behind her); (second row) Don and Alice Friedrich, George and Alma Johnson, James and Bernice Johnson, Elsie and Chris Jensen, Evelyn and Hugo Andersen, Evelyn Nielsen, Myrtle Abar, Arnie Nielsen, Bob Abar, and Harry and Metha Olsen. In the photograph below, Outlook men pay a visit to California's Knott's Berry Farm. Shown here are, from left to right, Orace Wagnild, Orrin Kleppen, Peter Melle, Herb Benson, Henry Walder, Clifford Paulson, and Marvin Wagnild. (Above, courtesy of Elsie Jensen; below, courtesy of Marvin Wagnild.)

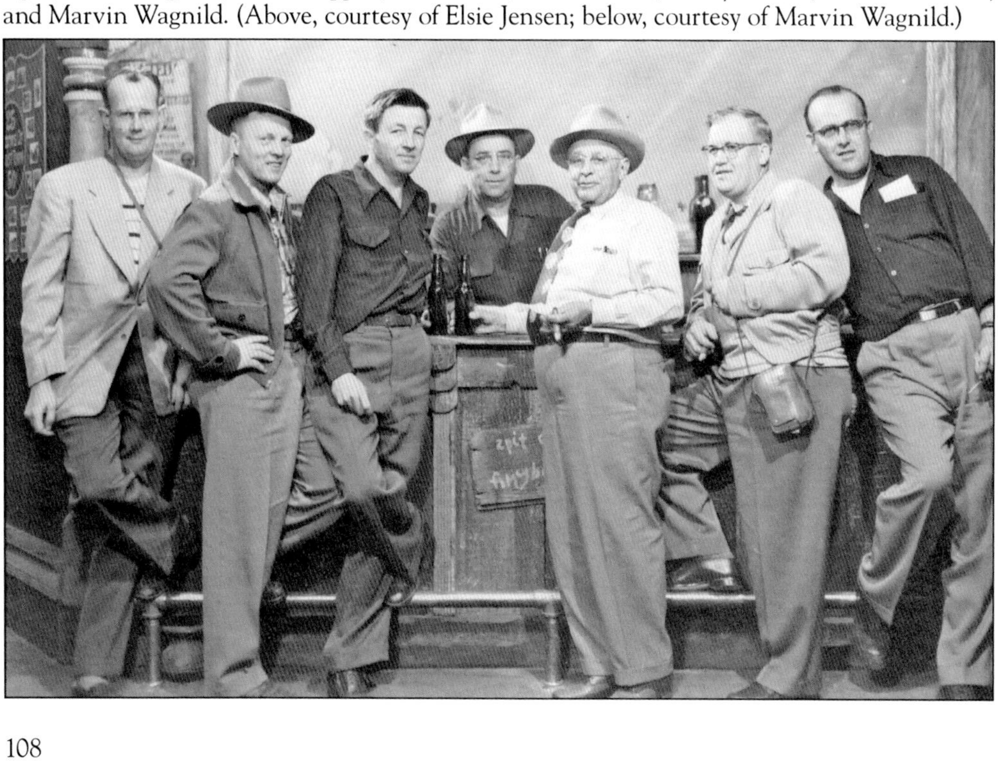

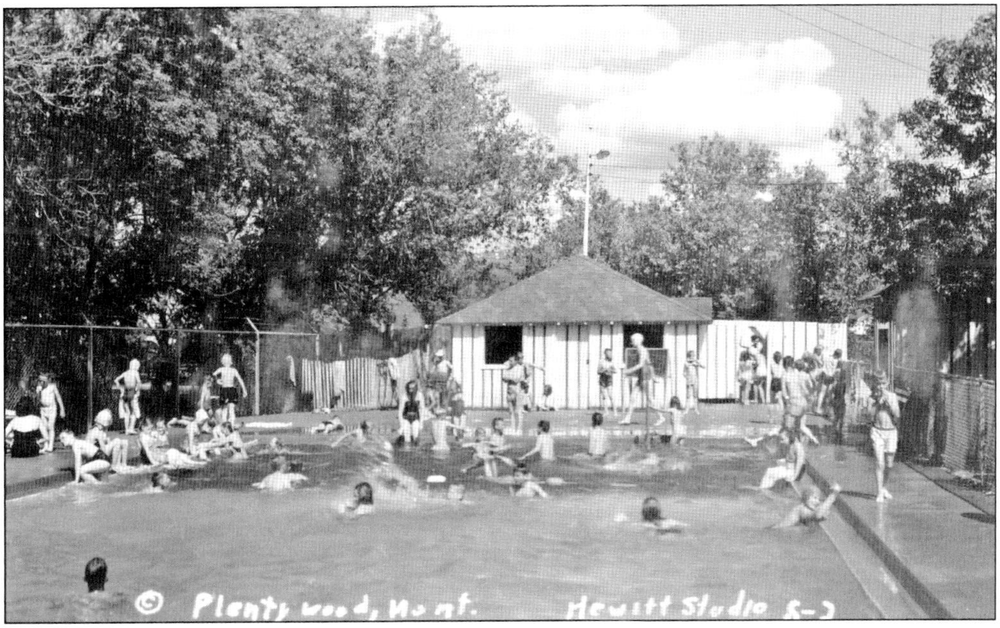

Generations of children growing up in and around Plentywood have enjoyed spending time at the swimming pool, the first of which was located in Wildwood Park, created by Harry DeSilva. The pool, pictured above in the 1950s or early 1960s, was finished around 1927. It measured 20 by 40 feet and, according to the book *Plentywood Portrait: Soil, Toil, Oil,* included a tower supporting three diving boards and, as seen above, a concession shack at the opposite end of the pool area. The trees that stand in the park today were planted by DeSilva and his son Harold. Musical talent ran in the family, and DeSilva oversaw the building of a band shell in the park (below). (Above, courtesy of Max Rasmussen; below, courtesy of Bernice Van Curen.)

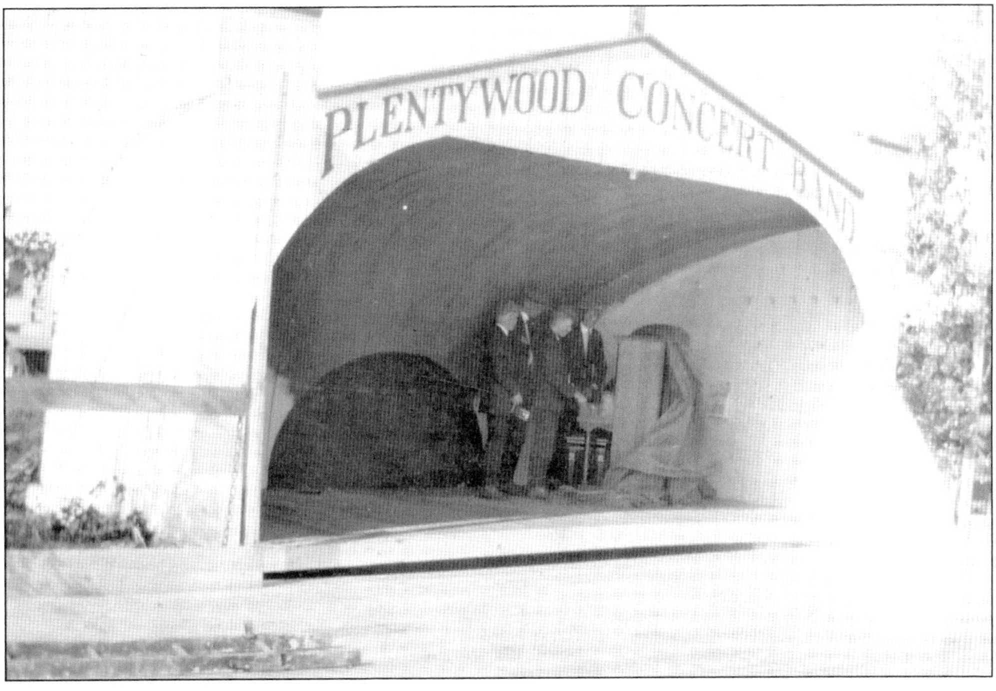

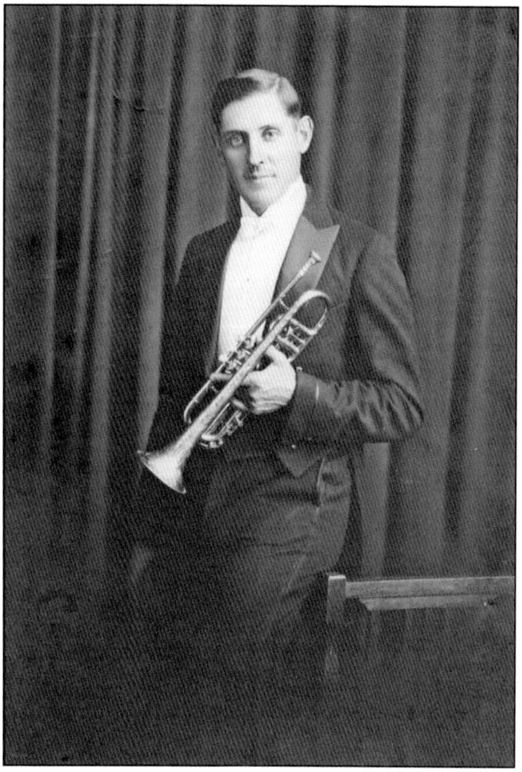

Harry DeSilva, his mother, Ethel, and younger brother Dwight came to Medicine Lake by horse and buggy from South Dakota. Harry married Minnie Larson of Medicine Lake, and they moved to Plentywood in 1913. A solo cornet player, DeSilva, shown at left in 1921, was hired for a salary of $70 per month to direct the Plentywood City Band. The band performed at various celebrations and was key in the barnstorming campaign for Plentywood to be named the county seat. DeSilva would later found the Wildwood Beverage Company, which he and Minnie, pictured below, operated until 1948, when they moved to California. (Both, courtesy of Lou DeSilva.)

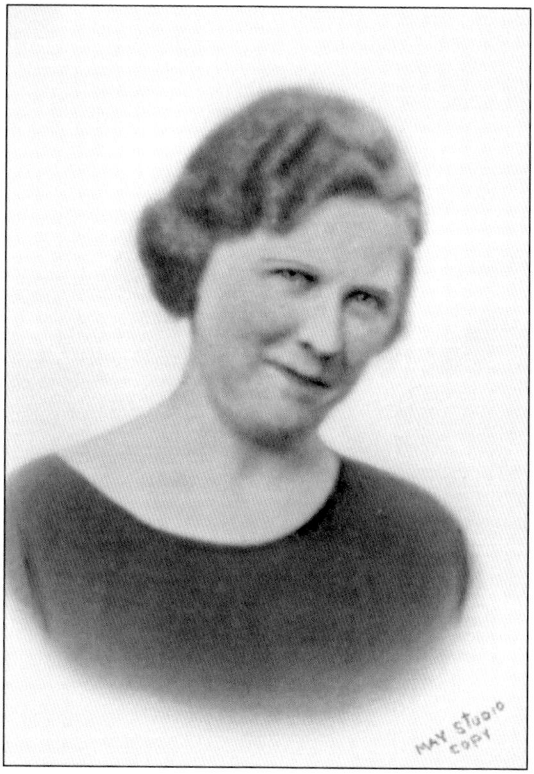

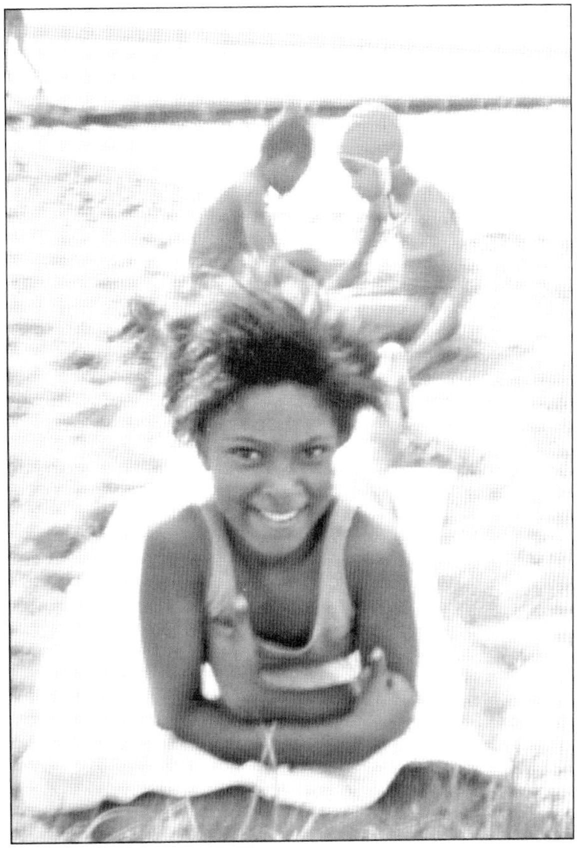

Public pools in Plentywood and Medicine Lake were not the only places to swim in Sheridan County. Brush Lake has been a popular destination for at least a century, serving as the site of picnics during the county's radical period, and as the location of 4-H and Bible camps and family gatherings. In 2005, it became Montana's 50th state park. Shown at right enjoying a day at the lake are Sharon Henry and other children from inner-city Chicago, who participated in the "Friendly Town" project sponsored by Nathanael and Volmer churches. She spent two weeks with Lloyd, Elice, and Marlene Anderson on their farm near Dagmar. Below, John Angvick swims in what is called a "dugout" on his parents' farm in 1937. Many farm families whose land was relatively flat excavated dugouts to collect water for feeding stock and, sometimes, entertaining the children on hot summer days. (Right, courtesy of Elice Nelson; below, courtesy of Marbea Lane.)

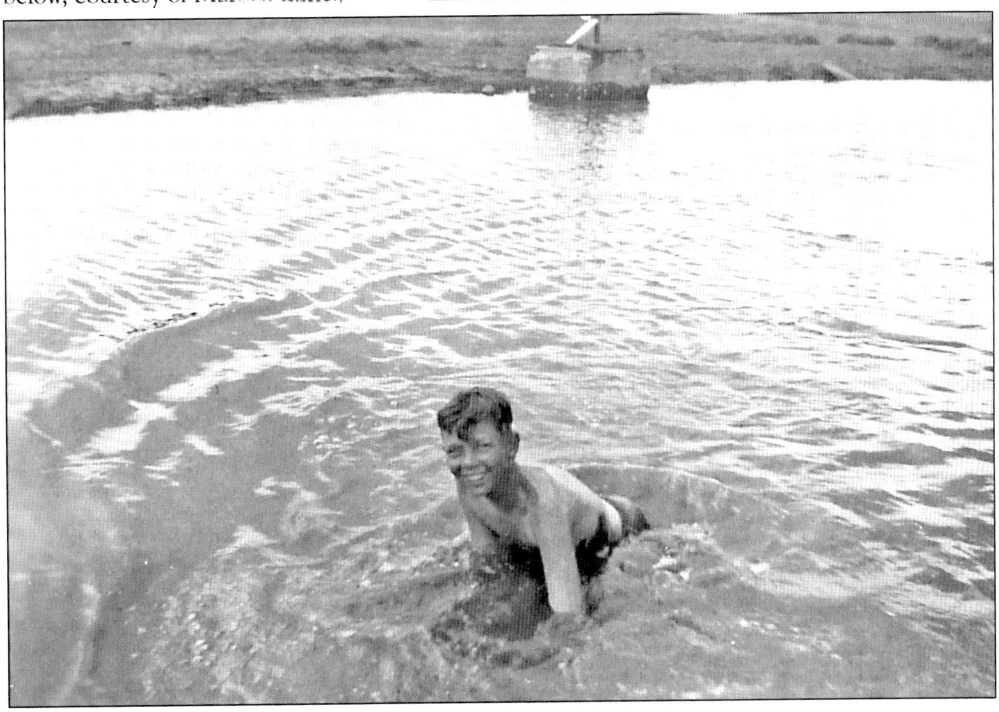

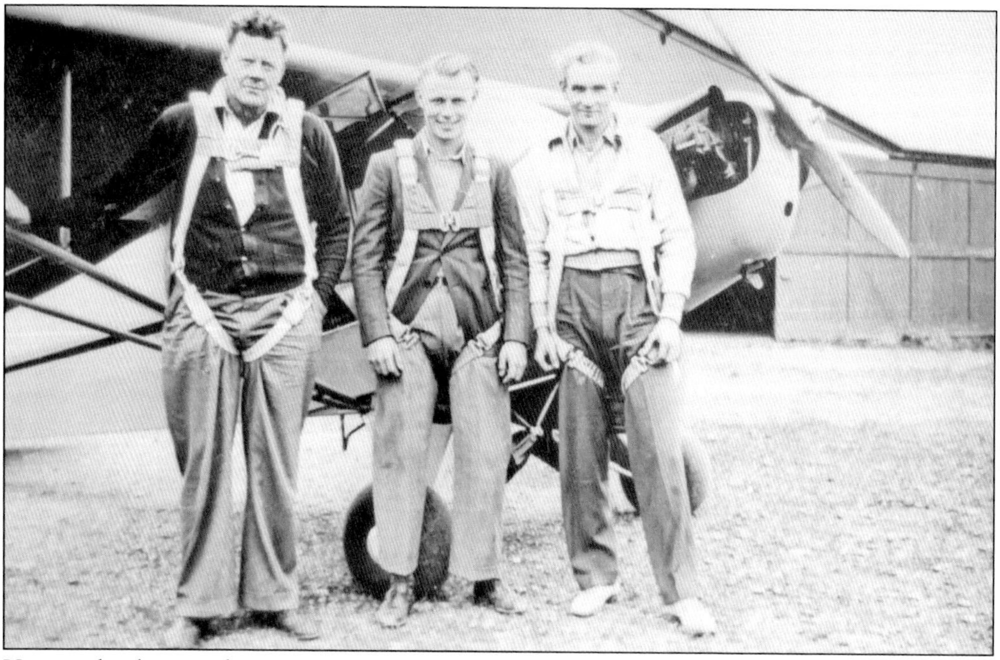

Hunting has been and continues to be a popular sport in Sheridan County. For some, it was more than a pastime; it was a job or the means of protecting their investments. Thor Thorstenson, at left in the above photograph, was a popular flight instructor. He is shown here with students Arlo Sampson (center) and Carl Sundsted. Below, Melvin Risa (left), Thorstenson (center), and Allen Bernau worked as a team to hunt coyotes from the air. In the 1940s, the animals were threatening calves, sheep, and other livestock, and the crew sought to reduce the coyote population. After killing coyotes, the men skinned the animals, earning $11 per pelt. (Above, courtesy of Jens Sundsted; below, courtesy of Sheridan County Museum.)

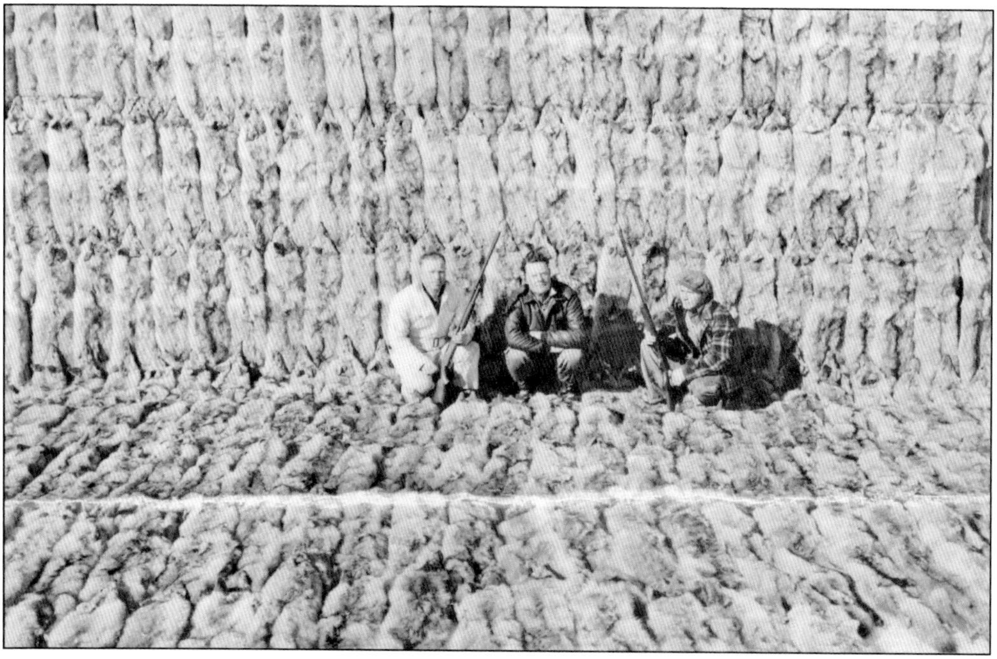

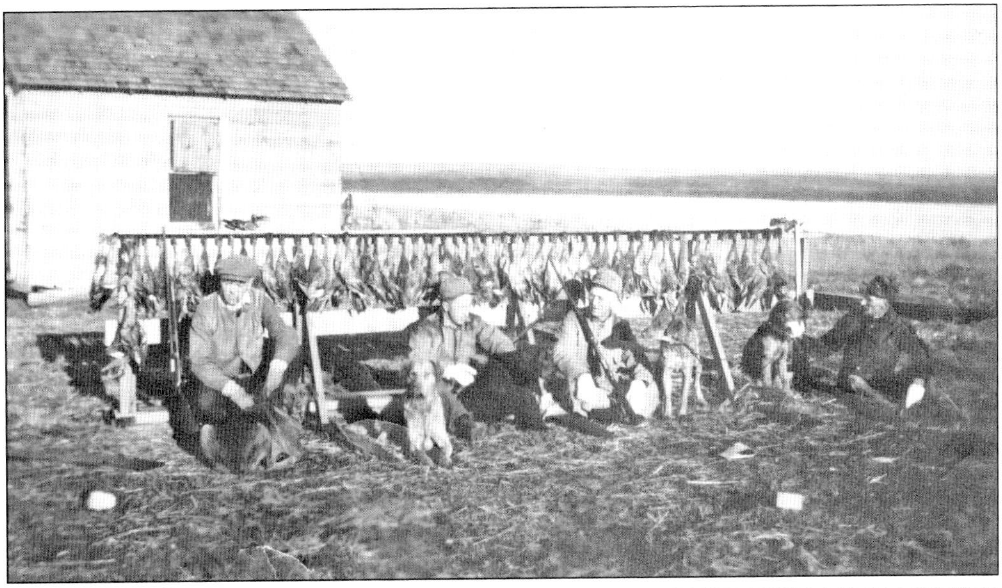

Unlike Thor Thorstenson, many Sheridan County residents hunted for sport or to supplement their family's food supply. In the above photograph are, from left to right, Mark Olson, Ed Powers, Frank Akers, and C.J. Poe. The men are on the shore of Medicine Lake with their hunting dogs and harvest of ducks. At right, Dave Mann displays the Canada goose he shot, probably on a hunting excursion with his father, Archie, who was an avid hunter and fisherman. According to his family biography in *Sheridan's Daybreak*, Mann was proud of having once bagged an albino mallard duck. (Above, courtesy of Virginia Carpenter; right, courtesy of Betty Mann and Mark Nelson.)

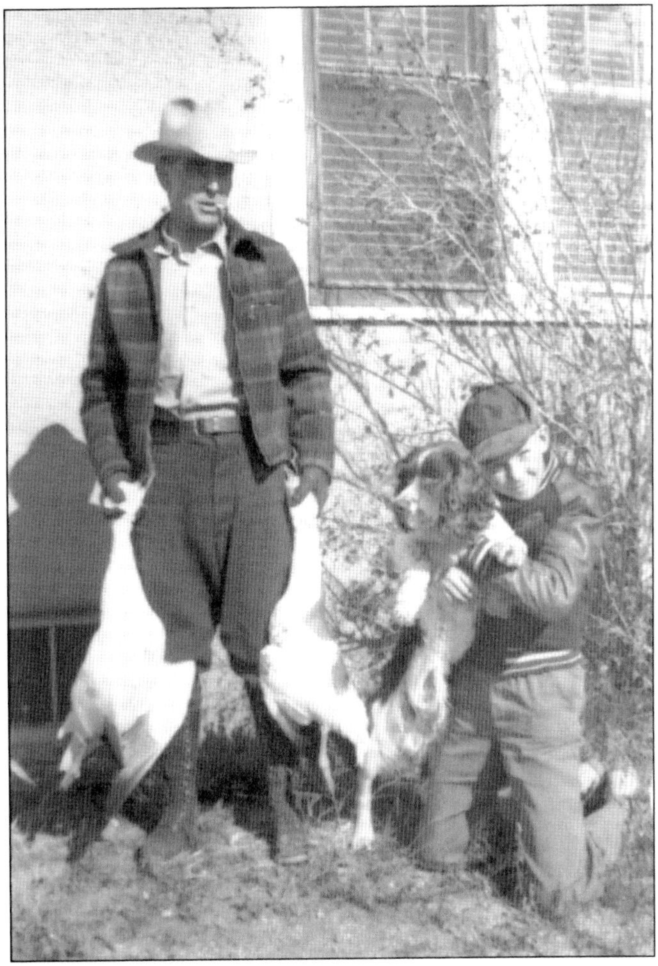

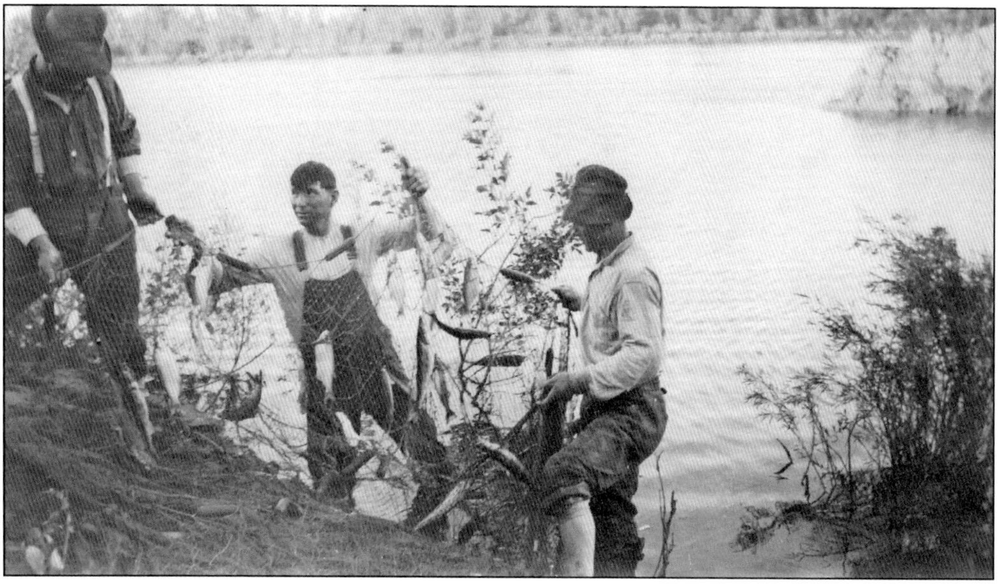

In the 1916 photograph above, Charlie Ross (center) and unidentified friends use a net to fish in a creek southwest of Plentywood. Below, a group of Plentywood friends is ice-skating near the home of Henry and Minnie Raaen, northwest of Plentywood, in the 1940s. They are, from left to right, Carolyn Enderson, Mina Raaen, Nelda Erickson, Dorothy Enderson, and Melba Erickson. The Enderson girls were the daughters of Rev. Jacob Enderson and his wife, Agnes, who served at Plentywood Lutheran Church from 1943 to 1951. The Ericksons were twins whose father, Arthur "A.C.," served as city and county attorney. (Above, courtesy of Millie Marsh; below, courtesy of Mina Mittelstaedt.)

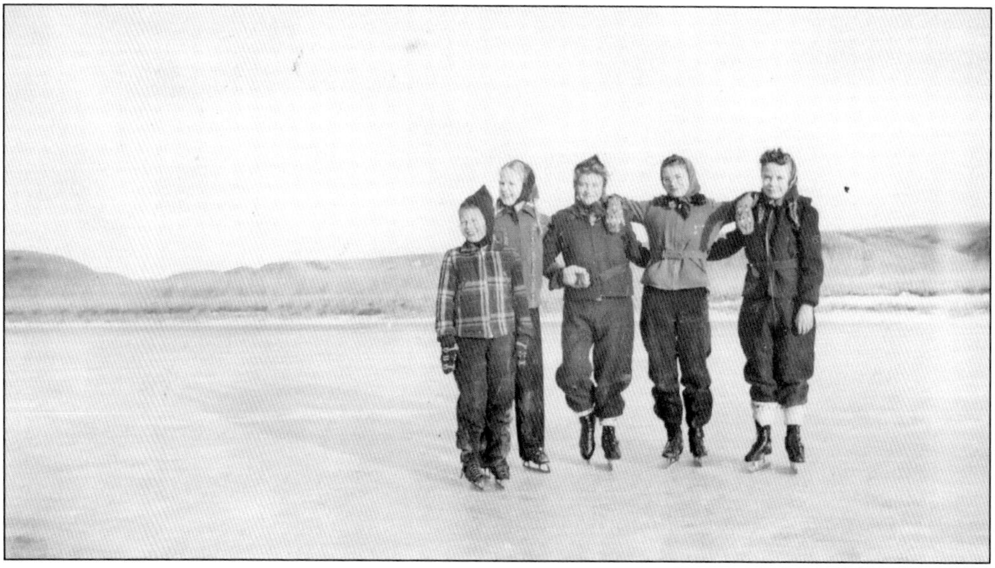

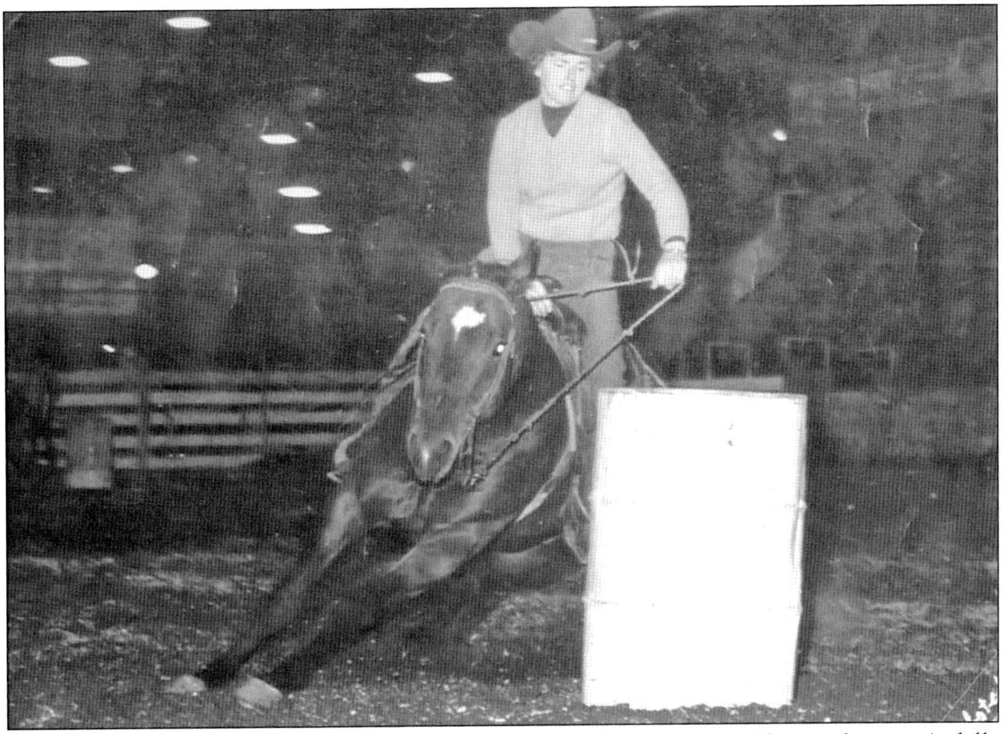

Rodeos have been a popular sport both for spectators and participants. Shown above is Ardelle Hart of Outlook in a 1970 barrel-racing competition in Red Deer, Alberta. Below is her brother, Leonard Nelson, of Raymond, competing in the saddle-bronc competition at the Wolf Point Stampede rodeo in 1972. Their mother was Martha McCoy Nelson, the first white child born in what would become Sheridan County. Horsemanship came naturally to both Hart and Nelson; their grandfather, George "Mac" McCoy, was allowed to go west with his uncles to become a cowboy at the age of 12. At a spring roundup in 1884, he met and was photographed with the famous painter Charles M. Russell. (Both, courtesy of Ardelle Hart.)

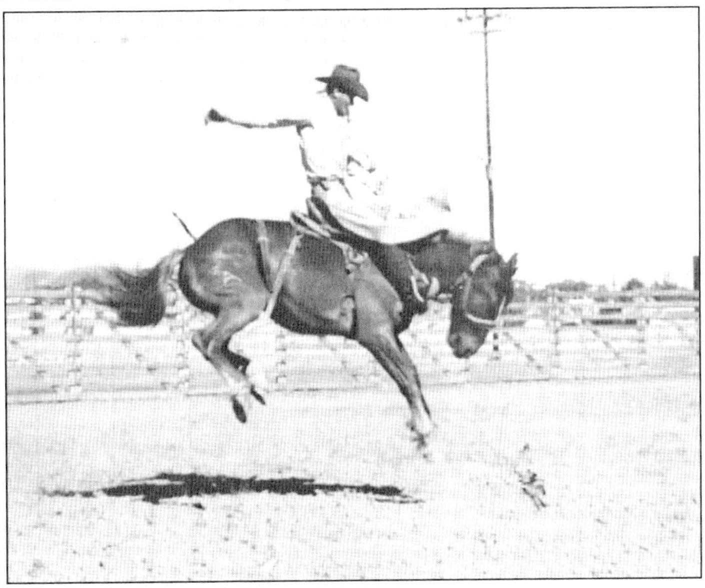

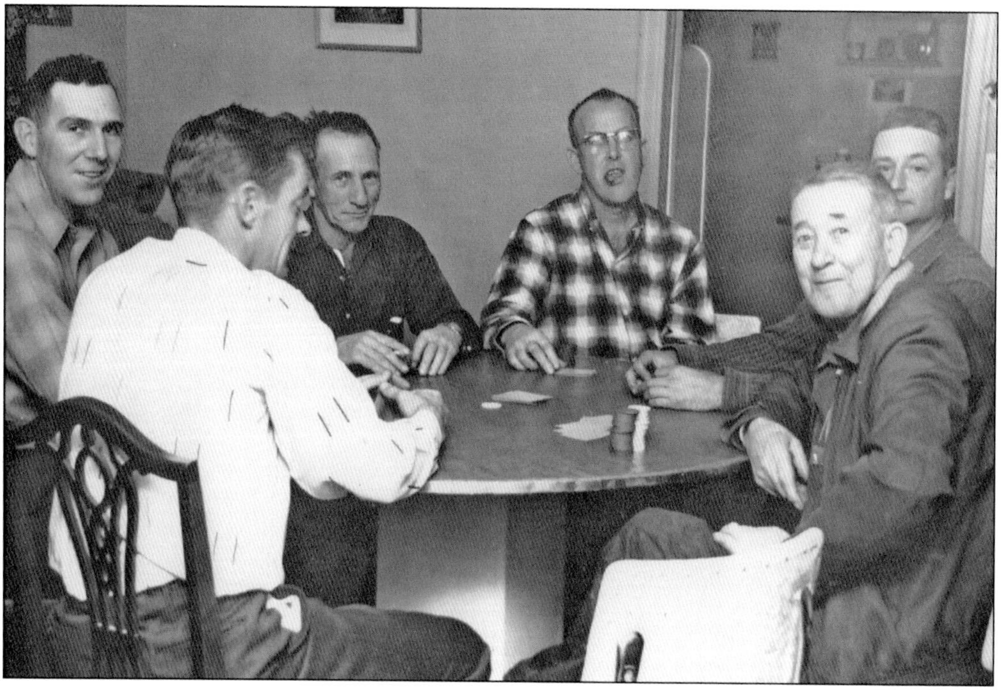

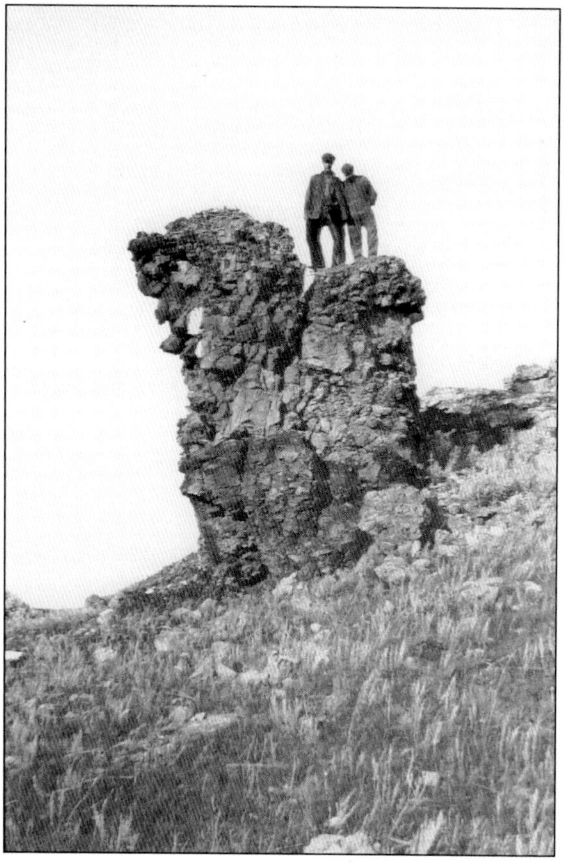

In the photograph above, a group of friends from the Outlook community partakes in a game of poker during the 1950s. The players are, clockwise from left foreground, Glenn Johnson, Wilf Fawcett, Francis Fellon, Marvin Wagnild, Bob Scott, and Bob West. At left, two unidentified young men of the Redstone community are shown on a stone formation south of town known as Cotton Rock. Generations of youngsters have enjoyed climbing and sometimes carving their initials on other Sheridan County rock formations such as the Carroll Dam chalk buttes, Writing Rock on Midby Road near Plentywood, and the Wankel's sandstone hills north of Raymond. (Above, courtesy of Jean West; left, courtesy of Bernice Van Curen.)

Nine

Celebrations of the Past and Present

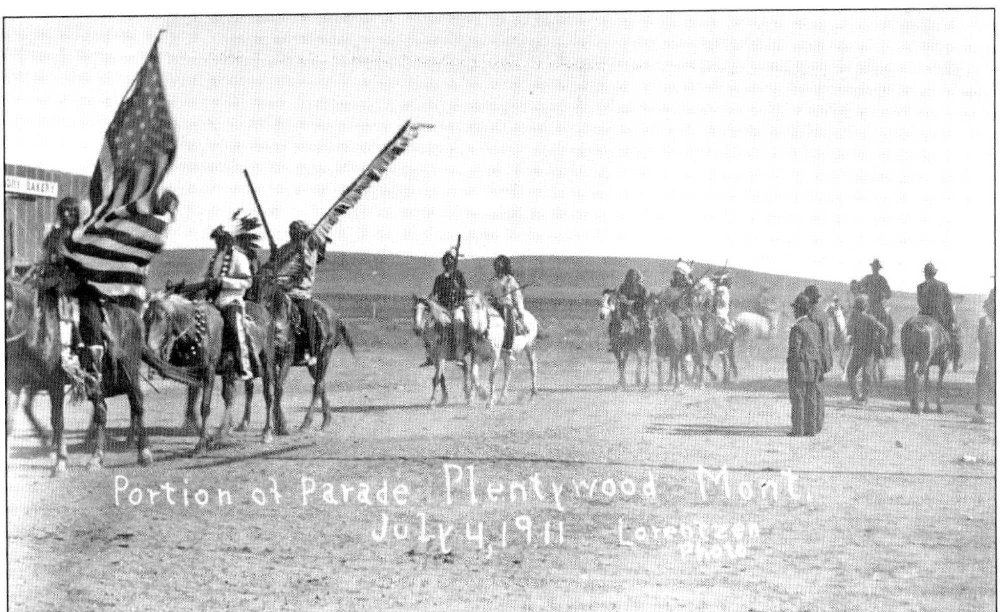

On July 3 and 4, 1911, Plentywood's celebration included members of the Sioux tribe. According to the *Plentywood Herald*, more than 300 tribe members set up tents and teepees just outside of town. The paper goes on to report that "the mounted Indians with their war paint and clothes headed the civics and industrial parade." (Photograph by Lorentzen, courtesy of Maynard Johnson.)

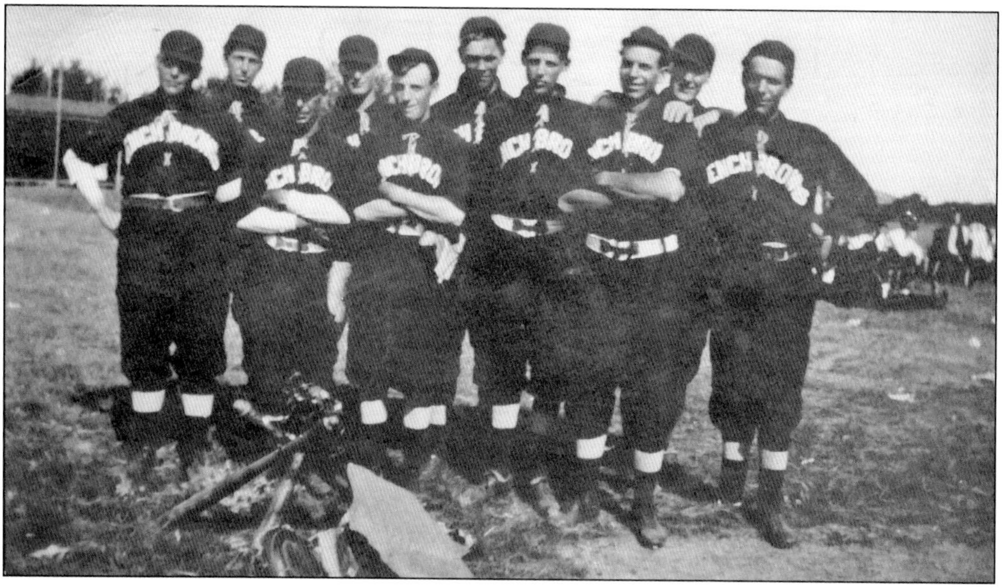

The Independence Day celebration of 1911 included a baseball game between the Outlook town team and the Outlook Bench Browns, which mostly consisted of men from farms in the community. The Bench Browns (above) trounced their urban opponents, 19-7. They are, from left to right, Archie Rasmussen, Earl Nickerson, George "Shorty" Bantz, Rex Scollard, Todd Downey, Harry Willard, Martin Knutson, Elmer Nickerson, Todd Scollard, and Ed Hill. Following the game, residents were treated to a barbecue (below). According to the *Herald*, 2,500 people "were filled to their hearts' content . . . and declared it the big thing of the whole celebration." (Above, courtesy of Jack Nickerson; below, photograph by Lindberg, courtesy of the Sheridan County Museum.)

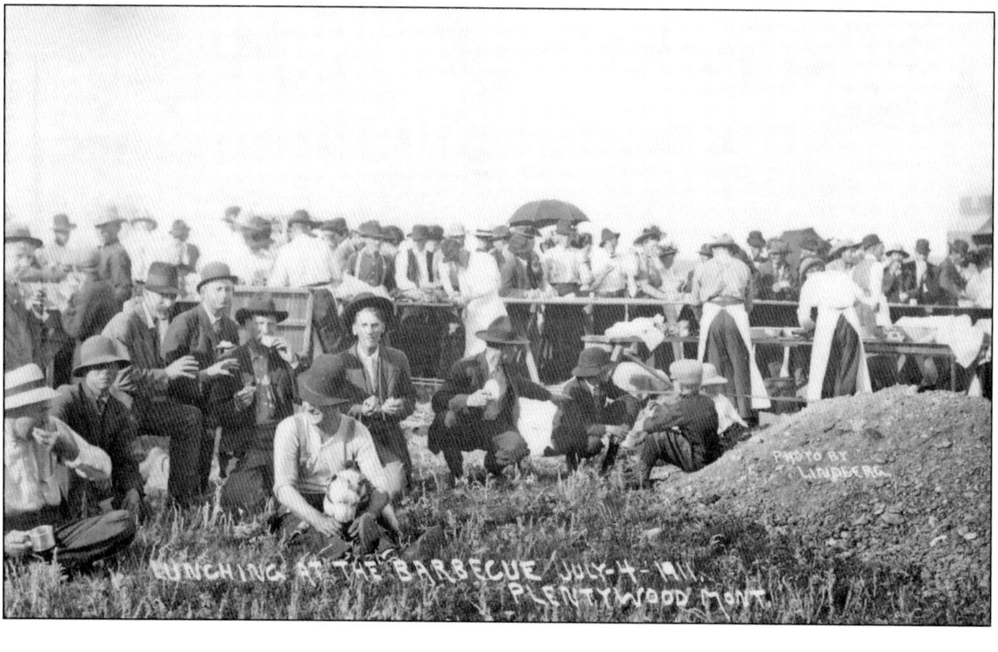

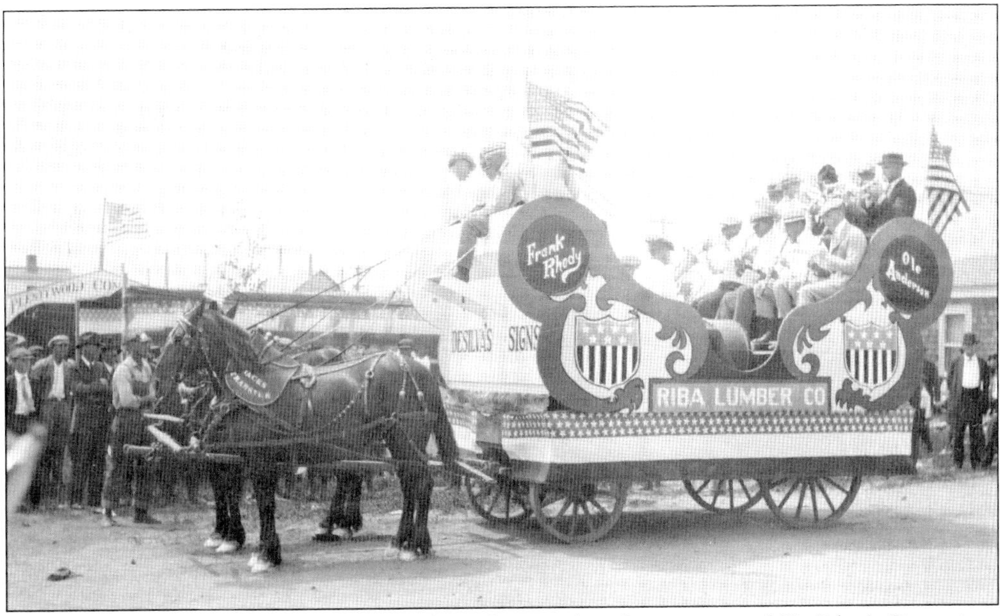

Shown above is a float sponsored by the Riba Lumber Company and DeSilva's Signs in a Plentywood parade. It carries the community band, under the direction of Dr. Steele. Visible in the background is the Wildwood Park band shell. Adolph Riba, whose business interests were quite diversified, hired brothers Henry and John Hill of Raymond to build his bank, pictured below, at the northwest corner of Main Street and First Avenue. The building still stands today, currently housing Michels Insurance Agency. Imbedded in the stonework on the south wall are two iron rings, which were used for tethering horses while their owners conducted transactions inside. If a longer meeting was required, horses could be stabled for a fee at the livery barn, which was located where Plentywood City Hall currently stands. (Above, courtesy of Sheridan County Museum; below, courtesy of Heather Shoal.)

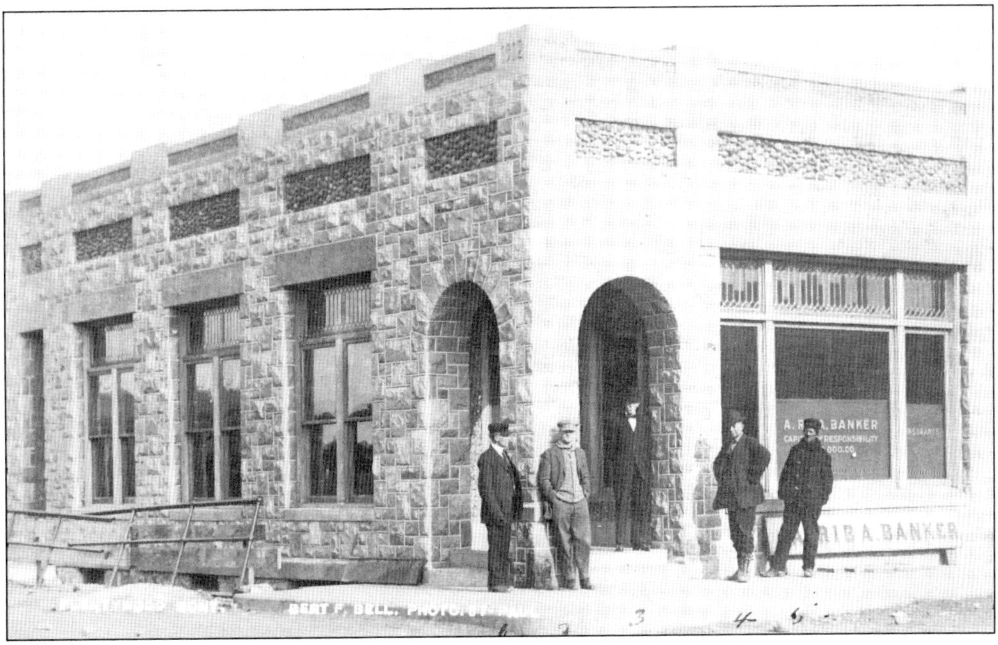

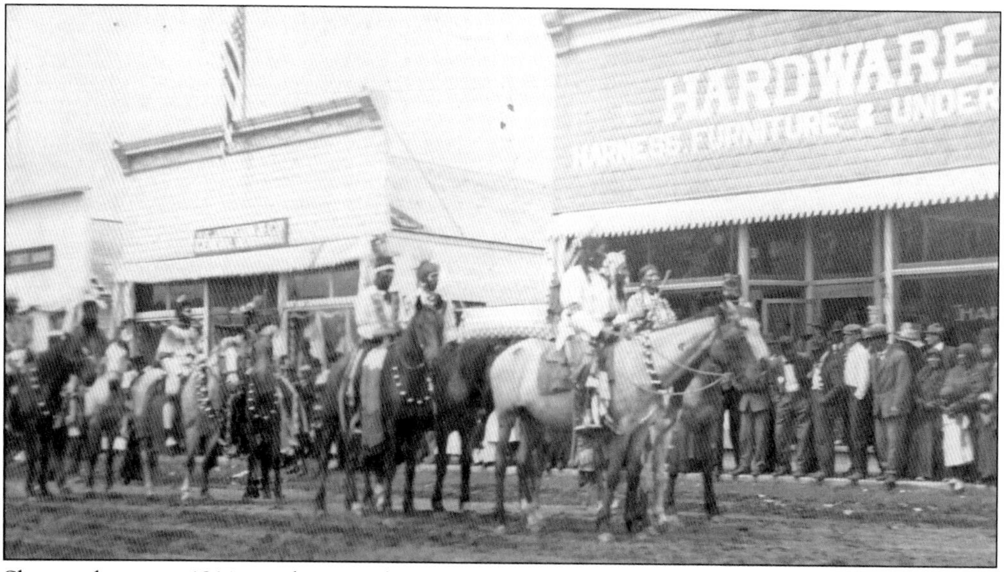

Shown above is a 1914 parade in Medicine Lake on Market Day. On the right, Native American women and children can be seen standing among Medicine Lake's white residents to watch the festivities. In the photograph below, Plentywood residents pose with members of the Sioux tribe, possibly around 1912. Louise Courtney McLaughlin, who is wearing a hat, was the sister of Tom Courtney, the first sheriff of Sheridan County. He and his deputy, Richard Burmester, were shot and killed while attempting to arrest a suspect in Mondak. A ghost town in Roosevelt County today, Mondak was just over the border from North Dakota's Fort Union Trading Post and, until 1919, was a part of Sheridan County. (Above, courtesy of Virginia Carpenter; below, courtesy of Sheridan County Museum.)

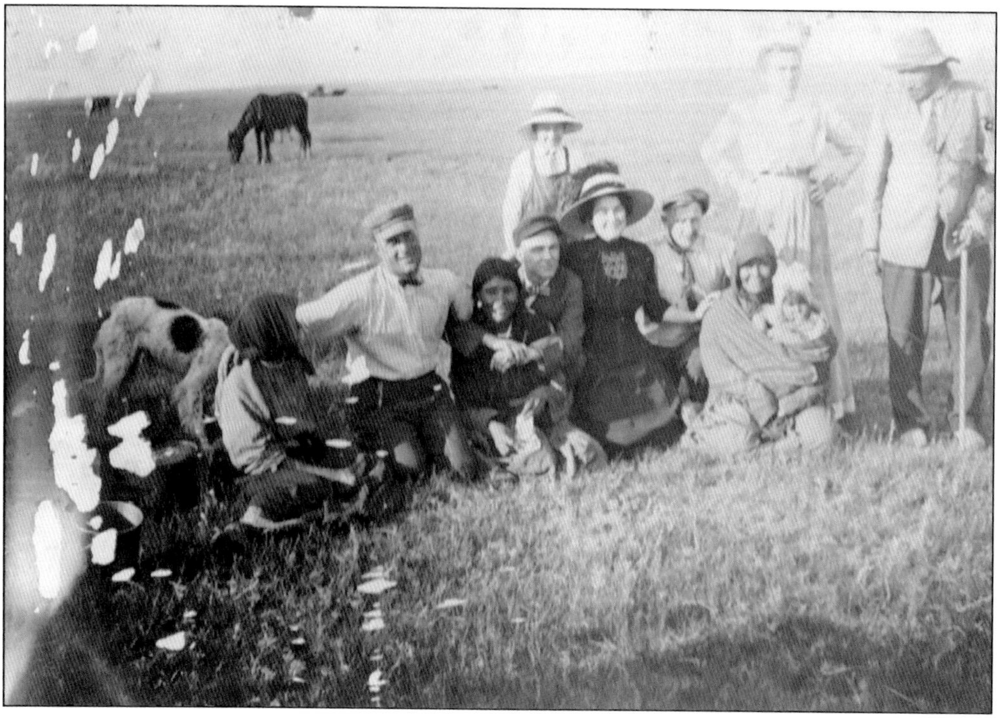

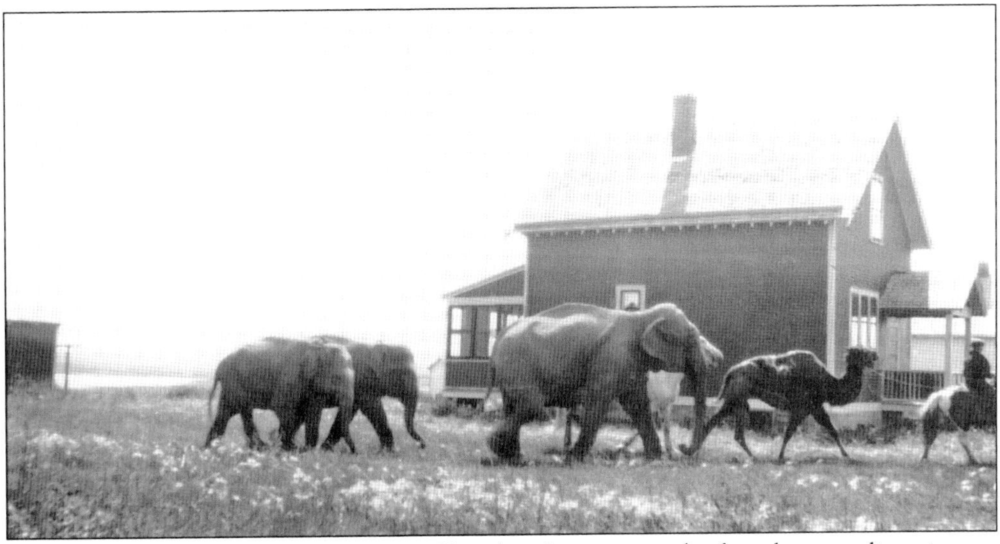

Among other surprising occurrences in Sheridan County was the fact that traveling circuses sometimes passed through. In this early-1920s image, elephants and camels, led by a man on a pony, parade through Comertown. Traveling circuses were anticipated not only by young children, but by local teenagers, who were sometimes hired to haul water or feed for the animals. The Sheridan County Democrats' float (below) participates in Plentywood's golden anniversary celebration in 1963. Shown in the car are, from left to right, (in back seat) Anna Rehmer, Lyle Medders, and Velma Aasheim; (front seat) Dorothy Anhalt and Sylvia Darland. (Above, courtesy of Merlin Rostad; below, photograph by Glyn Deem, courtesy of the Sheridan County Museum.)

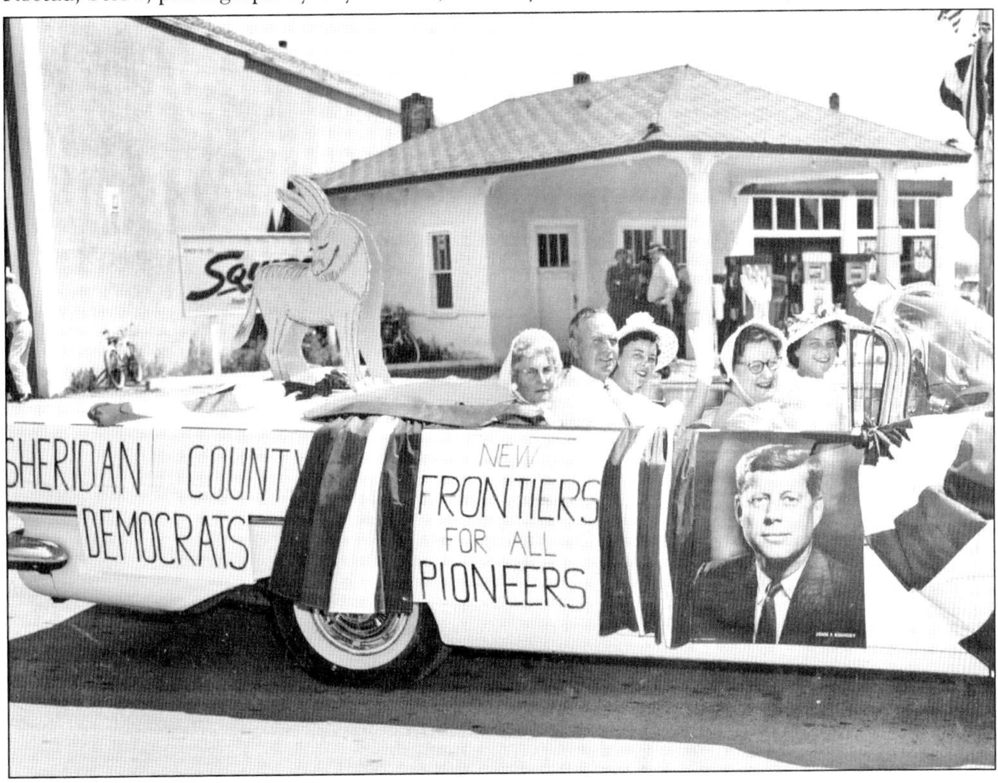

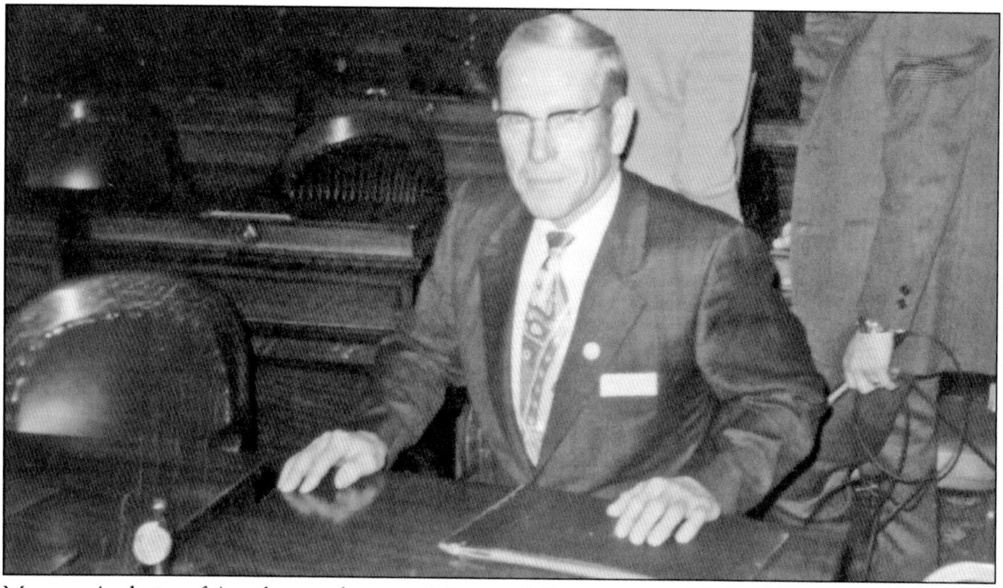

Magnus Aasheim of Antelope is shown at Montana's Constitutional Convention, to which he was elected as a delegate, in 1972. Aasheim was a teacher, farmer, and rancher who served four terms in the state house of representatives and was the driving force behind the production of two local history volumes, *Sheridan's Daybreak* and *Sheridan's Daybreak II*. Shown below at Medicine Lake's centennial celebration in 2010 are Ed Smith of Dagmar-Volmer and Irene McCallister Stageberg of Westby. Stageberg celebrated her 100th birthday in 2011. Smith, born on the farm homesteaded by his parents in the Volmer community, was engaged in public service over the years, serving on various boards and, notably, as state representative and, later, state senator. Smith was also the Republican candidate for governor in 1972. (Above, courtesy of Gary Aasheim; below, courtesy of Irene Stageberg.)

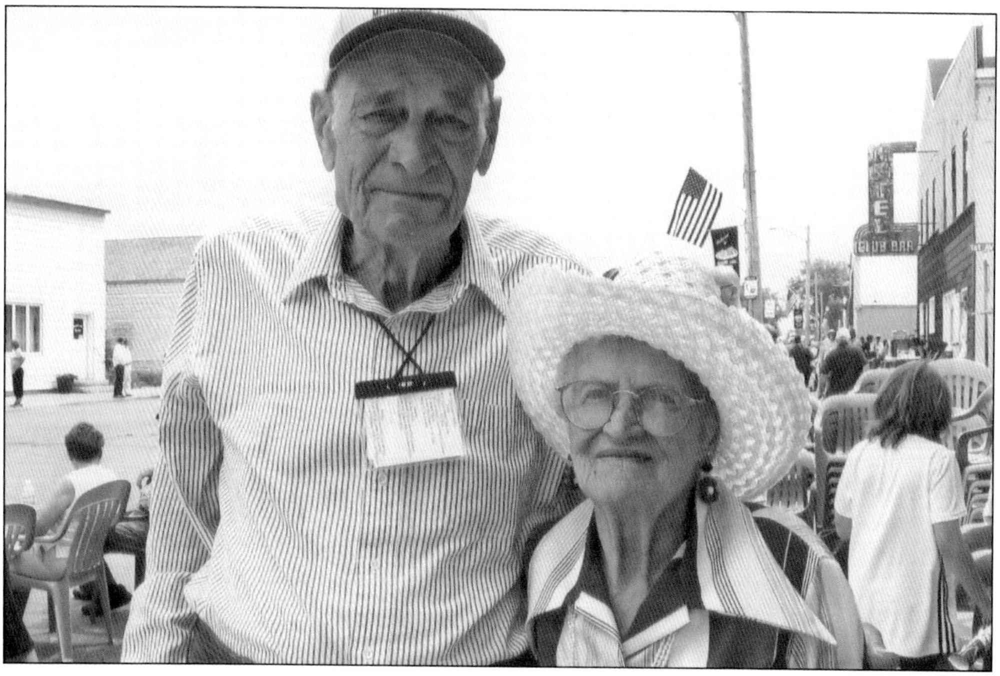

Sheridan County's bicentennial celebrations were elaborate and spanned an entire year. They included community variety shows throughout 1976 and a full slate of events for the July Fourth weekend. A time capsule (right) was buried in front of the Sheridan County Museum in Plentywood; it is to be reopened in 2076. Craig Saxton (center, holding stone map) of Antelope built the capsule from steel pipes that are 12 feet long and 12 inches in diameter. Filled with memorabilia stored in canisters, the capsule weigh about 500 pounds. The stone monument at the capsule site, with masonry by Ralph Parpart, includes an engraving of a contest-winning sketch by Bonnie McCrory (below) entitled *Beginning of Tomorrow.* (Right, courtesy of Helen Rippley; below, courtesy of Bonnie McCrory.)

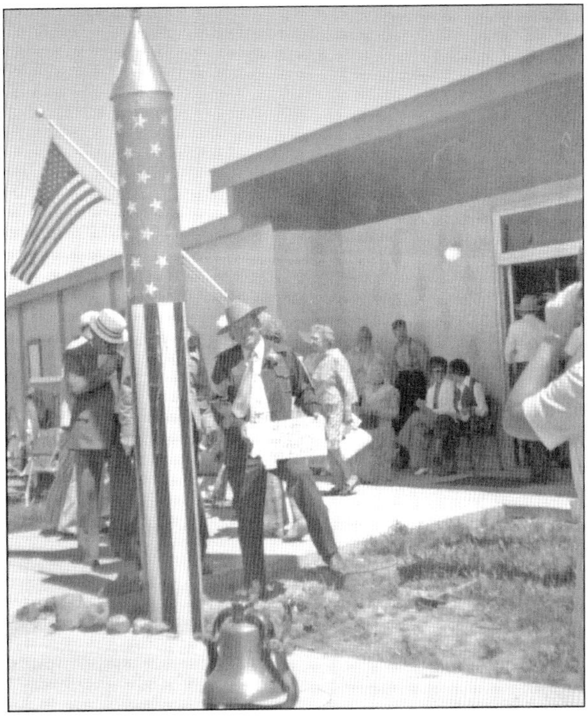

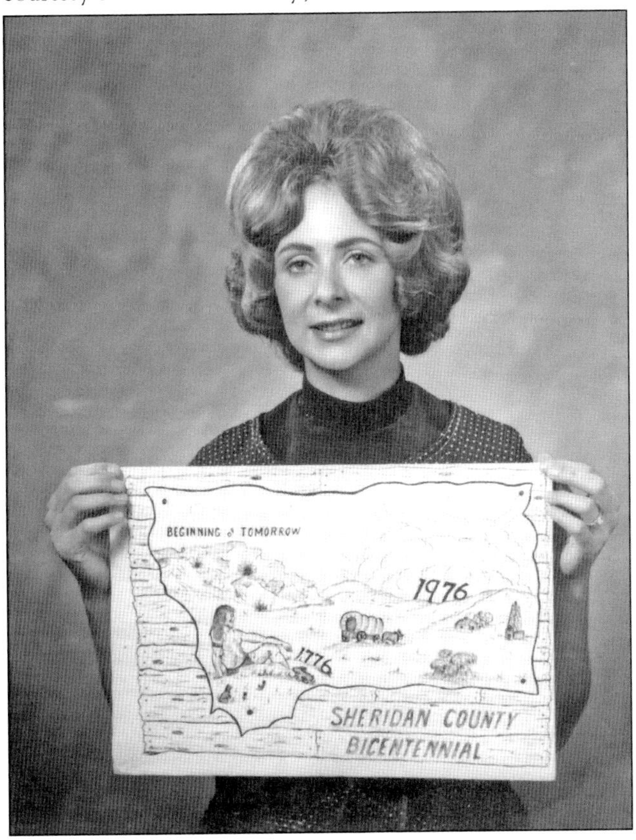

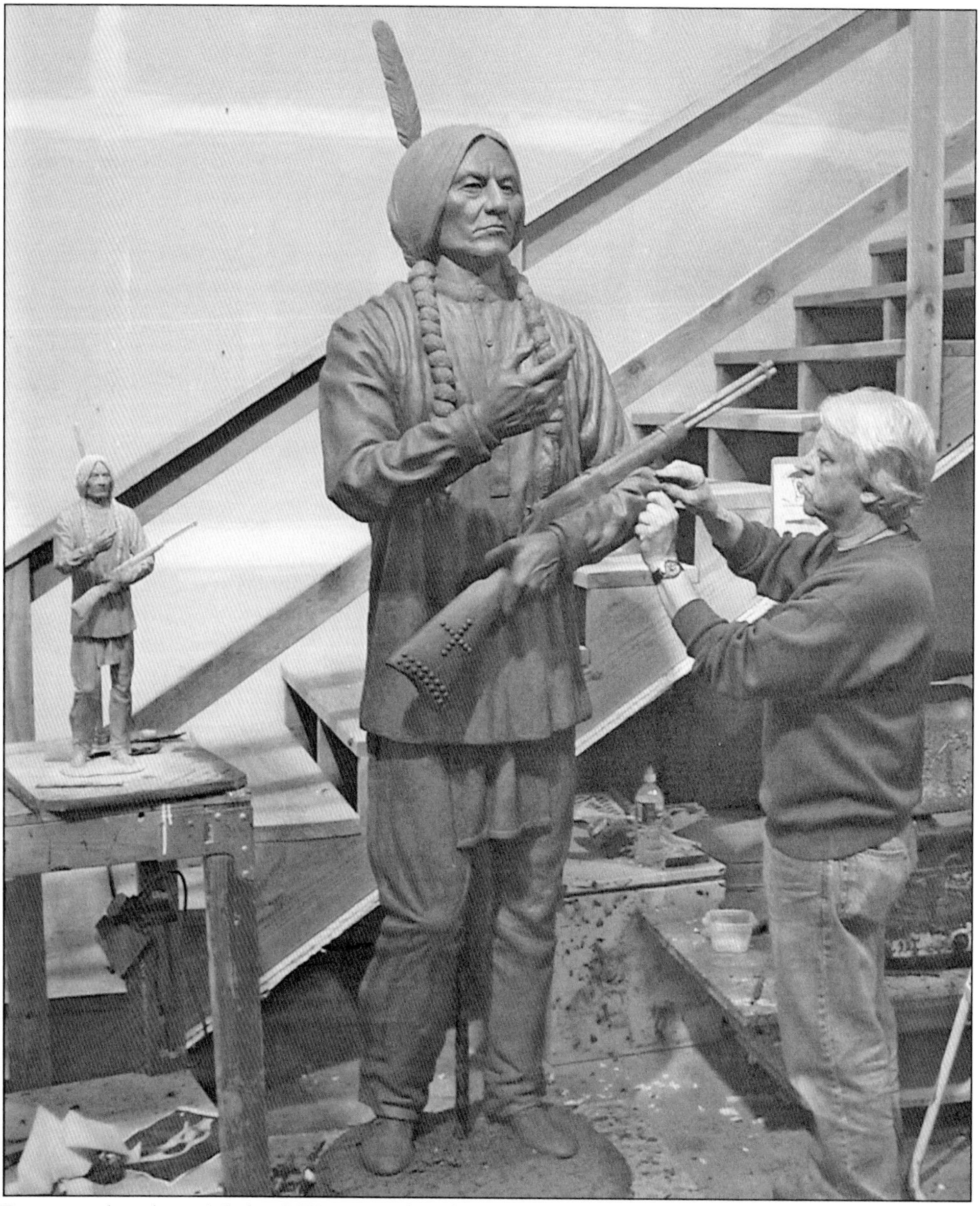

Renowned sculptor Michael Westergard is shown in 2011, completing the clay original for his bronze sculpture of Sitting Bull. The seven-foot, five-inch sculpture is located at the main entrance to Williston State College in North Dakota, roughly 20 miles from the scene of Sitting Bull's 1881 surrender at Fort Buford. Before traveling to the site of his surrender, Sitting Bull met with a military escort from the 7th Infantry in the area of present-day Plentywood. Westergard's sculpture captures the image of Sitting Bull just before he relinquished his Model 66 Winchester rifle, now housed in the Smithsonian Institution. In the course of creating his sculpture, Westergard corresponded and eventually met with Sitting Bull's great-grandson, Ernie LaPointe, who approved the final design. Westergard grew up with two brothers and his parents, Carl and Mary, on a farm in the Coalridge area. His work has received many awards and has been exhibited and purchased for collections all over the world. (Courtesy of Michael and Patricia Westergard.)

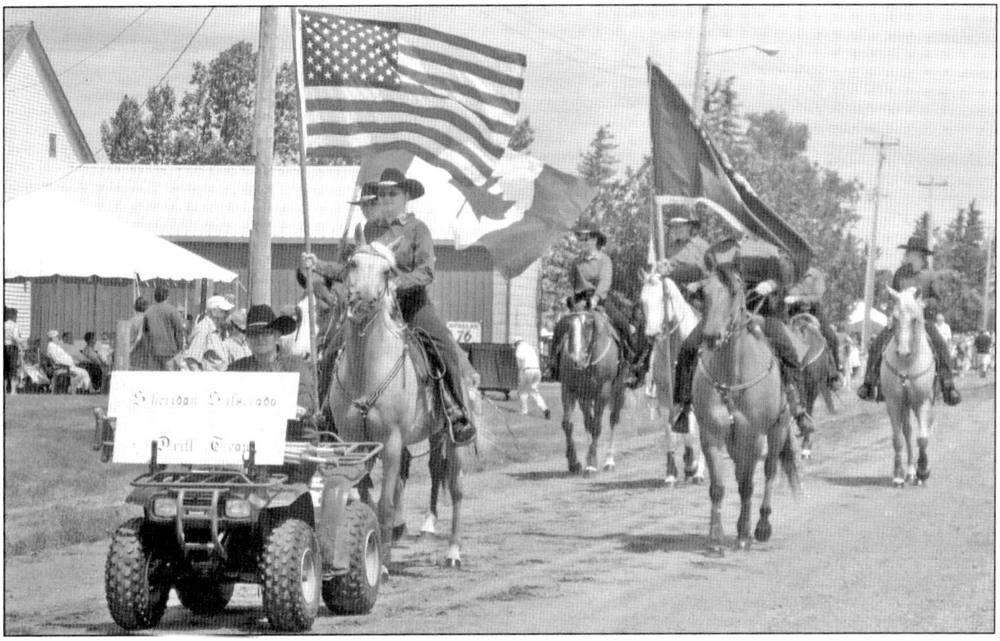

Above, the Sheridan Silverados drill team makes an appearance during Antelope's centennial parade in July 2010. Jacqueline Hendrickson rides the four-wheeler as flags are carried by Lacy Whipple (America), Holly Juve (Canada), and Louise Urdahl (Montana). Other riders are, from left to right, Rhonda Opp, Kathy Berntson, Dana Christensen, and Tanya Gobbs. The Sheridan County Fair is a treasured local tradition that began in September 1940. It was called the Harvest Festival for many years. Now held at the end of July, the fair features livestock shows, commercial exhibits, live music, a rodeo, and, often, a carnival. Shown below at the 2011 fair's livestock show for children ages 10 and under are Justin Olge and his son, Braden. (Above, courtesy of Dave Golterman; below, courtesy of Dona Osksa.)

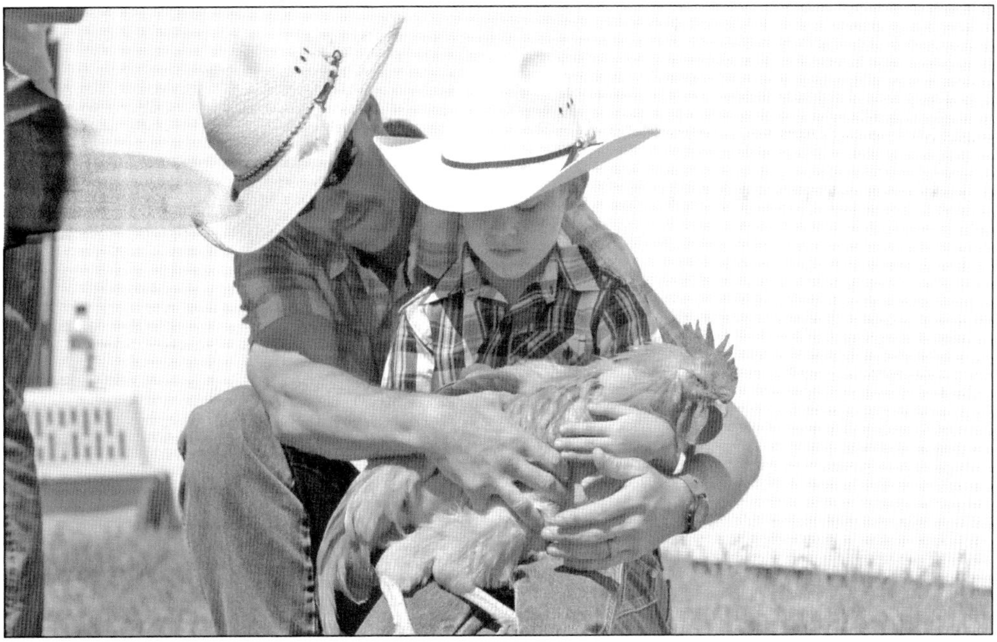

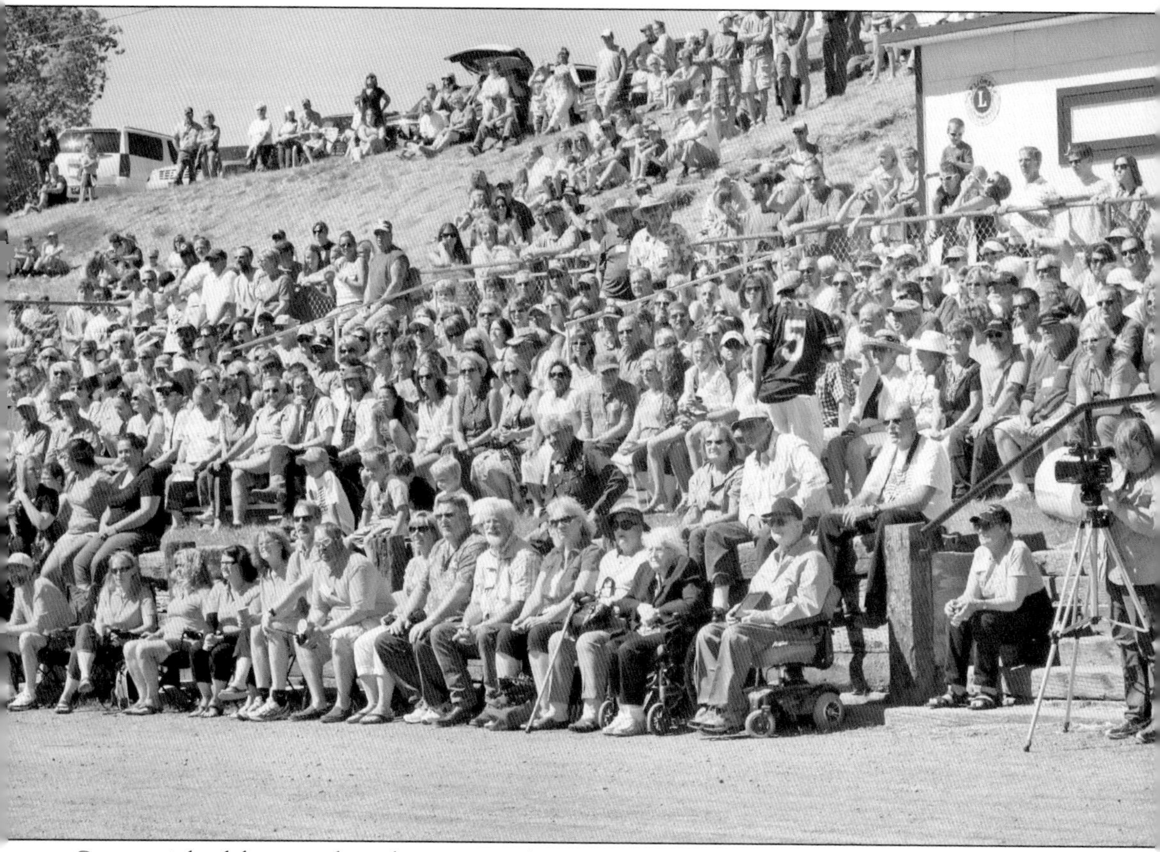

Centennial celebrations have become regular occurrences in Sheridan County since Dagmar kicked off the festivities in 2006. Plentywood's centennial will not be the last; Westby will celebrate its first 100 years in 2013, as will Sheridan County. Shown here is part of the audience at the first official event of the Plentywood centennial, a pep rally, on July 4, 2012. On the right side of the first row are members of the Bolster family, including Lloyd, the youngest son of Gertie and George Bolster, the "father of Plentywood." Bolster's son received special recognition at the rally, which drew a crowd of at least 2,300. To the left of the Bolster family are members of the centennial committee, whose planning process began in 2010 and resulted in four days of activities, ranging from a 5K run and an extensive parade to a multimedia historical show. (Courtesy of Dona Osksa.)

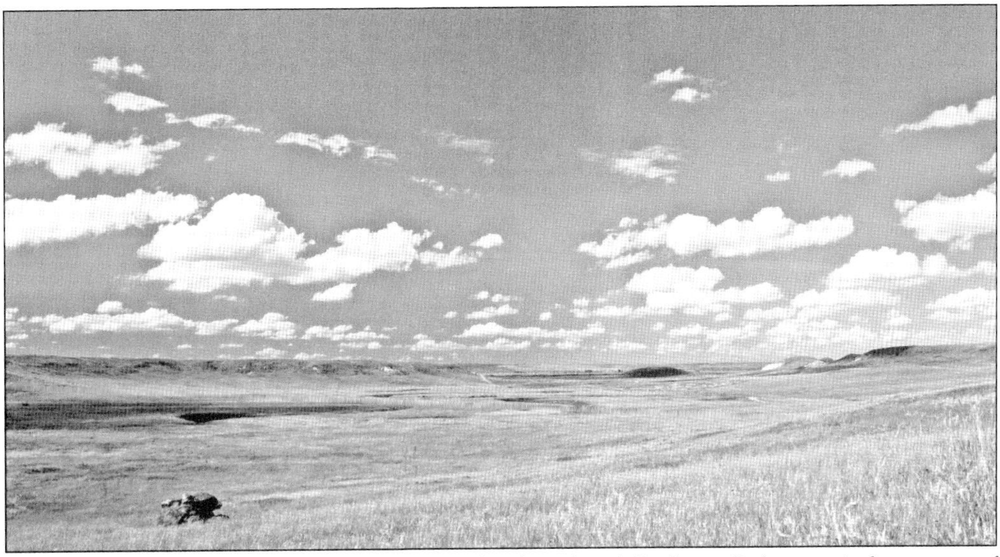

Above, the stark and beautiful pasture south of Paul and Barbara Golterman's farm west of Plentywood serves as a reminder that there are still many places in Sheridan County's approximately 1,700 square miles where the landscape remains virtually unchanged since the first homesteaders arrived. Below, artist Bob Southland is shown in 1989 completing a mural that depicts the county's history. The 74-foot-by-four-foot oil painting, displayed in the Sheridan County Civic Center in Plentywood, is thought to be the longest indoor mural in the state. Beginning with the period when American Indians roamed northeastern Montana, Southland's artwork captures images of the county's development and offers a visual testimony to the resilience, hard work, and community spirit of the people who have made Sheridan County their home for over 100 years. (Above, courtesy of Dave Golterman; below, courtesy of Betty Lee.)

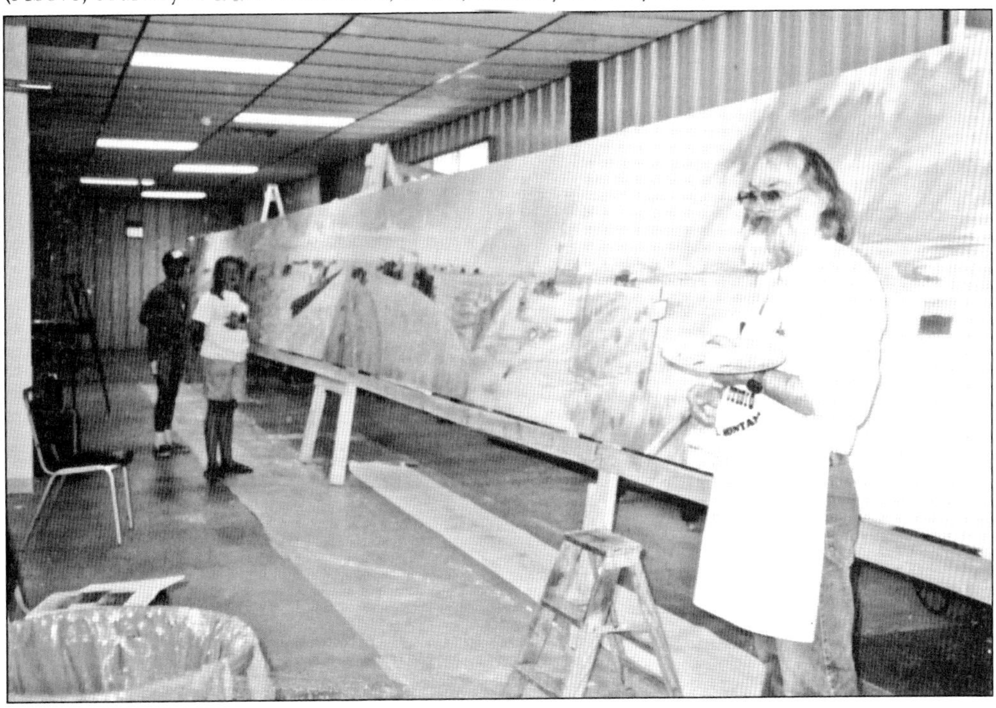